# JON SOPEL

# A Year
## at the
# Circus

BOOKS

3 5 7 9 10 8 6 4 2

BBC Books, an imprint of Ebury Publishing
20 Vauxhall Bridge Road,
London SW1V 2SA

BBC Books is part of the Penguin Random House group of companies
whose addresses can be found at global.penguinrandomhouse.com

Penguin
Random House
UK

First published by BBC Books in 2019
This edition published by BBC Books in 2019

www.penguin.co.uk

A CIP catalogue record for this book is available from the British Library

Hardback ISBN 9781785944376
Trade Paperback ISBN 9781785944383

Typeset in 12/17 pt Sabon
by Integra Software Services Pvt. Ltd, Pondicherry

Printed and bound in Great Britain by Clays Ltd, Elcograf S.p.A.

Penguin Random House is committed to a sustainable future for
our business, our readers and our planet. This book is made
from Forest Stewardship Council® certified paper.

MIX
Paper from
responsible sources
FSC® C018179

*To Rosalind, my wonderful sister*

# Contents

# Foreword

One of the things about covering the Trump White House is just how much is going on all the time – objects flying towards you 24/7, ceaseless noise, constant activity. It is exciting and relentless – and occasionally exhausting. But the frustration for most of us covering these events is how much goes unreported. My main outlet as the BBC's North America Editor is the *Ten O'Clock News* in the UK. That will on average contain eight to ten of the most important and interesting stories from around the world that day. If I am to find a berth in the running order, it is going to be on the one stand-out event.

That never does justice to all the stories that don't quite pass the threshold of being globally significant but which, nonetheless, are fascinating. So, when BBC Books asked me to come up with an idea to follow on from *If Only They Didn't Speak English*, my first thought was to try to find a mechanism to report some of the untold gems of this unique administration. That is what I have tried to do in the pages that follow. And thanks to my publisher

Yvonne Jacob (and publicist Claire Scott and copy editor Steve Dobell) and literary agent Rory Scarfe for their support. Likewise Malcolm Balen in the BBC for his input.

In this endeavour I have to single out Ron Christie. He is our in-house BBC analyst on this administration. He served with distinction in the Bush White House, runs his own political consultancy – and as well as being a Republican strategist also finds time to teach at Georgetown University and NYU. He also – somehow – found time to read my manuscript. And all I can say is lucky, lucky students to be taught by him. His incisive intellect picked up on any number of sloppy judgements, half-baked assumptions, weak arguments and occasional inaccuracies. And like all great teachers he managed to point all this out while being immensely encouraging too. Any errors that remain – are entirely down to me.

There are three other people I need to thank. In Washington we seem to have an astonishing procession of super-talented young Americans coming into the bureau, straight out of college – three of the best are Morgan Gisholt Minard, Cosima Schelfhout and Aiden Johnson: brilliant minds, good fun to have around, great colleagues with an unbelievable work ethic. I have no idea what they will end up doing – but I am sure they have stellar futures ahead of them. I am only grateful they found some time to help with vital bits of research and fact checking on this book.

One other shout-out: Jonathan Csapo is the logistics maestro of the office, and I cannot imagine how my life would function without him.

And last but certainly not least, my wife, Linda, for her constant encouragement and enthusiasm for this latest project; oh, and Alfie our miniature German Schnauzer – editorially he is still weak, but for companionship he is an A+: never complaining about going for long walks when my mind became a mushy mess and needed to be cleared; and just as happy to doze for hours on the sofa in my study while I wrote.

Jon Sopel
Washington, July 2019

# Introduction

It is 12 July 2018, and President Trump on a baking hot day has a much anticipated joint news conference with Theresa May at her official country house, Chequers, in the rolling Buckinghamshire hills. Much anticipated, because, the night before, Donald Trump has given a scabrous, freewheeling interview to the *Sun* newspaper, criticising Theresa May over her handling of Brexit, warning that America wouldn't be much interested in a trade deal with Britain if it was still in some way yoked to the EU, and then to add a good sprinkling of chilli powder onto an open wound, went on to say that Boris Johnson would make a very good prime minister. Well, if that was a game of darts in your local pub, those three barbs would have the scorer calling out 'one hundred and eighty'. Unerring darts, Donald.

Except he probably hadn't meant it, or at least hadn't calculated the fall-out. But this was day three of a tour which had already seen the US president clash with the leaders of NATO over the resistance of many member states to paying 2 per cent of their GDP into the collective security coffers. And while he was in Brussels he got into a fight with the leaders of the EU over trade. And then he came to London and gave Theresa May a mauling. In this topsy-turvy world, the President was going on to Helsinki in Finland on the last stop on his tour to hold a one-to-one summit with the Russian leader Vladimir Putin, which he predicted would be the easiest leg of his journey. The Trump circus was on the move.

But back to the news conference on the parched, dun-coloured lawn of Chequers. In a heatwave summer, Mrs May was feeling distinctly cool towards her visitor. And he knew it. He was in full contrition mode. At their private talks before they met the press, he was behaving as a man who knew he was in trouble. Gushing in his admiration for Theresa May, saying this time, and in contradiction of the *Sun* interview, there could still be a trade deal. One of those present told me that unlike on previous occasions, he listened attentively to what she had to say. No interruptions. No changing the subject and cutting her off. And he complained that the newspaper had not published all the flattering things he'd said about her.

This he repeated at the news conference. Repeatedly. From Chequers he was going on to meet the Queen at Windsor Castle and, from there, up to Turnberry for the weekend to play the championship golf course that bears his name. And then he started talking about the vote to leave the European Union, and the last time he'd been in Britain.

'If you remember I was opening Turnberry the day before Brexit,' he told us. 'They all showed up [the journalists covering the trip, myself included] on the ninth hole, overlooking the ocean, and I said "What's going on?" and all they wanted to talk about was Brexit.

'They asked for my opinion and I think you will agree I said Brexit will happen, and it did happen. Then we cut the ribbon.

'The reason I felt it was going to happen was because of immigration. One of the reasons I got elected was because of immigration, I felt that Brexit had the upper hand, and most people didn't agree with me.'

I am now listening intently, wondering whether I have misheard. As I say, I was at Turnberry with the then Republican hopeful for the presidency those unforgettable few days in June 2016. He wasn't there the day before Brexit. He didn't stand on the ninth tee and predict the result of the next day's vote. People didn't disagree with his forecast. And the reason that nothing of the kind like that happened was that Donald Trump didn't arrive in Scotland until 24 June, the day *after* the Brexit vote. It is a claim he would repeat again at length.

So onto Twitter I went and rather clumsily and hurriedly wrote this: 'Bizarre. @realDonaldTrump says he came to Turnberry the day before Brexit and he told everyone that he thought Brexit would happen. And that he predicted correctly what would happen the next day. Umm. Not true. He came the day after Brexit. I was there. June 24.'

I guessed that might get a bit of pick-up, but when I quickly got a reply to my tweet – from a woman called Stephanie Grisham – a small fire went 'whoosh'. After the election Grisham became the First Lady's director of communications, but during the presidential campaign she was one of Donald Trump's press officers, and she was with us on the 2016 trip. She tweeted this back to me: 'He did. It actually is true. I was there. June 23.'

So I replied to her: 'Stephanie – I hate to argue as we were there together. He was NOT at Turnberry on the day before the referendum, as he said at the news conference. He was not there on polling day itself. He was there the day after, on Friday 24th. These are indisputable facts.'

And back she came: 'Nope. I have photos. I also have a newspaper from the morning after Brexit. I remember sitting in a pub the night before, watching the results come in.'

So then I went scrolling back through Donald Trump's Twitter feed, and sure enough there it was, dated 24 June: 'Just arrived in Scotland. Place is going wild over the vote. They took their country back, just like we will take America back. No more games.'

Someone else found the flight manifest from the Trump plane, and that too proved he'd arrived the day afterwards. After that I heard no more from Ms Grisham, and I have emailed her a number of times to discuss it, but she has never replied. Now leave to one side the small fact that Scotland had voted decisively to remain, this was a most odd episode that I honestly still struggle to fathom. We all misremember from time to time things that happen. And I am sure I am not alone if I admit to occasionally being prone to giving some of my stories a light sprinkling of icing sugar. And I'm honestly not saying it's a big deal in the sweeping arc of history. It's pretty irrelevant. But what still leaves me scratching my head is why over something that was so easily disproved did the President choose to perpetuate a falsehood? And why would communications professionals in the White House seek to prop up an obvious falsehood?

At the end of June 2019, it was announced that Stephanie Grisham would take over as the White House Director of Communications and Press Secretary to the President.

In the circus these people are the illusionists or mentalists. But there's another word for this. In 1938 a British author, Patrick Hamilton, wrote a play called *Gaslight*, which was later made into a film with Ingrid Bergman. Set in Victorian times, the play concerns a celebrated opera singer who becomes a victim when fed continuous falsehoods by her evil, manipulative partner and ultimately starts questioning herself over what she thought she knew to be true. Today a whole discipline within psychology now studies this phenomenon, and in honour of the original play it is called 'gaslighting'. The best definition I have seen is this: 'Gaslighting is a form of psychological manipulation that seeks to sow seeds of doubt in a targeted individual or in members of a targeted group, making them question their own memory, perception, and sanity. Using persistent denial, misdirection, contradiction, and lying, it attempts to destabilise the victim and delegitimise the victim's belief.'

But before we get carried away with a single psychological theory to explain what the President and his inner circle does to bamboozle us, the reality is more complicated. Yes, there are things that happen where you do sort of think that maybe Donald Trump is a Bond villain, stroking a white pussycat, while carefully figuring out every move that will ultimately deliver him world domination. But there are other times when this presidency is more Austin Powers than Ernst Blofeld.

The one thing that you can be sure of, is that it will be rough, verbally violent – occasionally brutal. The appointment of Stephanie Grisham as the new press secretary came a matter of weeks after Donald Trump's state visit to the UK. The President had loved it; the White House entourage had been dazzled. On the eve of the 75th anniversary of the D Day invasion the leader of the free world went to Portsmouth with the Queen and spoke of the joint sacrifice. At a news conference with Theresa May standing by his side, he declared the bond between the US and the UK as the "greatest alliance the world has ever known."

Past criticism from the President of Theresa May was also discarded by Mr Trump at this press gathering at the Foreign Office. Mrs May had done "a very good job" in getting the Brexit negotiations to this point, he declared and with unusual generosity added: "she's probably a better negotiator than I am." This president best known for glowering was now glowing.

Much of the praise for the smooth running of this potentially awkward State Visit was given to Sir Kim Darroch, Britain's ambassador to Washington. It was him who had liaised with the White House on a daily basis to work through the programme and the different meetings that would take place. Three weeks after the state visit Linda and I went for Saturday lunch with him and his wife Vanessa at the magnificent Lutyens residence, which is home to the ambassador on Massachusetts Avenue. There were a few other people there – another foreign ambassador and his wife, a couple of people from the Washington Post, one of my British counterparts. The night before he and another senior British official who had played a key role in the organisation of the trip had been at a party thrown by Kellyanne Conway, the president's closest and longest serving advisor, at her house to celebrate the success of the visit.

Shares in Darroch were at a high. His posting was due to end at the end of 2019, but he had been told he might be asked to stay on a little longer. We spoke of his plans for the future outside the civil service after 40 years as a public servant. As you might expect from Britain's most senior diplomat he is super smart, not in the least bit pompous, good fun (though fiercely competitive on a tennis court) – and he was looking forward to his summer holiday - going sailing in Cornwall where he and Vanessa have a cottage. Life was looking pretty damn peachy.

A week later the world looked a very different place. For reasons that are almost entirely to do with the toxic political debate over Brexit (there are many conspiracy theories), someone wanted Darroch compromised, and a more keenly pro-Brexit ambassador put in his place. The method by which this was to be achieved was malevolent. Unprecedented. Someone in the Foreign Office chose to leak a pile of Sir Kim's cables that he had sent back to a very restricted circulation list, recording his impression of the comings and goings in the Trump administration. It is the very definition of an ambassador's job: to analyse what is happening in a foreign government and how it might impact on the foreign policy goals of your own administration. An important part of that is feeding back to your government the latest gossip and intel – and of course to keep ministers and officials appraised of the way key policy discussions are unfolding. Diptels – or diplomatic telegrams – are most definitely NOT written for publication or wider dissemination.

Given the swirl of gossip you get about the administration, what Darroch had to say in his telegrams could on one level be seen as pretty benign. Trump's White House was 'dysfunctional' and would be likely to remain so. No shit, Sherlock, as some might say. The Iran policy was in disarray (a commonly held view in Washington). The Trump administration was inept. In one cable he wrote for his very limited audience of senior mandarins and ministers that "We don't really believe this administration is going to become substantially more normal; less dysfunctional; less faction riven; less diplomatically clumsy and inept." At any Washington cocktail party, you will hear people – some of them Trump administration members - using much more colourful language, telling far more lurid stories.

In the diplomatic world though, this wholesale leak of the British Ambassador's memos was an exceptional breach of security. The odd cable has very rarely found its way into the public domain – but the journalist who had been the recipient of the leak, Isabel Oakeshott – had been handed something altogether more explosive. She is someone who has close links to the uber-Brexiteers, Aaron Banks and Nigel Farage. She co-wrote a biography (with another leading Euro-sceptic Lord Ashcroft) of David Cameron. The Sunday Times would point out she was in a relationship with the leader of the Brexit Party, who categorically denied being involved in or handling the information. Foreign Office staff I spoke to in the immediate aftermath of the leak saw their fingerprints all over it.

When the embassy got wind on the Friday before that the story was to break in the *Mail on Sunday*, British diplomats contacted the White House and the State Department to forewarn them. Darroch was assured it would blow over; it was small beer and not that grievous. That came from the Chief of Staff, Mick Mulvaney, no less. But in this White House what officials might say and what the president will eventually do are two entirely different things. Balm offered up by an underling counts for nothing.

The president had three options on how to respond. The first was – quite simply - not to respond. Does the leader of the most powerful country in the world need to dignify the leaked comments of an anonymous ambassador reporting back to his ministers and masters? The second way to respond was with humour and irony: 'Oh so the masters of the Brexit ominshambles at Westminster think *my* administration is dysfunctional and inept?' It would have hit the bull's eye. And, of course, can you imagine the cables that the US Ambassador to the Court of St James has been sending back to Washington on the daily road-crash on government and parliament?

There was of course a third option. And given the gossamer like thinness of the President's skin when it comes to criticism, it was always the most likely - and that was to go ballistic. Yes, Donald Trump went utterly ballistic. At Kim Darroch. At Theresa May too; the woman he had been praising a month earlier at their joint news conference in London. Onto Twitter he went:

"I have been critical about the way the UK and Prime Minister Theresa My have handled Brexit. What a mess she and her representatives have created. I told her how it should be done, but she decided to go another way. I do not know the Ambassador, but he is not liked or well thought of within the US. We will no longer deal with him."

No longer deal with him? Wasn't that in effect declaring Sir Kim *persona non grata*? Wasn't that the US more or less telling the UK who it could have as an ambassador? As the head of the Foreign Office, Sir Simon McDonald told MPs he knew of no precedent – even from unfriendly countries at difficult times to say such a thing. So much for the endlessly vaunted 'special relationship'; so much for the laying out of the red carpet, the piling on of royal charm; the ingratiating. It counted for nothing.

Sir Kim had been invited to a dinner that evening that the president would be at; he was promptly disinvited. Liam Fox was in the city. A meeting with Ivanka Trump that the Ambassador would normally have attended to, Sir Kim stayed away from. The calculation was – let the storm pass, and steer the ship into calmer waters. But Donald Trump wasn't done. He followed his first broadside with another. Sir Kim was 'wacky', 'pompous', and 'very stupid'.

When Boris Johnson, at that stage the runaway favourite to become Britain's next prime-minister failed to back Sir Kim, despite being asked four times to do so in a TV Conservative Party leadership debate, Britain's ambassador threw in the towel. A man who had served his country for over four decades, operating under governments of all political stripes, arguing against Brexit when it was British government policy to stay in the EU, and presenting the case for Theresa May's deal to leave once it had been negotiated had been ousted by a US president who wouldn't or couldn't turn the other cheek.

And then with an insouciance that you can only marvel at, Donald Trump, two days after he had brought about Sir Kim's demise said to reporters 'I wish the British Ambassador well. Someone just told me [that he had resigned] – too bad – but they said he actually said very good things about me.'

Not only is Donald Trump changing the way that America is governed, he is challenging the liberal democratic institutions (American and foreign) that have been built up over decades, and which depend on certain norms of behaviour. He is the norm shatterer *par excellence* – thrilling his supporters and terrifying opponents. Won't any ambassador to the US now think twice before committing unvarnished thoughts to paper about what is happening in the US, and about the way Donald Trump is governing? It's not just that he is behaving differently from any president who has gone before him, he is forcing other governments to wonder, to fret about how they need to behave towards him; whether their institutional apparatuses are any longer fit for purpose.

He can scent weakness from a mile away, and Britain needing a post-Brexit trade deal was just such an animal. Kim Darroch, a lifelong public servant, was its victim. The old rules are no longer Trump's rules.

This is a tale of two Kims, and it is instructive on a wider level. North Korea's Kim Jong-un, the leader of one of the most brutal regimes in the world today, with the worst human rights record, where citizens have been starved to death, is venerated for his toughness and wiliness; Kim Darroch, lifelong public servant, drawing a government salary from Europe's most enduring democracy, is to be torn to shreds. Leaders from the old democracies and America's historic partners and allies seem to fare a lot worse under this president than strong-men dictators and tyrants.

The chaos, the dysfunction, the totally unexpected, the endless bareknuckle fights and the unorthodox behaviour are what is the norm. When I was a child I loved watching *Batman*, where it always ended with the caped crusader and Robin facing imminent death – and you came away thinking there's no way they could escape from this, but miraculously in the next episode they somehow wriggle away. It often feels like that with this president. Or maybe if I am going back through my television watching childhood it is more the

*Wacky Races*. The Dick Dastardly *de nos jours* careering along some mountain road, crashing into other vehicles, brakes failing, the wheels about to fall off, body parts crumpled, the engine about to seize, black smoke belching out of the exhaust pipe – but somehow not only does the vehicle keep going, it often emerges as the winner, and out steps Donald Trump, hair unruffled and that half smile, half smirk firmly in place.

It is noisy and unrelenting, defying norms and convention, and paying no heed to history. And with seemingly implausible plot lines, all played out as if a made for TV spectacular. John F. Kennedy was described as the first president of the television age. Donald Trump is his own television director. And, make no mistake, he likes any drama that he is at the centre of. For this is a president who revels in the column inches and headlines devoted to him. The only thing worse than being talked about, it seems, is not being talked about.

Whether – like me – you are reporting on this president, or you are working within the administration to make a success of his term in office, or working to speed his downfall, or just an interested observer, it feels like we are halfway through the second season of a six series box set. But without any idea how the show can possibly go on for another four and a half seasons. I mean, what plot twists are left? 'Surely it can't carry on like this?' is the repeated refrain at Washington cocktail parties. But it does. And, in all likelihood, it will.

When speaking at a literary festival a little while ago, I was amused by a question from a young man who was the president of his students' union. (Many moons ago I had been the president of mine.) He wanted to know whether anything

I had done then as a student politician had prepared me for covering the Trump administration today. I replied – only half jokingly – that nothing in 35-plus years in journalism had prepared me for what we were seeing and reporting on.

And like any well-staged drama, there are a series of intriguing, complex characters, and a series of locations – rooms and buildings and places where the drama unfolds: the Oval Office, the Cabinet Room, the Briefing Room, the East Wing, on Air Force One, the Supreme Court – and most critically the Federal building where the publicity averse Special Counsel, Robert Mueller, went about his investigation into the president. As a BBC reporter my focus is on the main story, the one event that stands out above the others. Invariably, it is all about the President – the latest thing he has said or done. But every day there are intriguing sub-plots and twists, with a cast of characters that is every bit as unbelievable as the President himself. The former governor of New Jersey and confidant of the President, Chris Christie, wrote in a memoir that Trump has a 'revolving door of deeply flawed individuals – amateurs, grifters, weaklings, convicted and unconvicted felons'.

In Lin-Manuel Miranda's masterpiece *Hamilton* – a rap musical about the Founding Fathers of the US and the jostling for power within the fledgeling republic – one of the songs in the second act is 'The Room Where It Happens'. It is an ode to power: of the fear of being an outsider, of the need always to be in the room where the action is happening, where decisions are being made. This book will take you into the key rooms in the White House and buildings in Washington where power is fought for, bargained away and occasionally squandered; where the battles have raged, where his inner circle have pushed back against this unique president, and where sometimes they have conspired to circumvent him and thwart him too. And the terrible attrition rate of those in this administration who have been chewed up and spat out. As the refrain from the song goes: 'You've got to be in the room where it happens.'

# Chapter 1

# The Oval Office

Donald Trump loves the Oval Office. It satisfies him on every level: its storied history; its familiarity; its unmistakable symbolism as the epicentre of power – *world* power. We know that the British prime minister works out of Number 10, and the French president the Elysée Palace, and that Vladimir Putin has the Kremlin – but in any of those cases do we know *where* in those buildings they work? In Washington we know the exact bit of the floorplan where the president is based – his offices are the West Wing, and the name of the room he occupies: 'the Oval Office'. And in January 2017, improbably, it became Donald Trump's. For a man who is big on being given due respect, it says 'I've made it.' For a man who never likes to lose, it also says 'I won. I beat her.' And for the property man from Queen's – who always had to prove himself to his demanding and difficult father, and who, among the Manhattan elite was never quite accepted – it said 'Look at me now.' All of this is encapsulated in a story I heard from a senior aide. He had been with Trump in New York soon after he took office. They were sitting in 'the

Beast', the President's armoured Cadillac. The only vehicles on the normally heavily congested West Side Highway, that runs up along the Hudson river, were part of his motorcade. A path had been cleared for the President. Trump turns to his senior aide and says, 'Mark Zuckerberg wouldn't get this.' The brash, braggadocious outsider now had a four-year tenancy agreement – which, who knows, may be extendable to an eight-year one – on the Oval Office, the most famous piece of real estate in the whole of the United States, and perhaps the world.

The Oval Office first became oval in 1909. Until then it had been a round office, used by the secretary to the president (the position now referred to as Chief of Staff). The president had tended to work out of the residence – in the room that is now the Lincoln Bedroom. The first president to install himself in the West Wing was Theodore Roosevelt. But it was the 27th president, William Taft, who brought in the builders to turn it into an oval shape. It measures approximately 34 feet by 27.

Anyway, to press the fast forward button, fire ravaged the West Wing in 1929, gutting the original Oval Office – and much of the rest of the building. Franklin Delano Roosevelt oversaw renovations and he moved the Oval Office to the south-east corner – building on what was the laundry drying yard. History doesn't recall where the presidential underwear and damask tablecloths billowed in the breeze after that. The advantage of placing the Oval Office there was that it had much better light – looking out onto the Rose Garden – with windows facing to the east as well as south. And when your staff were driving you mad, it was easy to walk back to the residence in the East Wing.

Since its completion in 1934 the office has changed very little. Except in the way it is furnished, the room is the same. There are three large windows looking out onto the gardens at one end of the room and a door which opens onto the Colonnade linking the East and West Wings. At the far end of the room, opposite the presidential desk, is the fireplace. And that is where you will see the two armchairs, in one of which sits the president and in the other a visiting head of state as they chat in a somewhat stilted manner with the cameras clicking and a mass of microphones seeking to record the conversation between the two. We call this a 'pool spray'. Either side of the fireplace there are two doors, linking to outer offices. Set into the ceiling is the Presidential Seal.

An incoming president can choose the curtains and the oval rug, and what paintings to hang. Even what desk to use. John F. Kennedy's new décor was just being installed on the day he was assassinated. Barack Obama caused controversy with the British when he had a Jacob Epstein bust of Winston Churchill removed, to be replaced with one of Martin Luther King Jr.

When Donald Trump moved into the White House, the Churchill bust was restored to the Oval Office. Also moving in, at Donald Trump's insistence, was a portrait of the 17th president of the United States, Andrew Jackson – someone the 45th president seems to have an affinity with. When the remark is made that politics has never been so dirty, those making that assertion would do well to look back at the 1828 presidential election, in which Jackson defeated the incumbent, John Quincy Adams. 'Old Hickory', as Jackson was known, was described at the time as bullish, defensive, quick-tempered, thin-skinned, a populist and unfit to govern.

He felt that the world was against him, and that he was looked down on by the ruling élites. Jackson would talk about putting American interests first and warned against 'alien enemies'. Sound familiar? That said, so far (at time of writing!) Donald Trump hasn't killed anyone in a duel – as Jackson did.

The 45th president has replaced the carpet and brought in the rug designed by Nancy Reagan when her husband was president; the curtains now hanging were first used by Bill Clinton, and Mr Trump hasn't yet changed the beige and cream stripy wallpaper that Obama had installed. And the President is still sitting behind the Resolute desk, a gift to the American people from Queen Victoria – it is made from the timbers of HMS *Resolute*, which once upon a time patrolled the Arctic. Behind the desk on an occasional table are two photographs. One is of his mother, Mary, who came to the US from Scotland – and the other is of his father Fred. Aside from that – for the first year or so – there were few personal touches. A far cry from his cluttered office in Trump Tower, piled high with papers and walls decorated with magazine covers – all of which have one thing in common: they all have photographs of him on the front.

The other thing about the room – and it might sound counter-intuitive to say so given the grave global crises that have played out from the Oval Office over the decades – is that it feels like a place of serenity. Obviously more so when it is empty. Light streams in through the windows and you look out onto the wonderfully landscaped gardens with mature magnolia and crab apple trees, and beautiful lawns that go down to the ellipse and then on to the Washington Monument. It can feel more like the elegant drawing room of an upscale country house than the crackling nerve centre of global power.

One former aide to George W. Bush told me that one of the really intimidating things about the room was the imposing grandfather clock – a Seymour long case clock, built at the end of the eighteenth century – which ticks very loudly. If you are there presenting some argument on why the president should do this or that, and you know your time is extremely limited, that clock had a way of unsettling you. Not helped by President Bush being an impatient man. When you were in a meeting with him, and Marine One, the presidential helicopter, landed on the lawn he was wont to say with a twinkle in his eye, 'My ride's waiting for me. You'd better hurry.'

When Donald Trump speaks to acquaintances on the phone, or meets new people he wants to impress, one of the first things he will ask is, 'Have you visited the Oval Office?' If your answer is no, he will invite you. And who doesn't want to go to the Oval Office? One well-known American CEO who received the invitation, told me that when he was arranging the visit a White House staffer advised him to bring someone else along with him. The counsel was unusual – better to have a witness with you who can back up your account of the meeting, in case the President makes claims about it you don't recognise. Another corporate titan told me how the President was almost childlike in his excitement at showing him his new office. 'Can you believe I'm here?' he asked his guest in wide-eyed wonderment.

He also likes to show off the power that is at the fingertips of the Commander in Chief. On one occasion when the press was allowed in, the President had been due to take a call from the then Mexican president, Enrique Pena Nieto. We had been called in to witness what was meant to herald the start of a new chapter in trade between the US and Mexico. The cameras rolled, the President looked at the speakerphone, and this happened.

President Trump presses a button on his phone, and after waiting a moment, says 'Enrique?' There's more silence, followed by Trump telling someone off camera, 'You can hook him up.' That is then followed by more dead air – Trump says 'Tell me when' to the mysterious, out-of-vision person – and then more awkward silence. 'It's a big thing, a lot of people waiting,' Trump says. More buttons are pressed. He says 'Hello?' multiple times. Eventually he suggests people 'be helpful'. And then someone comes over to help, who, miraculously, is able to properly set up the speakerphone and the call begins. As these things tend to, it went viral on the internet.

The one button that Donald Trump knows how to work is housed in a small wooden box on the Resolute desk. It is the red button. And as he has noted wryly, it can cause guests some anxiety when he moves to press it. However, this is not an order to launch nuclear Armageddon. It is a call to one of the White House butlers that the Commander in Chief is in need of another Diet Coke. The President is famously teetotal, having seen the damage that booze did to his brother, who died an alcoholic in 1981. And he is also famously un-famous for being self-deprecating, but he did crack a joke over what his relationship might have been with alcohol: 'I'm not a drinker. I can honestly say I never had a beer in my life. OK? It's one of my only good traits. I don't drink. Whenever they're looking for something good, I say, "I never had a glass of alcohol." I've never had alcohol … Can you imagine if I had, what a mess I'd be?' But Diet Coke he can't get enough of – apparently drinking up to 12 cans a day.

Something else that I have picked up from any number is how well he treats the foot soldiers who work at the White House. Not so much his generals. There was a telling moment when the President was doing an interview with one of the US networks in the Oval Office,. His acting chief of staff, Mick Mulvaney, has a cough, and out of vision he splutters a few times. It is barely picked up by the microphones. But Trump stops the recording and berates Mulvaney, telling him to get out. "I don't like that you know," says the President. "If you're going to cough, please leave the room. You just can't. You just can't cough." And shaking his head adds "boy oh boy." The most senior official in the White House skulks off, tail between his legs, publicly reproached and humiliated. It was a vivid example of what it must be like to serve this President.

But the lowlier staff? Well they can't speak highly enough of the Trumps. He remembers people's names, is appreciative when things are done for him, asks how they're doing – and I have heard from ordinary household staff that he and the First Lady are much easier to work for than the Obamas, who were apparently never at ease with all the flunkies around. The most junior staff, the housekeepers and gardeners get the politeness and the respect that his most senior officials don't.

I don't know whether logs are kept for the sheer numbers who have visited Donald Trump in the Oval Office, but I would wager under this president it has been more than under any other. 1600 Pennsylvania Avenue is the People's House, and to his great credit he likes to throw open its doors – even if on occasion it is with slightly chaotic results.

There have been the visiting heads of state. When Angela Merkel came for her first visit since Donald Trump took over, he just scowled at the woman who had been Barack Obama's closest ally. And when she leans over to him, as camera shutters click and TV cameras record the moment, and says, *sotto voce*, 'Should we shake hands?' Donald Trump ignores her and keeps his hands firmly between his legs, palms planted together, fingers out straight. He clearly has no intention of going near his German guest.

With Emmanuel Macron, the French president, the body language couldn't have been more playful – you almost felt like saying, 'Get a room.' Donald Trump struck up an early rapport with him, and he was afforded the first state visit of this presidency. Mr Trump summoned up his inner European, and everywhere you looked he was kissing M. Macron on both cheeks (goodness knows what his macho, not ever so metrosexual, redneck base made of that). They had arms round each other. But there was also – unmistakably – the assertion of seniority by the US president. As they stood together in the Oval Office, Mr Trump started picking dandruff off the French president's lapel. 'In fact, I'll get that little piece of dandruff off – you have a little piece. We have to make him perfect. He is perfect.' If there were any silverback gorillas watching their flat-screen TVs in the forests of sub-Saharan Africa they'd have said, 'You see, those humans aren't so very different from us.' Stephen Colbert, the late night TV satirist, would joke that it wasn't dandruff. 'After two days in Donald Trump's company,' he said, 'it was cocaine.'

And can you imagine the preparation that goes into these meetings for the visiting head of state? What you might be asked, where the president might try to blindside you. When Portugal's president, Marcelo Rebelo de Sousa, came to call on Donald Trump in the Oval Office, what was the subject of discussion? Cristiano Ronaldo. The President wanted to know on behalf of his son Barron how good a footballer he was. The best, his Portuguese visitor confirmed. And then Mr Trump asked whether he thought Ronaldo would ever run for office against him. White House staff always prepare briefing notes for the President ahead of these meetings, complete with talking points – and Mr Trump rarely, if ever, looks at them. Many guests leave utterly bewildered.

Though something extremely unusual happened in October 2018. Into the Oval Office swept the rapper, Kanye West. And it was full Kanye. Over a period of ten minutes he went on a rambling soliloquy, covering such subjects as space, race, his favourite comic book hero – and not letting President Trump get a word in edgeways. The Trump show had been superseded. I was in the office when I got the first 'pool report' from the meeting – this comes from one of the small group of journalists, rotating on a daily basis, who cover the President when he is holding a meeting in his office. These are the scribbled notes taken down while the talks are taking place, and is a sort of 'heads up' to newsrooms before the full audio and video is played out.

This 'pooler' noted: 'Kanye went on extended monologues, banged on Resolute desk many times. Says his MAGA [Make America Great Again] hat makes him feel like "Superman". Says "bullshit" and calls himself a "motherfucker". Hugs Trump and says "I love you."' I am going to hazard a guess: this is the first time in the course of an Oval Office meeting that a pool report has included the word 'motherfucker'. And another guess: there's never been a meeting like that one.

The week that Kanye came to call ended equally unortho-doxly with the visit of an evangelical pastor, who had just been freed from a Turkish prison. He had become a *cause célèbre*, and Donald Trump had made strenuous efforts to get him freed, mindful no doubt of the importance of the evangelical vote in getting him elected. Sitting in one of the yellow chairs normally reserved for visiting heads of state, Pastor Andrew Brunson – TV cameras rolling, naturally – knelt down, put his left arm round the president's back and prayed. He asked for God to give Donald Trump 'supernatural wisdom' and to 'protect him from slander from enemies'. In the course of three days we had run the gamut in the Oval Office from the profane to the sacred. From 'mofos' to supernatural wisdom. Neither particularly normal.

OK, there was that time when Elvis Presley just pitched up at the door of the White House in 1970, high on drugs, and asked to see the president. Yes, that was pretty crazy too. Elvis arrived in a purple velvet suit, gold belt, and carrying a Colt 45 revolver, and a letter. 'I have done an in-depth study of drug abuse and Communist brainwashing techniques and I am right in the middle of the whole thing where I can and will do the most good,' the then 35-year-old singer wrote. 'I would love to meet you just to say hello if you're not too busy.' Nixon, then not yet tainted by Watergate, was riding high having promised to bring American troops home from Vietnam, and to desegregate schools. Elvis was on a big comeback, and was selling out wherever he went. So, the two men met.

No actual transcript of the meeting exists in the archive, though President Nixon agreed that Elvis could be a force for good in the war on drugs; Elvis, who collected badges, wanted one that declared he was a narcotics agent at large. A memo was drawn up by a Nixon aide who'd been in attendance, and it noted there was one important respect where Elvis was seeking to undermine one of the cultural ties of the special relationship between the US and UK. 'Presley indicated that he thought the Beatles had been a real force for anti-American spirit. He said that the Beatles came to this country, made their money, and then returned to England where they promoted an anti-American theme. The President nodded in agreement and expressed some surprise.'

I noted earlier that I suspect records will show no president has had so many visitors to the Oval Office as Donald Trump; equally I suspect no president will have had the television cameras in the Oval Office as often. Hardly a day seems to go by without some iteration of the Trump show, the Trump circus. Sports stars, celebrities, Kim Kardashian pushing criminal justice reform, unknowns with poignant stories to tell, traffic cops, servicemen, people of faith, people of none. The President will sit behind the Resolute desk, they will congregate behind – and Donald Trump will make sure that every visitor gets the photograph of their dreams to go with it. The days when the 45th president goes off the grid are few and far between.

Early on in Donald Trump's presidency, a friend from a rival news organisation went to interview the President. They had received an invitation to interview him in the Oval Office. Or they thought they had. Bosses flew in. The Washington correspondent was there to meet them. But when they got to the security gate on Pennsylvania Avenue, there was no record of an appointment. The rain was hammering down, and if the system says there's no scheduled meeting, you don't get in through the gate, and that in turn means there is nowhere to take cover. So they got wetter and wetter. Other news organisations have experienced similar things.

Staff in the White House seemed vaguely aware of the interview, but no one seemed to know who had authorised it. Certainly, the press office and the communications team didn't have anything written down. Nothing was joined up. Eventually they were told to come in. They were told they would be able to see Mike Pence, and he would seek to find out if they might get a word with the President himself. Eventually they go into the Oval Office, and not only does the President agree to be interviewed, it will be on the record. No one has discussed with him subject matters, areas of interest, subjects that might be out of bounds. There had been no talk within the White House itself of what *they* wanted to get out of the discussion. Or even why they were doing the interview. Strategy? There was none.

When I interviewed President Obama in 2015, we had had pre-meetings with his staff about the ground we might cover and why it would be good for him to be interviewed by the BBC, rather than one of the American networks. The President was about to go on a trip to Africa, and the BBC World Service has a particularly strong reach in Africa with its English language broadcasts, and its Somali and Swahili service. It was agreed that questioning would start with Africa, but after that I could go where I wanted. It was also agreed that clips of the interview would go out immediately, but the whole interview would be embargoed to coincide with African breakfast shows – a source of huge irritation to the American broadcasters.

One other extraordinary difference worth noting: when I interviewed President Obama, the only other people in the room from the White House were the President's press secretary, Josh Earnest, a junior press officer, and a rather large secret service officer. When journalists conducted their interviews with President Trump, there would be the journalists from the media outlet – but that wasn't all. Virtually every senior White House staffer would find reason to be there. The Chief of Staff, the Press Secretary, the Communications Director, the Treasury Secretary, the Director of Strategy, the Chief Economic Advisor, the Staff Secretary (and probably the gardener, the cook and chief bottle washer too). And others. It would be standing room only.

In this disorderly White House, the only way to find out what the President is thinking on any given day is to be in the room as he speaks; and in a chaotic White House, with a president who can change his mind fundamentally on any given issue, you also wanted to be the *last* person in the room. So, meetings would come to an end, and the participants would gather up their papers incredibly slowly; they would find a reason not to leave their chair, and as everyone else filed out they would try to be the last person to cup their hand over the President's ear – and seek to influence his thinking. It was musical chairs without the music.

On one occasion when the President was giving one of these 'standing room only' interviews, the presidential diary had started to fall apart. A large group of US Navy submariners had been invited into the Oval Office to meet the President. The corridors of the West Wing are decidedly cramped and pokey, so they were shown straight in while the interview was going on. Now in the Oval Office you had the President, a group of journalists with notepads poised, the entire senior staff of the White House – and a couple of dozen sailors. They stood patiently in their dress uniforms, and probably vowed never again to complain about space being cramped underneath the oceans in their nuclear submarine.

This was a White House largely without rules, largely without structure. One person who'd been in the Oval for a meeting with the President wrote in an email afterwards: 'I saw twenty different people. Omarosa came by; Tiffany Trump was there. Bannon, Priebus, Kushner. Everyone. People walked in and out like it was a shopping mall. There was no paper trail of who had said what to whom. There were no appointments. No diary. There was no formal minuting. People just came and went.'

Omarosa Manigault Newton (though she was only ever known as Omarosa) was one of the more colourful characters in this crazy set-up. She had been appointed to a senior position at the White House on the basis of ... err – well, no one was quite sure what, other than – at that time – a ferocious loyalty to the boss. She had first come to public attention as a contestant on *The Apprentice* and had many Trump-like qualities. In the show she displayed cunning aplenty, chutzpah galore and brashness by the bucketload. But policy expertise? Political acumen? Knowledge of the inner workings of government? Not so much. She was also African American in a White House that was, well, very white. Tall and physically quite imposing, she also sensed that her tenure would be relatively short – if ever you were going to put money on someone flaming in and flaming out it would be on her. And so she made a habit of secretly recording her conversations with other senior staff. It made for great listening when eventually – and inevitably – she was fired.

And with a firing comes a book. Omarosa's account of life in the White House has a glorious story of her walking into the Oval Office to find the President and his then personal lawyer, Michael Cohen, locked in conversation. He is the man who facilitated the $130,000 payment to buy the silence of a former porn star who wanted to sell her story of an alleged affair with Donald Trump. Something the President has always denied. According to Omarosa, the moment the President saw her he stuffed the piece of paper he was reading into his mouth and started eating it. 'Since Trump was ever the germaphobe, I was shocked he appeared to be chewing and swallowing the paper. It must have been something very, very sensitive.' That story, I should add, has been denied. Michael Cohen said it did not happen. The White House said the book was riddled with lies.

But there was no doubting the veracity of the call that President Trump made to her just after she had been fired. It is almost funny, as the President seeks to feign ignorance about the circumstances of her dismissal by the then chief of staff, John Kelly. Or of the conversation she recorded with General Kelly as she was being fired. That conversation really did seem to hold out the prospect of work for her on any future Trump campaign if she kept her mouth shut and didn't make waves. She chose waves.

But if she was eccentric, many of the other staff inside the White House were part of distinct power bases. In any

'court' there will be different factions, different groups jock-
eying for power or prestige. That is politics. But it seemed
in this White House – at least in the early days – all the
senior staff mistrusted each other. There were rival groupings, which would occasionally overlap. Broadly it shook
down into three groupings. First there were the 'more Trump
than Trump radicals'. This was the grouping led by Steve
Bannon, the populist, provocateur, economic nationalist –
and supposedly the brains of Trumpism. And also Donald
Trump's young speech writer, Stephen Miller – a man who
was particularly keen on the crackdown on immigration –
has been a significant force.

Then there were the orthodox Republicans, who, though
they had their misgivings about Donald Trump's brand of
populism, wanted to help him deliver economic reform,
reverse Obama-era health policies, and ensure proper
conservatives would fill vacant court positions. Their obvious
leader was the Vice-President – the pro-life, anti-abortion,
socially conservative evangelical, Mike Pence.

Finally, there was the Wall St/New York/globalist gang.
They were internationalist, free-marketers, and deeply antagonistic to the President's views on tariffs and trade, and
socially quite liberal too. There was a raft of people who
had joined the administration with Wall Street backgrounds –
Steve Mnuchin, the Treasury Secretary, Gary Cohn, the head
of the National Economic Council, and Dina Powell, who
was Deputy National Security Advisor, were all graduates
of the Goldman executive floor. The president's daughter
Ivanka and her orthodox Jewish husband Jared – both of
whom were appointed to senior White House positions
(remember this US presidency still has many of the charac-

teristics of a family run business) – were also at the forefront of this grouping.

Incidentally, Jared and Ivanka's observance of the Jewish Sabbath was an opportunity not to be missed in this scheming, conniving court. They have been cast – and cast themselves – as one of the restraining influences on the President. They were the brake as he wanted to put his foot on the accelerator. They are family and can therefore say things to him that others dare not say. But from sundown on Friday to sundown on Saturday they are out of the loop. Their mobile phones are switched off. In the early months of the Trump presidency some of the most controversial things that happened – the signing of the executive order banning travellers from mainly Muslim countries, the accusation that Barack Obama had tapped Trump Tower, the President's bizarre self-aggrandising speech at CIA headquarters – all happened during Shabbat. As the *Huffington Post* noted – when the Jews are away, Steve Bannon can play.

In the early stages it was a White House where everyone was leaking and briefing against each other. Sieves look like positively robust and solid structures when compared to the administration in these formative months. Sometimes transcripts of whole conversations would emerge – as happened with a call between the then Australian prime minister Malcolm Turnbull and the President. After the Russian foreign minister Sergei Lavrov visited the White House the official minute of that meeting emerged in its entirety. Everyone inside the building condemned the leaking, while carrying on leaking prodigiously.

One of the communications professionals brought in to help deliver the Trump revolution was a man called Cliff

Sims. Like Omarosa he would depart, and like Omarosa he would write a memoir of his five hundred days there. Its title tells you everything you need to know. It was called *Team of Vipers*. In an article he wrote for *Vanity Fair* he noted: 'The inner circle of Trumpworld was not always a pretty picture. Too often, it was a portrait of venality, stubbornness, and selfishness. We leaked. We schemed. We backstabbed. Some of us told ourselves it was all done in the service of a higher calling – to protect the president, to deliver for the people. But usually it was for ourselves.' And he went on: 'Lincoln famously had his Team of Rivals. Trump had his Team of Vipers. We served. We fought. We brought our egos. We brought our personal agendas and vendettas. We were ruthless. And some of us, I assume, were good people.'

Sims recalls a meeting with the President where Trump asked him to draw up a list of the people who were leaking, and those who were loyal. It wasn't that simple: there were leakers who were also loyal. And don't forget one important point: when you read in an article that 'a source close to the president has told us ...' – who do you think that might be? This is the most media savvy and media obsessed president there has ever been. You think he doesn't leak?

In a way that's how the President likes it. He is a non-politician, unused to and impatient of the boring and plodding ways of bureaucratic committee structures and inter-agency cooperation: working groups reporting to subcommittees, subcommittees funnelling up their findings to full committees, minutes prepared and signed as a true and correct record. Dotted lines, straight lines, direct reports, organograms were not his thing. This is not who Donald Trump is. He is an irascible alpha-male who barks orders, and expects people to act accordingly. Nor is he a military man, with a strong sense of the chain of command. He does what he wants. Even when discussions have taken place and agreements reached, he'll still feel free to undercut them. He will do things his way. People can be in favour one day, and languishing in the Siberian wastes the next. He will say things that make officials wince. He will routinely ignore advice. He will not be corralled. And that unorthodox, devil may care, screw the rest of you, take a poke in the eye approach is what fires up his base.

And one other important thing: he doesn't often read the briefing documents presented to him by his Cabinet officers and White House staff. His attention span is limited. He is easily bored, and very easily distracted. In meetings the TV is often on in the background – *Fox News* naturally. Sims tells of another occasion when the Speaker of the House, Paul Ryan, was briefing the President on the complex plans to reform healthcare in the US. After 15 minutes Donald Trump spent a brief time staring out of the window, and then stood up without saying a word and walked out of the room and into his adjacent private dining room where he has installed a giant, flat screen TV on the wall, and sat down and turned the television on. Meeting over, Mr Speaker. Briefing papers are kept, well, extremely brief. A paper prepared for the President will ideally be one sheet of A4, with bullet points, diagrams and pictures. Officials talk about giving him the Reader's Digest version of events.

The President's second National Security Advisor was a bald-headed, thickset general, H.R. McMaster. He was a warrior (the President loved that), and an academic (the President was less impressed by that). And H.R. McMaster liked to do things by the book, and do things formally. Before giving the President a recommendation, the carefully prepared paper would first go into the background, setting a historical context of the issue, then he would give an overview of the different options, the pros and cons, the risks and advantages. And eventually he would reach his conclusion and tell the President of his recommendation. It drove Donald Trump nuts. They never hit it off, and stories would keep on emerging of Trump becoming increasingly frustrated with McMaster during meetings. He droned on too long and was too rigid in his thinking, the President would tell friends. In one instance, when McMaster entered the Oval Office over the summer, Trump complained that he had already seen him that day.

The *Washington Post* put it thus: 'President Trump consumes classified intelligence like he does most everything else in life: ravenously and impatiently, eager to ingest glinting nuggets but often indifferent to subtleties.' And so new ways were devised to communicate the nation's secrets to the Commander in Chief. Dreary, formal documents, with appendices and referencing, now had maps, charts and pictures. There were videos, as well as 'killer graphics', as the then CIA Director, Mike Pompeo, put it. 'That's our task, right? To deliver the material in a way that he can best understand the information we're trying to communicate.'

Chris Christie recounts an occasion during the presidential campaign when they were meeting to prepare for one of the debates, when a new member of the team put a four-inch thick binder in front of where Trump would be sitting at his luxury Florida Gold Coast retreat. Christie asked what it was. The earnest staffer told him it was detailed research on every topic that might come up, lines to take, background research, historical context, facts and figures. Weeks of work had gone into it. Christie told him it was destined to become the most extensively researched coaster in the history of Mar-a-Lago. A few minutes later Trump came in, sat down, ordered breakfast and, sure enough, when his orange juice arrived, he took it from the waitress and plonked it on top of the binder – and never once peered inside at its contents. Christie had been right.

But because Trump doesn't like to read, don't mistake that for him not wanting to learn. What he loves to do is talk. Chatter to endless people – many nothing to do with the administration – to bounce ideas off, to be challenged – occasionally, to hear what people are thinking on the outside – often calls that are conducted in the evening when he is back in the residence, on his old unencrypted Blackberry – a source of constant worry to his security people.

And for all the chaos, don't think that means important decisions aren't being made. Donald Trump loves to brandish his Sharpie to sign some new executive order that will hack away at the thicket of Obama era regulation and red tape that – to his mind – has stopped industry producing and growing. Bans on building pipelines, forget it. He even issued an executive order making it a requirement for government departments to cut two regulations for every one they introduced. It is from the Oval Office that he signed the Tax Cuts and Jobs Act, a sweeping legislative change that saw corporations being given big tax cuts, and gave a massive sugar rush to the US economy. That was his signature legislative achievement. It was also the marquee achievement of his chief economic advisor, Gary Cohn, who has told friends that the key to success was giving Donald Trump only four key bullet points about the legislation (and no more); and ensuring he was away in Asia during the two vital weeks when Congress was considering it.

As befitting a man who is not exactly a stickler for orthodoxy, on all manner of issues over the years Donald Trump has flipped and flopped. He is not what you would call ideologically rigid; indeed, he prides himself on his almost contortionist-like dexterity. He has been pro-choice for women and their right to have an abortion, and is now ardently pro-life. He has given money to Democrats and given money to Republicans; he has supported an NHS style health system, and sought to undo anything that smacks of socialised healthcare. He has seemed to back gun control, only to change his mind a day or two later. He can march purposefully in one direction, and then turn through 180 degrees without so much as blushing or breaking step.

But on one thing he has been utterly consistent: his belief that globalisation and free trade have invariably been at the expense of the American worker. If American manufacturing jobs have gone abroad, that is the reason; if coal mining is in decline; if steel mills are shuttered; if factories are mothballed; if companies have gone offshore, that is where the finger of blame should point. At rallies during the election campaign he called it a 'politician made disaster'. None of it was down to increased investment from abroad, cheaper labour or increasing automation – it was all the fault of the politicians who went before him, and who had allowed themselves to be mugged in trade deals by smarter, savvier opponents: 'the consequence of a leadership class that worships globalism over Americanism', he would tell audiences.

He will not be budged from the view that if there is a trade deficit, it is because America has been swindled. His economic worldview is of a zero-sum game. There are no win-wins. There are only winners and losers. The North Atlantic Free Trade Agreement, which has transformed trade between Mexico, Canada and the US? A con. Trans Pacific Partnership? Don't go near it. And the reason is that all his predecessors and their trade negotiators and commerce secretaries were idiots, and only he can be trusted to do the deals that will put that right. And he is an economic nationalist. His job is to protect the American worker, to stop companies moving offshore. And for the first year of his presidency, battle raged in the White House between the 'Wall Street brigade' and the 'protectionist insurgency'. The Sharks and the Jets – all that was missing was a score by Leonard Bernstein.

Gary Cohn, the former top man at Goldman Sachs and at the White House heading the National Economic Council, would try on a near weekly basis to school the President on the structural shifts in the US economy. It had moved – as most of the advanced societies had – away from manufacturing to a service economy. He dealt in facts, charts and detailed numbers to show that deficits were not automatically a bad thing. He led the Wall Street free traders. The old joke is that if you put twelve economists in the room you will come out with thirteen different opinions. But about 99.999% of economists would agree about the importance of free trade to global business and stable economic growth. In Peter Navarro, the President had found that rare 0.001%. He stands way outside the academic mainstream. As an academic who loathed free trade as much as the President, he saw his job very clearly: 'This is the president's vision, my function really as an economist is to try to provide the underlying analytics that confirm his intuition. And his intuition is always right in these matters.' Navarro, who earned a PhD in economics from Harvard was now the director of the White House National Trade Council. And he headed up the 'protectionist insurgency'.

If this is a circus, Donald Trump sees himself as the charismatic, brilliant master of ceremonies. The person who, when he is in the arena, will always be directly under the spotlight, centre stage. The ringmaster. The greatest showman on earth. A modern P.T. Barnum – the impresario who, incidentally, also flirted with politics, spending two terms as a Republican congressman in the Connecticut legislature in the nineteenth century. And though the phrase 'fake news' is distinctly twenty-first century, Barnum liked creating his own hoaxes and designing his own reality. In 1842 he spoke of having discovered an exotic new creature – the Feejee – an animal with the head of a monkey and the body of a mermaid. When asked about his somewhat tenuous relationship with the truth, Barnum said that his claims were advertisements to draw attention to his museum. 'I don't believe in duping the public,' he claimed, 'but I believe in first attracting and then pleasing them.' Some things just seem to echo down the ages.

But not all those who worked most closely with the President saw him in the same light. They accepted that they must never try to steal his limelight – that was a sure-fire way of being evicted from the circus – but they balked not only at the way this president would take decisions and make policy, but often they were horrified at the policy decisions themselves. And so the central guiding narrative of this exceptional administration has been the battle between a president who sees himself as the all-powerful ringmaster; and those around him who see their role as akin to the circus's lion tamers. A battle of wills. A fearsome, untamed, king of the jungle versus the cunning of those who want to suborn the animal to their will.

All of us who cover the White House on a daily basis know about the different factions, and the all-out battles on policy that have been waged. Early on I was told that among the so-called 'adults' (that equates to the generals McMaster, Kelly and Mattis, and the Wall Street wing – represented by Cohn and deputy national security advisor Dina Powell – and others more junior) there was an agreed policy that there could never be a time when all were out of Washington at the same time. Someone had to be there to keep the President in check, someone needed to stop him from allowing gut instinct to become implemented policy. There had to be a grown-up in the room. It should be noted that by the beginning of 2019, the White House had been gutted of all the so-called 'grown-ups'.

It wasn't until the publication of the book *Fear* by Bob Woodward that the extent of this 'chaperoning' of the President became clear. When the book first emerged, the first instinct of the White House would have been to rubbish it, deny its contents, call it fake news and move on. But Woodward has a track record that is not so easy to dismiss. Having been one half of the legendary duo that played a critical role in bringing down Richard Nixon, and having written a number of hard-hitting, well researched books on the presidents who've succeeded him, this would not be swatted away so easily.

The initial headlines would have caused Donald Trump anguish enough. Apparently the chief of staff John Kelly had referred to the President as unhinged and an idiot; Jim Mattis apparently called him a fifth or sixth grader (in other words a ten-year-old); while the chief economic advisor, Gary Cohn, was just 'astounded' at how dumb the President was. It was manna from heaven for the cable news networks and the headline writers. But there is much more to this book than name-calling. What is immediately apparent the moment you delve into its contents is that a lot of very senior staff, after donning the latex gloves to leave no fingerprints, had spilled the beans on life on the inside. Indeed, for hours after publication there was that rarest thing – silence from the comms team at the White House as they figured out what to do or say.

The Woodward book gives a remarkable insight into the White House battle to impose tariffs, in which the President was ready to blow his whistle and order his men to climb the ladders out of the trenches. First, though, there was the internal dispute to resolve, which had become a long-term, attritional battle. On one side was the free trade globalist Cohn, arguing for the existing order in world trade; on the other the protectionist Navarro, urging Trump on to try the wrecking ball – and each also had his own surrogates within the West Wing, backing their man every inch of the way.

The character who found himself at the centre of this was Rob Porter, the President's Staff Secretary (he would later be forced out after former partners alleged that he had been violent towards them, charges he called 'simply false'). If 'staff secretary' sounds a rather dull, workaday grunt job, don't be mistaken. The staff secretary is the funnel through which all paper passes that will end up on the Resolute desk for the President to sign. Anything the President sees, the staff secretary will have read first, and in many cases helped draft. And the situation he often found himself in was walking into the Oval Office to find Steve Bannon handing the President his proposal, or Kellyanne Conway handing over hers. None having gone through the normal filtering and straining process. Random bits of paper flying around and landing on the President's desk – which no one else knew anything about.

On trade, Porter was allied with Cohn. As well as getting rid of NAFTA, the deficit with China and Japan, and what Donald Trump perceived to be the unfair trading relationship with the European Union, the President was incredibly vexed about KORUS – the South Korean US trading relationship. According to Woodward, allies of the President had prepared documents for Trump to sign that would herald an American withdrawal from KORUS, a free trade agreement setting the rules for $150 billion worth between the two nations. But the trade deal could not be disentangled from the security relationship with South Korea, and many in the White House saw the trade deal as a small price to pay for the military presence it allowed the US. Jeopardising KORUS was about much more than Samsung TVs and smartphones flooding the US market. National security was at stake. Porter alerted Cohn, and Cohn resorted to desperate measures. Woodward says he stole from Trump's desk the letter that was sitting there awaiting the trademark signature. Remarkably the President didn't seem to notice. And on this occasion the protectionists backed off.

In this skirmish it was a win for the free traders. But it wasn't over. Donald Trump was growing impatient about the foot dragging over removing the US from the NAFTA agreement: 'Why aren't we getting this done? Do your job. It's tap, tap, tap. You're just tapping me along. I want to do this,' Trump reportedly told his then staff secretary Rob Porter.

So Porter did as he was instructed. He drew up a letter notifying NAFTA officials that the US would withdraw. But he was fearful of what the consequences of this precipitate action would be. So once again, he spoke to Gary Cohn that doing so could trigger an economic crisis. Cohn is a thick-set, bald, physically imposing man (he and H.R. McMaster looked comically similar when they shared a platform together, as they sometimes did in the White House Briefing Room), and he was one of the few who openly confronted Donald Trump on policy. Cohn said, according to Woodward, 'I can stop this, I'll just take the paper off his desk.' And he did. In the spring of 2017 that draft communiqué went missing from the Resolute desk.

The first excerpts of the Woodward book, with its detailed accounts of how staff were flagrantly ignoring the President's will, or just quietly blocking, caused a sensation in Washington. But something altogether more earth-shaking would appear the next day. The *New York Times* – or the 'failing *New York Times*' as the President would have it – had something rather unusual on its op-ed page. This was an anonymous article, written by a senior administration official, setting out in explicit, toe-curling detail the extent to which some of those in the President's inner circle had deep concerns about Trump's temperament, his ability to govern, his grasp on reality. It would have been journalistic suicide for the *New York Times* to have agreed to grant someone the cloak of anonymity unless it could be properly justified; unless there was no other means for the individual to express him or herself. Whoever wrote it must have been very senior indeed.

The headline accompanying the piece read: 'I am part of the resistance inside the Trump administration.' The headline and the piece tipped the President over the edge. He hated everything about it: the paper it was published in, the disloyalty of whoever wrote it, the unflattering portrayal, the suggestion that he was losing his marbles. It presented the complete opposite image of how the President – who once declared himself a 'very stable genius' – liked to see himself. He wanted blood. He wanted a head on a platter. That night on the cable news channel MSNBC the credits rolled and the veteran news anchor Brian Williams sat behind his desk and read a headline that seemed to capture the chaos engulfing the man brooding in his Oval Office: 'The portrait of a volcanic president who wants a newspaper to hand over a mole in his own government. Or, as we call it, Wednesday night.'

There are no quiet days and no calm weeks in the Trump presidency. No period where the whirring machine of government takes a roughly hewn idea and hones it into a carefully assembled and thought through policy, whose roll-out proceeds effortlessly. At one point in that tormented week, the President's long-suffering press secretary, Sarah Sanders, even seemed to admit as much when she said it's not always pretty, and that it was unconventional how this White House functioned.

There are times when you can just feel it. There was a press briefing I was at where Sarah Sanders looked like she hadn't slept a wink. She probably hadn't, as a new hurricane was blowing through the West Wing. There have been any number of occasions where the White House staff agree what line they're going to take – only for the President to contradict it. Talk to officials and they either shrug their shoulders with a 'What can I do?' or, after a few drinks, they will unburden. It's exhausting enough reporting on this President. But working for him? Well, that requires saintly levels of patience, or heavy doses of prescription pharmaceutical products. I was in Sarah Sanders's West Wing office to discuss some matter or other and asked how she coped with the endless drama. 'Bourbon,' she replied without a nanosecond's hesitation. I don't think she was joking.

When I had my famous clash with the President, and he called me 'another beauty' it was over precisely that. I had challenged him over whether this administration could be described as a smooth-running machine. He has always insisted it is. But the pretence was now gone. It is worth quoting at length from the anonymous piece because of its incendiary nature:

> The dilemma – which he does not fully grasp – is that many of the senior officials in his own administration are working diligently from within to frustrate parts of his agenda and his worst inclinations. I would know. I am one of them.
>
> To be clear, ours is not the popular 'resistance' of the left. We want the administration to succeed and think that many of its policies have already made America safer and more prosperous.
>
> But we believe our first duty is to this country, and the president continues to act in a manner that is detrimental to the health of our republic.

And it goes on:

The root of the problem is the president's amorality. Anyone who works with him knows he is not moored to any discernible first principles that guide his decision making ... From the White House to executive branch departments and agencies, senior officials will privately admit their daily disbelief at the Commander in Chief's comments and actions. Most are working to insulate their operations from his whims.

Meetings with him veer off topic and off the rails, he engages in repetitive rants, and his impulsiveness results in half-baked, ill-informed and occasionally reckless decisions that have to be walked back.

And then the *coup de grâce*, which almost reads as a call for a *coup d'état*:

Given the instability many witnessed, there were early whispers within the cabinet of invoking the 25th Amendment, which would start a complex process for removing the president. But no one wanted to precipitate a constitutional crisis. So we will do what we can to steer the administration in the right direction until – one way or another – it's over.

The 25th Amendment is the hitherto never used provision in the Constitution to remove a president from office if the cabinet believes he is mentally incapacitated or unable to carry out his functions and duties as head of state.

Critics of Mr or Ms Anonymous would say this: the country voted, 62 million of them for Donald Trump, and by the rules of the electoral college he was the duly elected president. Furthermore, no one could say he wasn't doing what he promised. Renegotiating trade deals, tougher immigration laws, cutting taxes, exiting the Iran nuclear deal and winding back regulations. These are precisely the policies he promised during the campaign. And as Sarah Sanders noted, while it may not always be pretty, the economic policies were paying dividends, with growth up and unemployment at record lows.

So what legitimacy did the writer have in declaring that s/he is the guardian of US democracy? For better or worse, the ballot box is where elections are decided, and in November 2016 the American people spoke. If someone is that unhappy about the direction of travel of the administration, they have the honourable choice of resigning, and fighting the Trump agenda at the next election. Or stay and fight their corner. But if they lose the battle while fighting from within, then surely their duty as a public servant is to remain and enact the policy that the head of state is constitutionally entitled to decide.

There are two other things that Donald Trump said repeatedly during the campaign, which were designed to appeal to those who always love to smell conspiracy in their nostrils: that there was a deep state, and that Washington was a swamp that needed to be drained. The deep state is the idea that there is a self-perpetuating élite of lawyers, lobbyists, industrialists and politicians who are the unseen resistance to change, whose only guiding principle is to keep their hands on the levers of the state so that they continue to get rich, keep power and see off anything that might curdle their gravy train. According to this theory, lurking in every marble corridor and around every neo-classical column were malign actors whose allegiance was to the status quo, who would thwart the newly elected president and scupper him as if their lives depended on it.

I thought it was tendentious in the extreme – a ploy designed by Donald Trump to show that he was the non-politician in the race, the change maker and people's tribune taking on the deeply entrenched élites. But that article can be seen as the very definition of the deep state. I started thinking conspiratorially whether the article might have been penned by Donald Trump himself as a means of justifying a crack-down on those around him, while demanding greater, unfet-tered power in decision making. The clincher that stopped me believing it was *him* – I just couldn't see him writing those nasty things about himself. But the article had the net effect of the President becoming even more distrustful of those in his court, with fewer being allowed to be brought into the inner circle of decision making. Presumably completely counter to what the author would have wanted.

Also, just on a slightly practical note, if you are part of a deep state conspiracy, don't you keep your mouth shut about it and get on with the business of conspiring, rather than advertise what you are doing in the pages of the *New York Times*? I know that in spy-craft hiding in plain sight can be mighty effective. But this? What did s/he hope to achieve?

'Anonymous' still hasn't been unmasked. Anonymous is presumably still functioning within the administration – thwarting, blocking, subverting and laying booby-traps wher-ever possible. The hashtag of 2018 across the United States was undoubtedly #metoo. But at the highest altitudes of the Trump administration it brought into being the #notme move-ment. Senior officials, from the Vice-President downwards, were falling over themselves – almost racing each other to Twitter and the microphone – to be the first to say 'I didn't do it', 'it wasn't me guv, honest', 'my nose is clean', and 'don't try and fit me up for this' – and any number of other cockney phrases you would never hear in Washington. It was as if Donald Trump had given them all a class detention, and no one was going home from school until the miscreant in the form had owned up to letting off the stink bomb in the headmaster's office.

It gave rise to a good cottage industry in textual analysis. Sleuths were cracking their knuckles and working late into the night looking for clues; uncovering motives. Washington was playing Cluedo. The author had used the word 'lodestar' – a word often used by the Vice-President, Mike Pence, in his speeches. Aha. Swift denial followed. Who had motive? Well, lots of people, it seemed. Who disliked the President? Again, quite a few people. Who harboured ambitions of their own? Everyone. Why now? Well, why not?

It was around this time that I took a transatlantic flight, and a bit bored I settled down to watch Kenneth Branagh's high camp remake of *Murder on the Orient Express*. And then, like a flash, an epiphany, it came to me. 'Anonymous' wasn't a person. It was joint endeavour. They'd all written it. Kellyanne, Sarah Sanders, Mike Pence, the FBI director, the CIA director – you name them, they were in on it. I'd cracked it. It was all the senior administration officials, in the Oval, with the lead piping.

Life would change for Donald Trump in November 2018, although at the time he didn't realise just how profoundly. The midterm elections were the first full report card on how Donald Trump was doing. A third of the Senate's hundred seats were up for grabs, and the full House of Representatives. In the key Senate races, Trump had cause for satisfaction. Some rock-solid red states returned to trend and the Republicans increased their Senate majority. But more significant were the nationwide results in the House. Here there was a 'blue wave' (confusingly in US politics the more right-wing party – the Republicans – are ascribed the colour red; while the more left-wing party, the Democratic Party, has blue as its colour) and the Democrats overturned a big Republican majority to take back control easily.

Again, the Oval Office was the immediate backdrop for this new political reality, and needless to say, the cameras were invited in. But the Chuck and Nancy show was different from anything else we had seen. Nancy Pelosi, who was then the frontrunner to become the Speaker of the House (and she would subsequently be confirmed in that post by the Democratic Caucus), and Chuck Schumer, the Senate minority leader, had not come as supplicants, like so many other people we had witnessed passing through. They had not come to tell the President how marvellous he was, they had come to plant a flag in the ground. The contested issue was Donald Trump's belief that the only way to secure the southern border of the United States was by building a wall. Of course, in the campaign he had said repeatedly that Mexico would pay for it. But – surprise, surprise – they hadn't ponied up the money. So instead it would be the American taxpayer footing the bill.

They quarrelled. They fought. Nancy Pelosi and Chuck Schumer immune to the President's exhortations and threats. Eventually an exasperated Donald Trump said he would be 'proud' to shut the government down over this issue, and happy to call it a Trump shutdown. And Chuck and Nancy smiled. Big smiles. Big knowing smiles. These two veterans of legislative battle had got the President to agree ownership of something that invariably turns into a smelly bucket of ordure.

Just before Christmas 2018 the government did shut down. No budget had been agreed – and just shy of a million federal workers were laid off without pay. The President talked tough. There would be no reopening of the government until there was a $5.7 billion line in the budget towards the border wall. Nancy and Chuck were unmoved. The closure dragged on. White collar workers in Washington, living pay-cheque to pay-cheque, were lining up at food banks. Families were choosing between vital medicines and keeping their homes warm. It had become the longest government shutdown in history, and as Chuck and Nancy had correctly calculated, it was hurting the President far more than it was the Democrats. Airport security staff and air traffic controllers were required to work unpaid – but once they started calling in sick, and some of America's biggest airports had to shut, or at least severely curtail flights, the game was up. After 35 days Donald Trump had to hoist a white flag. The government would reopen temporarily, but without a single cent pledged towards his wall. It was a chastening lesson to him in how much more difficult life was set to become. He'd got himself into an arm wrestle with this slightly built Californian grandmother, the 78-year-old Speaker of the House, Nancy Pelosi – and had come second. She had delivered a lesson on governance. And a warning shot to the executive of what power she now wielded as the leader of one part of the legislature.

The President now either had to admit failure or go for the nuclear option. He did the latter, and early in February

2019 sat in the Oval Office and signed the declaration that the situation on the southern border was a National Emergency, allowing him to raid other departmental budgets to pay for his wall. And in the process he set off a constitutional battle between Congress and the White House. The emergency powers law, passed in 1976, had never been used for anything as overtly political as this – and this was a naked attempt to steal the budget-setting power of Congress.

Just before the midterms and the government shutdown Americans had become transfixed by something other than the fireworks of the administration. There was a real firework show to watch. A volcano had started to erupt in Hawaii. The Kiluaea volcano was putting on a spectacular show. It was belching hazardous gases, there were molten lava flows, smoke rose menacingly and at night the sky was lit up with luminous red flames, as volcanic rock was fired out of the crater over great distances. Seventeen hundred homes were abandoned. What was occurring in Hawaii brought a revelatory *aperçu* in Washington. A staffer told me earnestly that events in Hawaii had brought a change in how the White House staff would treat its president. The policy had gone from resistance to strategic surrender. You can't change his mind. No point trying. He is what he is. But perhaps you can manage him, as the volcanologists and civil emergency people were doing on Hawaii's big island. You may not be able to stop the President from blowing his top and erupting on this or that point. He will spit with anger at times. All you can do is manage the lava flow. Keep the molten rocks from landing where they will do most damage. Try to funnel; try to direct. But don't think you can stop the man in the Oval Office from doing what he wants to do.

# CHAPTER 2

# The Office of the Chief of Staff

If you get up from behind the Resolute desk in the Oval Office, and you take the first door out on the left-hand side, you go past the President's study – which in reality is where he does most of his work – past the Dining Room, where Donald Trump has installed a huge flat screen television, so he can watch Fox News – which he spends a lot of time doing – and at the end of the corridor, after a couple of small rooms, is the Chief of Staff's office, occupying the south-west corner of the West Wing. It is spacious enough. There is a long table for meetings with staff, and above the fireplace hangs an oil painting of Abraham Lincoln. It has none of the grandeur of the Oval. The Chief of Staff, it has often been said, does the grunt work for the president. Or to use a nautical metaphor, this is the engine room, not the bridge.

The title is relatively new. Before the Second World War the description was President's Private Secretary; in 1946 it became Assistant to the President; and then in 1961 it finally became Assistant to the President and Chief of Staff. It is one of the senior jobs entirely in the gift of the president, requiring no Senate confirmation. And it is not a legally required role – if President Trump chose to do without one, he would be free to do so.

At various times Donald Trump has openly mused about doing away with the role altogether. As with so many senior White House roles, this president fundamentally believes he could do the job better than anyone else, therefore why have someone else doing it? But in reality, the chief of staff is the man (there has never been a female chief of staff) with the oily rag, the socket set and a screwdriver, immersed in the detail, adjusting the tappets, making sure the cylinders are firing, the engine isn't overheating and the oil is sluicing round the vital components. However else you might describe Donald Trump, he is not a greasy-fingernailed, under the bonnet man, with a thumbed copy of the owner's manual. And so, like every president since Harry Truman, he accepted the need for a chief of staff.

H.R. Haldeman, Richard Nixon's chief of staff, is quoted in the book *The Gatekeepers: How the White House Chiefs of Staff Define Every Presidency*, by Chris Whipple, reflecting on his appointment: 'Eisenhower had told Nixon that every president has to have his own son of a bitch. Nixon had looked over everyone in his entourage and decided that Haldeman was pluperfect SOB. And because of that somewhat unflattering appraisal, my career took a rise.' Nixon soon found himself plagued by endless leaks and palace intrigue. He was a man who always had a keenly developed sense of paranoia, and he announced at a cabinet meeting in 1971, 'From now on Haldeman is the Lord High Executioner.

Don't come whining to me when he tells you to do something. He will do it because I asked him to and you're to carry it out.' Leon Panetta, who was Bill Clinton's chief of staff, put it slightly differently: 'You have to be the person who says no. You've got to be the son of a bitch who basically tells somebody what the President can't tell him.'

And you are the person who behind closed doors might have to tell the President some home truths, and even, when the cameras are rolling, whisper in his ear. That is literally what happened on 11 September 2001 when George W. Bush's chief of staff, Andy Card, had to approach the President, as he was reading to schoolchildren in Florida, to tell him about what was unfolding in New York. The first Bush and Card knew about a crash came just before the President walked into a second-grade classroom. Initial reports were of a small prop plane hitting the Twin Towers. Card waited in another room while the President spoke to the class. Then a US Navy captain told Card that, in fact, it was a commercial jet that had slammed into one of the towers. A few minutes later, Card recalled, the captain exclaimed, 'Oh my God, another plane hit the other tower.'

Card would later recount the experience to Congress, where he had once served. He had decided, he said, to 'pass on two facts and one editorial comment and to do nothing to invite a dialogue with the president'. He walked into the classroom and whispered into the President's ear, 'A second plane hit the second tower. America is under attack.' Card said he was convinced that his words to Bush 'caused the president to reflect on his job; not the speeches he had given, but the oath he had taken … to preserve, protect and defend'.

Accepting the need for the chief of staff role, as Donald Trump had done, is one thing; willing the holder of the post the means to do the job most effectively is quite another. And that is where the problems were most conspicuous for this president's first two chiefs of staff. Unlike being Secretary of Defense or Secretary of State, where the job description is more or less displayed on the tin, here there is nothing constitutionally laid out, fixed and immutable, no document detailing where responsibilities begin and end. Former President Gerald Ford once said that the ideal pick for the job should be 'a person that you have total confidence in, who works so closely with you that in effect he is an alter ego'. The flippant remark would be that Donald Trump is Donald Trump's own alter ego. How could he have total confidence and trust in anyone else, when no one is as smart as he is? For Donald Trump the only person that would closely resemble that would be one of the family members – say, daughter Ivanka, or her husband Jared Kushner. But that would fuel suspicions about the White House being run as an unaccountable family business, not the pre-eminent global superpower.

That said, there have been common features about how the various chiefs of staff have done the job, and what they saw as the common threads of it. You are the centre of managing the vast federal US bureaucracy, ensuring the policy priorities that the president has set out are enacted, so keeping an eye on the disparate government departments and agencies. You are the person liaising with Congress to get bills passed; you are the person through which everything is funnelled in the White House. You are the eyes and ears of the president: the rat-catcher when there is a rodent in the building; the progress chaser when things are moving slowly;

the ultimate arbiter when disputes break out. You are the diary keeper, so you know who the president is seeing and speaking to – don't crowd the schedule with people who don't need an appointment; keep a record of what the president has discussed, so that on any given topic, at any given time you know what is in the president's mind, or what ought to be in the president's mind. You are also the person who might need to do the president's dirty work: to tidy up messes that might arise; fire those who have transgressed; be the smoother of ruffled feathers when plumage has been disturbed. It is a job which it is probably impossible to do properly because there simply aren't enough hours in the day to get it done.

Seeing as Donald Trump had never really expected to get elected president, he hadn't given a whole lot of thought to who should be his chief of staff. And the Trump organisation, for all its global reach and ubiquitous branding – visit one of his golf courses and the number of times you see the word 'Trump' is truly astonishing – is ultimately run as a family business, with few formal structures.

Trump's choice of Reince Priebus to be his chief of staff after the election was in some ways a very traditional and conservative appointment – and yet simultaneously wipe-your-eyes-with-amazement surprising. It was traditional because Priebus was steeped in Republican politics and during the election campaign had been the chairman of the Republican National Committee. That meant they had worked together closely, and not only on Trump's campaign. Priebus had been the point person for the Republican party on all the 'down ticket' races – for the House and Senate, for state legislatures and the myriad other vacant seats. Priebus also hailed from Wisconsin, where he'd cut his political teeth, and which was also the home state of the Speaker of the House, Paul Ryan. Though Priebus hadn't held elected office, the fact that he had a close relationship with Ryan was an undoubted boon given the legislative battles that would lie ahead. The party establishment, wary of what a Trump presidency might look like, given that he had surrounded himself with iconoclasts who seemed as antipathetic to the establishment Republican Party as they did to the Democratic Party, found the choice of Priebus reassuring. 'Phew' was the most common reaction.

Why it was so unexpected, though, was that, to put it mildly, they were not exactly natural soulmates. In fact, let me go further: the two men have absolutely nothing in common – the billionaire property guy, and the geeky bureaucrat. Trump's people were typically exceptionally wealthy, or they were kindred spirits in populist politics, or they had a background in the military. Priebus was none of those things. And during the one major crisis of Donald Trump's freewheeling campaign they came to starkly different conclusions about what should happen next.

*Access Hollywood* is a hugely popular programme in the US, a kind of *Hello* magazine of the airwaves. It is full of celebrity guests, has the latest Hollywood gossip, and comes on after the nightly news bulletin on NBC. The programme had been out on the road in a tour bus. And on the bus, Donald Trump – long before he was running for president – was discussing women with the programme's host, Billy Bush (ironically, a scion of the Bush family and first cousin to George W. Bush and Governor Jeb Bush). It was a discussion that, had Trump remembered he was wearing a microphone, he might not have had. The property man and host of *The Apprentice* was telling Bush what he could and would do to women as a result of his fame. He could grab them 'by the pussy'. He described how he would just start kissing beautiful women. In essence, he was bragging about being able to commit sexual assault.

The tape emerged on a Friday afternoon, with just weeks to go before polling day. On the Saturday there was a council of war for leading figures in the Republican Party. Priebus tried to convince Trump that it was all over; he had to withdraw from the race with as much dignity as he could muster. There was a strained atmosphere in Trump Tower as this all played out. There were different people on different floors of the building, each with their own take on what should happen next. Eventually a meeting bringing everyone together was called.

One of the chief iconoclasts, Steve Bannon, who was then running the campaign and would go into the White House as Chief of Strategy, described after he was fired what unfolded at that fateful meeting following the *Washington Post*'s release of the *Access Hollywood* tape. Priebus had already issued a public statement through his chairmanship of the RNC saying, 'No woman should ever be described in these terms or talked about in this manner. Ever.'

In what passed as the Trump Tower 'situation room', Trump according to a number of sources opened up the conversation. He went around the room and asked those present what they thought the percentage chances were of him still winning and what their recommendation was. Priebus was the first to wade in. He was blunt, telling the presidential candidate: 'You have two choices. You either drop out right now, or you lose in the biggest landslide in American political history.' Trump, with deadpan humour, replies, 'Well, I'm glad we're starting off on a positive note.' Bannon now spoke up, declaring the Priebus analysis total bullshit. Priebus, meanwhile, had brought in the top TV anchor from one of the networks to stand by in another room for the interview at which Trump would make the bombshell announcement that he was pulling out of the race.

Except that, by the end, Bannon had convinced Trump to fight on. And fight on he did in characteristic style. Instead of giving an interview to announce he was going, he released a tape that evening during which he spoke directly to camera. Yes, he expressed regret for what he had said during 'pussy-gate', while also dismissing it as 'locker room banter'. And then alleging that whatever his transgressions, Bill Clinton's had been far worse. Not for the first time in Donald Trump's life he had chosen to meet fire with ire!

It was a pivotal moment in the campaign. The moment where once again this exceptional candidate would raise a middle finger to the party and to the media. But it was crucial in another respect too. It demonstrated vividly how much Donald Trump valued Priebus's judgement. Not a whole lot. His alter ego? Forget it. Trump thought the party apparatchik was spineless and too much in thrall to a Republican establishment that the insurgent candidate held in disdain. So, it was quite a surprise on the night of Trump's stunning election victory to find the president-elect seeking Reince Priebus out from the crowd.

The man who quarrelled repeatedly with candidate Trump, imploring – forlornly – the New York tycoon to tone down his rhetoric, was being given the big, warm embrace. 'I tell you Reince is really a star and he is the hardest-working guy,' said the president-elect in the wee small hours of that

Wednesday morning. The bureaucrat and functionary was clearly being lined up for greater things.

The other person that Trump considered to fill the chief of staff role was Steve Bannon, the polar opposite of Priebus in every way imaginable. Where Priebus was cautious, Bannon was cavalier; where Priebus was a respecter of tradition, Bannon wanted to tear the walls down; where Priebus was a product of the Republican Party, Bannon loathed it. One was an internationalist, the other isolationist. Where Priebus was small, neat and dapper and would feel stark naked if he wasn't wearing a tie, Bannon was large and lumbering, and had the rumpled look and rheumy, watery eyes of someone who had just been woken from sleep on a park bench after a particularly heavy night on the sauce. And, ultimately, where one was trying to rein Trump in, the other was trying to egg him on.

This was the angel that Trump had on one shoulder and the devil he had on the other. And there was quite a lot of swivelling of the head between the two before he finally selected Priebus. But it would turn out to be a short-lived victory for establishment Republicans. No sooner had Trump confirmed Priebus as the chief of staff than he appointed Bannon to a newly created post of Chief Strategist at the White House. Not only that, but they would be of equal rank, and work next door to one another in the West Wing. The press release making the announcement listed Bannon first.

For a while the two partners did their best to show they could get along. In the early weeks of the Trump presidency they even tried to project the idea that far from them having been yoked in a shotgun wedding, this was an affair of the heart. At one get-together of hundreds of conservative activists Priebus said, 'We're just buds ... we share an office suite together. We're basically together from 6.30 in the morning until 11 at night.' And he went on to claim that everything people had said about their relationship was wrong. In one interview for *New York* magazine, so much did they profess their affection for each other that it all felt a little bit creepy:

'We talk a lot, pretty much all day long,' Priebus said. 'And then we communicate at night –'

'Until we fall asleep,' Bannon interjected with a laugh.

Priebus cut in, 'Until somebody falls asleep ... You fell asleep last night.'

'I did,' Bannon said.

'I think, like, a quarter to 11,' Priebus added.

'I did,' Bannon said.

'He became unresponsive,' Priebus laughed.

But even if this bromance was ever real, it wouldn't last long. A month after the inauguration, *Time* magazine put Bannon on the front cover, with the headline 'The Great Manipulator'. The headline used for the associated article was 'Is Steve Bannon the Second Most Powerful Man in the World?', alluding to Bannon's perceived far greater influence in the White House than Priebus's. It was bad for Priebus, making the chief of staff look as though he was some bit part player in someone else's drama. Ultimately it was even worse for Bannon. In the President's mind there should only be one face on the cover of *Time* magazine from the administration – his. If the Rasputin figure was daring to think he was as important as the tsar he would need to be pulled down a peg or two.

Priebus could only dream of having the same problems. No one was talking about him having too much power. Quite the reverse. Weak and ineffective were the adjectives that most frequently attached themselves to the Wisconsin man. And to be a successful chief of staff that is fatal. You need to be seen as the top of the tree, the highest point in the evolutionary food chain. You are the person that every subordinate needs to respect, and if not respect at least fear – and therefore aim to please. Because ultimately if you displease the chief of staff, you are displeasing the President. One other thing needed for success in the role is for America and the world to know that when you open your mouth, you are speaking for the Commander in Chief. You are his master's voice.

This was the core of the problem for Priebus. Trump would never allow him to accrue that sort of power; the man in the Oval Office didn't seem to respect the judgement of his appointee down the corridor. This wasn't just a matter of Priebus's shortcomings – the truth was Trump really didn't want anyone to change his freewheeling ways. The President didn't want to submit to order, discipline and structure; he wanted things to carry on, much as they had at Trump Tower. The only final arbiter on anything would be Trump himself.

The one thing that the President had hoped Priebus would achieve, thanks to his close working relationship with Paul Ryan in the House, was a successful overhaul of healthcare. They persuaded the President that this should be his first legislative battle, before then going on to other key priority areas like infrastructure renewal and tax reform. It ate up most of the effort in the first year of Trump's presidency – before running aground.

Trump would now openly disparage him in meetings with staff – referring in mocking terms to the man he now dubbed 'Reincey'. Once executive branch workers picked up on that, what little authority he had drained away very quickly. In a White House roiled by factional infighting, Priebus seemed incapable of banging heads together and showing some stick, or of recruiting the President to sort out the turf fights. The sunbed king seemed to rather enjoy his court fighting for his attention and preferment, even though to the outside world it conveyed an image of dysfunction and disorganisation.

It all came to a head in a glorious Tarantino style bloodbath in the summer of 2016, with Priebus having only been in post for six months. The catalyst for the fast-moving events which followed was the President's appointment of a New York friend of his, Anthony Scaramucci, as White House director of communications. Scaramucci – or the Mooch as he enjoyed being called – was a fast talking, aviator sunglass wearing, slicked back hair pantomime villain if ever there was one. He looked as though he had strayed from the set of *Goodfellas* or *The Sopranos*. He had been a Trump fundraiser, having come from the world of finance, but he had a score or two to settle when he alighted off the Acela train at Washington's Union Station.

Trump had intended to appoint him to a senior White House post when he formed the administration. But he was blocked – by someone telling the President that Scaramucci's sale of his fund SkyBridge Capital to a Chinese buyer was, well, a bit dodgy and could turn out to be problematic. The person who had dripped this poison into the President's ear was none other than Reince Priebus.

Priebus was not alone in being alarmed at the President's choice of new communications director; so too was the press secretary, Sean Spicer. Like Priebus, Spicer had come from Republican Party HQ. And Spicer was one of Priebus's last remaining allies in the White House. It was too much for Spicer to have to answer to the Mooch, who had zero professional experience in the communications field, save his own appearances on TV as a Trump surrogate. Spicer made it clear he would quit if Scaramucci was appointed.

But as if to bear out Spicer's concerns about the Mooch not being a seasoned media professional, the new communications director made the mistake of calling a well-known Washington journalist, the *New Yorker*'s Ryan Lizza, to demand the names of his White House sources for a story he'd just written about a dinner that the President had been hosting. Scaramucci was on a mission to track down and evict the leakers from within 1600 Pennsylvania Avenue. A noble enough ambition. But no journalist is going to reveal the names of his contacts when to do so would result in their contacts' certain firing, and the journalist's own integrity disintegrating. Aside from the ethics of a duty to protect your sources, why would you do something that would end up in you having no sources to talk to? The new comms chief made one other egregious error of judgement in this conversation: he failed to say it was 'off the record'. Oops.

Oh, how their exchange, which Lizza had recorded, enlivened a steamy Washington summer's day. Scaramucci is a wonderful, entertaining communicator. He couldn't be boring and dull if he tried. And therein lay the problem. He said of the chief of staff – the man he would now answer to in the chain of command – that he had leaked information to hurt him and called him a 'cock-blocker' (there's an image). But he wasn't done. He's 'a fucking paranoid schizophrenic, a paranoiac', the Mooch unloaded to the astonished *New Yorker* journalist. I mean, how do you spin your way out of that one? 'When I said fucking paranoid schizophrenic, I shouldn't have used the word fucking ...' No, there was no easy way around any of this.

Just to give some context, Priebus wasn't the only target of the Mooch's colourful invective. Bannon copped a load too. 'I'm not Steve Bannon, I'm not trying to suck my own cock. I'm not trying to build my own brand off the fucking strength of the President. I'm here to serve the country,' Scaramucci went on. When this emerged, what was immediately apparent was the unsustainability of these disparate characters working together under one roof. Someone would have to go. As it turned out everyone went.

First out the door was the press secretary, Sean Spicer. True to his word, he quit soon after Scaramucci was appointed. Next to go, a week later, would be the chief of staff – extraordinary that when faced with a choice, the President sided with the man who called Priebus a paranoid schizophrenic, rather than his long-suffering chief of staff.

On the way back from New York, where he'd given a speech to police officers, the President decided enough was enough. And, so, sitting in his office suite aboard Air Force One, Trump stunned people aboard and the rest of America with this tweet: 'I am pleased to inform you that I have just named General/Secretary John F. Kelly as White House Chief of Staff. He is a Great American ...' And then this: '... and a Great Leader. John has also done a spectacular job at Homeland Security. He has been a true star of my Administration.'

For a few minutes there was simply no mention of Priebus. It was as though he had been erased from the history books as if the victim of some latter-day Stalinist purge. Reince who? But then came a rather desultory tweet from the President: 'I would like to thank Reince Priebus for his service and dedication to his country. We accomplished a lot together and I am proud of him!' It didn't exactly glow with warmth or appreciation. And that was that.

When they arrive back at Joint Base Andrews – with Priebus aboard – a moment unfolds as though from a movie. The rain is hammering down, the tarmac is glistening from the downpour, and as is normal there is a fleet of black SUVs waiting to ferry the President's party back to the White House. The senior administration officials run to the cars to avoid being soaked to the skin. Two staffers, who clearly haven't checked their Twitter feed, run up to Priebus on the tarmac to see if they can ride with him. 'No,' he says, 'I'm being driven home.' And without a moment's hesitation they turn their back on the former boss and look for a ride with someone else. And as the presidential motorcade turns left on leaving the gates of Joint Base Andrews in Maryland, with its panoply of motorcycle outriders and ambulances and heavily armed special agents, Priebus turns right. All alone in his car. In Washington you pass into history exceedingly quickly. Priebus was the past.

John Kelly was barely ten minutes into the job the following Monday morning when he made his first decision of conse- quence. Scaramucci's scabrous interview could not be allowed to stand. The Mooch would have to go. He had lasted ten days as communications director. A 'mooch' in Washington- speak now had a new meaning: it became a unit of time – if something had gone on for three mooches, it meant that it had lasted a month. So when someone says, 'We're going on holiday for half a mooch,' that equals five days away. As was noted at the time, a pint of milk lasts longer before going off. John Kelly was not done, though. A couple of weeks later Bannon was forced to walk the plank, this time with insults flying. When it emerged that Bannon had been a source for an unflattering book written by Michael Wolff about life in the West Wing, Trump turned on his one-time campaign chief and chief strategist: 'Sloppy Steve Bannon, who cried when he got fired and begged for his job. Now Sloppy Steve has been dumped like a dog by almost everyone. Too bad!'

In the space of a month the chief of staff, the chief strategist and the communications director had been fired, and the press secretary had walked out. The John Kelly era had started, and with the unmistakable smack of firm discipline. It was time to shape up or ship out. A new broom was sweeping through the West Wing – and across Washington there was a general feeling of 'not before time'.

John Kelly had spent most of his life in the US Marine Corps, enlisting in 1970, and rising to the rank of general. This no-nonsense, plain-speaking son of Boston, Massachusetts, served in Iraq with the 1st Marine Division as assistant division commander. His last military posting before being recruited to the White House was as head of SOUTHCOM – in other words, he was responsible for Guantanamo Bay, and all US military operations in South and Central America.

One diplomat who had very close dealings with him described him to me as serious, honourable – and with an unmistakable sense of melancholy. Kelly's two sons, John and Robert, had also served as marines. In November 2010, Robert stepped on a landmine in Afghanistan and was killed, aged 29. He would talk about the loss of his son at a White House briefing when there was controversy over the way Donald Trump had handled a call to the family of a fallen soldier. Defending the President, Kelly said, 'In my case, hours after my son was killed, his friends were calling us from Afghanistan, telling us what a great guy he was. Those are the only phone calls that really matter. If you elect to call a family like this – and it's about the most difficult thing you could imagine – there's no perfect way to make that phone call.'

Kelly exuded authority and integrity. He was also part of that small group referred to as the 'Axis of Adults', meaning those people in the Trump administration who were not afraid to stand up to their boss and 'speak truth to power'. But this description – which, as you might imagine, Trump detested – carried an implication that they were all, somehow, at odds with the President over policy too. A few were, but it would be a mistake to overstate that in the case of John Kelly. He had come from the Department of Homeland Security, where he was every bit as tough on the need to secure the border as the President.

What he wanted was order in the way business was transacted. This was the great advantage he brought as chief of staff. Here was a general who knew about the chain of command, who understood the need for discipline. And there was something about his bearing and demeanour – military, straight back, no nonsense – that ensured staff did not mess with him in the way they did with Priebus. A lot of the activities that were so prevalent before now came to a stop. At least in the short term.

People would no longer be able to wander in and out of the Oval Office as though it were some kind of communal water-cooler space, where you just stopped by for a chat. There would be appointments, and he would police who went in and out, and why they were going in and out. A lot of the leaking subsided too as a result of the staff changes that he made. It didn't stop completely – that would be impossible. And the president, having endured months of adverse headlines about the way the White House ran, seemed – for now at least – pleased with the recognition that the place was transitioning from playground to a heel-clicking parade ground.

But if Kelly brought the necessary order and structure that the job needed, there was one area where he was a novice. He may have spent forty years in the military, but he was relatively unprepared for Washington's asymmetric warfare that is waged between the executive branch of government and the legislature. Aside from a brief spell as the congressional liaison for the Marines he had little experience of DC politics. The deal-making, horse-trading, pork-barrel politics – the things that are the lubricant to the workings of Capitol Hill – were things he had scant experience of. Priebus may have lacked authority but he knew what the Republicans on the Hill wanted or needed from the President. Kelly was on a steep learning curve.

His main problem was that while in theory Donald Trump loved the sense of order that Kelly seemed to bring, it was questionable how much he appreciated it in practice. Within weeks of Kelly taking the post, well-sourced reports started to emerge that the President was 'chafing' at the controls being placed on him. He was missing the gossip, the informality. He hated it that when friends telephoned, their calls would now be routed through the chief of staff's office. And when other chums were in town with time to kill, where once they would apparently drop by the Oval, just to sit and chat, now they would be told the President was unavailable.

This is, of course, what Kelly was employed to do, but when this new formality and structure was reported in the media it had an unintended consequence. Yes, it was good for the President that what was now being said was that the White House was running more smoothly; but what he hated was the notion that people might get the impression that he was somehow being managed, or, worse still, controlled. And so well-known Trump surrogates started feeding stories that were unhelpful.

Roger Stone, a long-time Trump confidant, whose views are as provocative as his clothes are flamboyant, told the *Washington Post*: 'Donald Trump resists being handled. Nobody tells him who to see, who to listen to, what to read, what he can say … General Kelly is trying to treat the president like a mushroom. Keeping him in the dark and feeding him shit is not going to work. Donald Trump is a free spirit.' Anthony Scaramucci also joined in, saying that Kelly 'hurt the morale of the place. And he's hurt the president … and he [Kelly] has hissy fits.'

Kelly had also made two unfortunate enemies. His attempt at exerting iron fist control over who got to speak to the President, and who was allowed to go into the Oval Office, did not go down well with Jared Kushner and Ivanka – or Javanka as Steve Bannon had disparagingly dubbed them. During the campaign I was told by someone who spent a lot of time at Trump Tower that anyone and everyone going to see Donald Trump had to knock before entering his lair, except Kushner. He had an 'access all areas' pass and came and went as he pleased. For these family members it rankled now to be told that they, like everyone else, would have to go through the office of the chief of staff.

What Kelly admitted he had no control over was the President's use of Twitter, even though there were those who implored him to try. Kelly said he would not waste time and effort on a pointless task. 'Believe it or not, I do not follow the President's tweets,' he told reporters. And even attempting to control who he spoke to on the phone had its limitations. In the evening the President would retire to the East Wing, where he would use his old, unencrypted cell phone and freely chat to whoever he wanted.

But if John Kelly couldn't exert complete control over Donald Trump, nor could the President totally manage his independent-minded chief of staff. I remember a rally that Trump addressed in Phoenix, Arizona, in the summer of 2017, where the President was particularly wild in some of his attacks – on the media, on black American footballers who 'took a knee' during the national anthem. He attacked Congress, and was clearly furious that he had been talked into sending additional troops to Afghanistan. He'd also had a fight with Kelly before the rally started. At one point during his address he tried to call Kelly up on stage. 'Where's John?' he asked. 'Where is he? Where's General Kelly? Get him out here. He's great. He's doing a great job.' But Kelly did not appear. He wasn't going to play to the crowd; he wasn't going to pander to his boss or 'reward' him when he was behaving badly.

And Kelly would have made a lousy poker player. On numerous occasions he would be caught on camera, almost wincing at what the President was saying. During some of the most contentious episodes of the Trump presidency there would be photographs of Kelly looking pained. When Trump spoke about there being 'very fine people' on both sides during protests in Charlottesville where neo-Nazis clashed with anti-racism protestors, Kelly could be seen folding his arms and hanging his head. Photos of Kelly looking unimpressed when Trump was referring to Kim Jong-un as 'Rocket Man' very quickly went viral.

Kelly's background was very different from predecessors who've held the role. Most White House chiefs of staff are former politicians, and many go on to continue their political careers in other senior roles. So, Alexander Haig, who was one of Richard Nixon's chiefs of staff, went on to become Secretary of State under Ronald Reagan. Dick Cheney, who was chief of staff to Gerald Ford, became a Wyoming congressman, then a Secretary of Defense to George H.W. Bush and then Vice-President under George W. Bush. Rahm Emanuel, chief of staff to Barack Obama, had been in Congress, and after leaving the White House became Mayor of Chicago. Jack Lew, President Obama's fourth chief of staff, was later appointed Treasury Secretary.

When I interviewed Obama back in 2015 in the West Wing – I had a slightly surreal conversation when the President asked whether I wanted to go out and walk in the Rose Garden with him. Of course, I said, trying to sound nonchalant, as though that was quite the most normal thing in the world to be doing on that Wednesday afternoon. 'Yeah, sure thing Barry ...' We walked together out of the Roosevelt Room, and down the corridor that leads to the doors which open out onto the famous colonnades. In front of us were two men. To get between the President and the secret service staff who act as a sort of force shield around him, you have to be fairly senior. Obama introduces me to them. 'Jon, this is my chief of staff Dennis McDonough, his job is to keep me out of trouble. And this is my general counsel, Neil Eggleston, his job is to keep me out of jail.' It was a neat and succinct description and distinction between the two roles.

General Kelly did his best to keep Donald Trump out of trouble, even if that meant there were times when telling an impulsive and determined president what he could *not* do led to fairly incendiary clashes. On almost every occasion these eruptions would solely be heard by the staff in adjacent West Wing offices. A bust-up over immigration between the National Security Advisor, John Bolton, and Kelly was so loud that word of it quickly spread. But there was one row which, though the voices did not carry out onto the street, you could chart quite clearly by watching the movement of the flagpole above the White House.

It was regarded at the time almost as a moment of black humour, but what this episode conveyed was a brutal arm wrestle between an impetuous president, who nursed and tended his grudges and grievances with a care that a gardener might show to a herbaceous border, and a military man who believed in respect, honour and decency. The flashpoint for what became a defining battle was the death of someone who was widely revered as an all-American hero.

Senator John McCain was someone whom Donald Trump had a thing about – and not in a good way. McCain was an old school Republican who had run for the presidency himself against Barack Obama in 2008, but could do nothing to resist the tide of hope and 'Yes we can' that was sweeping America. Trump thought he'd run a lousy campaign. But it was McCain's background that made him such a role model in most people's eyes.

He was from a military family with a storied history. Both his father and grandfather had risen to the rank of admiral in the US Navy. He followed them into the navy, where he became a naval aviator. In 1967, during his 23rd bombing mission over North Vietnam when he was *en route* to take out a power plant, a surface-to-air missile struck his plane, knocking one of the wings off. As the plane corkscrewed at terminal velocity towards earth, he was forced to eject. In the process he was knocked unconscious, broke both his arms and a leg. Grainy black-and-white photos show North Vietnamese soldiers pulling the 31-year-old from Truc Bach Lake in the centre of Hanoi, where he'd ended up. After being beaten and stripped to his underpants he was taken to HoaLò prison in the city centre. HoaLò translates as 'fiery furnace'. The building of yellow stone, surrounded by high concrete walls, was nicknamed by Americans 'the Hanoi Hilton'. At the Hilton you would never want to stay at, soldiers dumped McCain's stretcher on the floor.

He would have been left to die, so serious were his injuries, but for the discovery of his family background. Here was a high value catch. Radio Hanoi boasted of the capture of 'air pirate McCain, son of Admiral McCain'. McCain was still badly disabled from the crash and the inadequate medical treatment that followed. Because of his importance the means were there to negotiate his swift return. But McCain wouldn't hear of it. He chose instead to adhere to the POW code that you wait your turn. He refused to be repatriated ahead of other American prisoners who had been in captivity longer than him. He wouldn't budge, despite it being made clear to him what this would mean. His guard told him, 'Now, McCain, it will be very bad for you.' He was tortured for his defiance, and ultimately spent more than two years in solitary confinement. The original injuries from the crash, the negligent and negligible treatment, and the physical abuse by his captors all left a physical mark on McCain. A physical mark that would stay with him until his dying day.

So, it was one of the most stunning and shocking moments of the presidential campaign when Donald Trump – a man who managed to perform a body swerve around the draft to go to Vietnam because of 'bone spurs' in his feet – spoke of McCain in the most disparaging terms: 'He's not a war hero. He's a war hero because he was captured? I like people who weren't captured.' Trump's disrespectful poke-in-the-eye drew gasps. But though the pundit class predicted this would be the end of the Trump candidacy, that this would be the moment when the air went out of his balloon, it barely left a mark. If anyone wants to pinpoint a single moment to demonstrate that the cultural unity around the things which Americans were thought to hold dear shattered, this was probably it. Trump had mocked self-sacrifice and demeaned honour, and blithely got away with it. Among those who might have been expected to find this unforgivable, there was a barely concealed shrug. Politics was now being played by Donald Trump's insurgent rules.

There was mutual disrespect, which would carry on through the campaign and into the White House. A media savvy senator from South Carolina, Lindsey Graham, would later try to broker a peace between the two men, but it never got very far. Graham, a close friend and ally of McCain, had been equally critical of Trump, but had come around, and felt there was more to be gained from trying to school the inexperienced President in matters of defence and foreign affairs than there was in standing on the outside hurling stones.

In truth, though, McCain seemed to enjoy tweaking the President's tail: pointing up his shortcomings, not seeking to mask policy differences. But things changed when the Arizona senator was diagnosed with brain cancer. With characteristically phlegmatic courage McCain would carry on coming to Capitol Hill, to speak on key issues and to vote. One of the most crucial votes was on Trump's efforts to repeal and replace the Affordable Care Act – or Obamacare as it was more widely known, the signature health reform from the Obama era. The policy had given millions more Americans insurance cover, but it had raised premiums for the middle classes and reduced choice. It was seen by many Republicans as unconscionably bureaucratic, unwieldy and, heaven forbid, a dangerous, slippery step towards the socialist nightmare of a National Health Service.

The vote was evenly tied in the Senate and, very deliberately, with the cameras running on the unfolding test of Trump's authority, McCain made sure he was the last to vote – and as he went towards the tellers he held his arm out, and left it there with a deliberate, dramatic pause. The eyes of the nation were on him; the eyes of the White House were burning into his back. He kept the pause going, just as the presenters on a TV talent show would do before announcing whether it is the fire-eating contortionist or the magician and his lovely assistant who would be going through to the finals, the cameras cutting quickly between their anxious, nervous-looking faces. All that was missing from the Senate floor that night was the roll of the drums.

This was McCain's moment – and he knew it. Then, finally, like a Roman senator deciding whether a slave who's given his all on the floor of the Colosseum should be spared or thrown to the lions, McCain, with the flicker of a smile playing on his lips, turned his thumb down. He was now tired and weak, his face scarred by the medical interventions to tackle his brain cancer. He was dying and he knew it – but he hadn't lost his sense of the theatre of politics; nor had he mellowed enough to acquiesce and just toe the party line. He thought the new health plan was flawed, and he was damned if he was going to just be meek lobby fodder. The former naval officer had torpedoed the Trump plan, and holed it below the waterline.

The froideur between McCain and Trump was now Arctic – penguins would have struggled to survive in this icy, wind-blown tundra. All of which was awkward, as the one-time presidential candidate was fast reaching the end of his life. Not that that brought any softening from the President. When it became clear that McCain was planning to oppose a Trump nomination for a post requiring Senate confirmation, one of Trump's loyal West Wing aides retorted, 'It doesn't matter. He's dying anyway.' This lion of the Senate, war hero and independent-minded statesman would soon be gone. The McCain family kept lines of communication open to the White House through John Kelly, keeping him informed of the senator's deterioration. The chief of staff would in turn brief the President. Kelly and McCain were friends. They had known each other well, and with their shared military background there was a huge amount of mutual respect.

Then Kelly had the call from Cindy McCain that he had been expecting. The doctors thought the time had come to turn off the life support machine. The family had concurred. The news would be announced that John McCain had passed. That day came on Saturday, 25 August 2018.

Kelly has told friends that he relayed the news to the President, and wanted him to engage on what should happen next. How did the President want to mark this death: would there be a period of mourning, was there to be a state funeral, and so on and so forth. But the President wouldn't engage. And in this impasse the chief of staff decided he would go it alone. He ordered that the flag over the White House should fly at half-mast to mark the death of this great American. That was Saturday evening.

When Trump realised this on Monday morning, he apparently went berserk at his chief of staff. I'm told the air was thick with F-bombs and with language so salty that it could clog your arteries. Kelly may have been a general, but Donald Trump was the Commander in Chief, and he decided the time had come to show who was the boss and who gave the orders. He commanded that the policy be reversed. So up went the Stars and Stripes, back to the top of the White House flagpole. Kelly has told friends that he said to the President in no uncertain terms, 'You can fire me if you want, but I am always going to do the right thing.'

The President had got his way. But it was turning out to be a pyrrhic victory. The White House was now out of kilter with the rest of Washington, where on public buildings flags were still at half-mast. The cable news channels had their cameras trained on the White House roof. Social media lit up. Donald Trump had picked an argument with a newly deceased American hero and statesman – and it very quickly became apparent he was losing. The President wasn't only fighting his chief of staff; he was fighting a good chunk of US public opinion. Lawmakers from both parties were calling on Donald Trump to show respect. Veterans' organisations piled in too. That morning the President repeatedly avoided journalists' questions on the subject. But by Monday lunchtime it was battle over, and the Stars and Stripes returned to half-mast. Trump had relented and issued a statement saying, 'Despite our differences on policy and politics, I respect Senator John McCain's service to our country, and, in his honour, have signed a proclamation to fly the flag of the United States at half-staff until the day of his interment.'

Throughout Kelly's tenure there were repeated stories that he was about to leave or be fired, only to be followed up by a Trump tweet that it was all nonsense, and they got along just fine. There would be further reports that his influence in the White House was on the wane, and he was becoming a marginal figure.

Then came the reports going in the opposite direction: the repeated suggestion that Kelly thought Trump was an idiot – and that he, John Kelly, was the one that was saving the country, not Donald Trump. Friends of his told me that the four-star general thought his period in the White House bunker had been the most demanding he had faced in his career. In June 2018 there were suggestions that Kelly had given up trying to save Trump from himself. That he had concluded he should let the President act unilaterally, even if that would result in impeachment – a threat that became more real after November 2018, when the Democrats made sweeping gains to take control of the House of Representatives.

Support for that view was provided by former White House communications staffer Cliff Sims in his tell-all description of life in the White House. He offers a lurid account of Kelly fulminating in his office. 'This is the worst fucking job I've ever had,' he says to a group of aides. The chief of staff was sitting in his office, with the White House swimming pool just visible beyond the French doors. 'People apparently think that I care when they write that I might be fired. If that ever happened, it would be the best day I've had since I walked into this place,' Kelly tells them. 'And the President knows it, too.'

But then came the most extraordinary news of all. Kelly said he had accepted Trump's invitation to remain as chief of staff through to the 2020 election. Really? Are you kidding? No one believed that was going to happen. And sure enough, at the end of 2018, with relations severely strained, and the chief of staff exhausted and disillusioned from his 18 wearying months of trying to hold the reins at the White House, it was agreed he would go.

The chief of staff job certainly has its rewards: the signature pieces of legislation passed when all seemed lost, the triumphant bits of diplomacy, the disasters averted through the chief of staff's acuity and diligence. But ultimately the job leaves most holders of the post burned out and frazzled, which is why it is a position where the tenure tends to be exceptionally short, and turnover is high. When Barack Obama was getting through his chiefs of staff at quite some rate, Donald Trump took to Twitter to berate him: '3 Chief of Staffs [sic] in less than 3 years of being President: Part of the reason why @ BarackObama can't manage to pass his agenda.' By the end of 2018, Donald Trump was on his third chief of staff inside two years. In political circles when you have the job of chief of staff you are known as the 'javelin catcher'. And for a reason. You are the person that has to interpose himself between the troublemakers and the bruised ego brigade who are intent on hurling a sharpened metal spear in the direction of the president with as much force as possible. You can only catch the javelins for so long in this high stress, no respite job.

Kelly and the President agreed a statement that would be put out on a Monday morning announcing his departure. But perhaps inevitably it was pre-empted by Trump himself, who announced it 48 hours early. The White House was doing nothing to steer journalists away from the suggestion that the 68-year-old Kelly would be succeeded by a 36-year-old wunderkind, Nick Ayers, who had served as chief of staff to the Vice-President, Mike Pence. He would be the political brain needed by the President in the run-up to 2020. There would be a renewed focus in the White House on campaigning and messaging – a common approach for a president halfway through his first term and starting to eye what needed to be put in place to win a second. In this Trump had the strong backing of daughter Ivanka and son-in-law Jared.

A fine plan – except Ayers had got cold feet. He wanted to 'spend more time with his family'. He was going back to Georgia to see more of his triplets. What is interesting is how the story was allowed to gain traction that he was a shoo-in for the post, and that it was almost a done deal. It made it look as if the President wasn't the master of his own destiny. More damaging, it made it appear that the President, far from being able to pick and choose from the brightest and best, was being rebuffed. In the normal course of events the greatest honour that could be bestowed upon an American patriot is to get the call to serve the country and the president. But Ayers chose to give it a miss. Things would go from bad to worse in the search for chief of staff number three.

A number of other names started to be bandied around. Some were put out there as kite flying exercises – you see what reaction their name provokes before you take it any further. Others were fantasy names, just as you might pick your fantasy football team. One name, though, started to get proper and due attention. Chris Christie has been in and out of favour with Donald Trump over the years. Back in 2015 when Trump launched what people thought would be a quixotic attempt to get the Republican nomination, Christie had been told that Trump would pull out, having milked the publicity for branding purposes – and the property tycoon would get behind the New Jersey governor. Christie is a heavyweight in every sense of the word. He knows politics. As a former federal prosecutor, he knows the law – although the fact that he put Jared Kushner's father away in prison a few years back didn't exactly endear him to the President's son-in-law. (The father pleaded guilty to 18 counts of tax evasion, witness tampering and illegal campaign contributions and was sentenced to two years in federal prison.) Christie also shared the President's pugnacious and pugilistic approach to politics, and the two men knew each other extremely well.

On paper he was the ideal candidate, particularly with Donald Trump facing multiple legal challenges wherever he looked. We were told that the meal that he and the President had at the White House had gone very well. And then, bang. Christie had turned down the job as well. 'I have told the President that now is not the right time for me or my family to undertake this serious assignment,' Christie said in a statement. 'As a result, I have asked him to no longer keep me in any of his considerations for this post.' As with the Ayers refusal, this is pretty extraordinary and would have never happened in the Bush or Obama White House. You just do not get out in front of the president and publicly contradict him. It breaks all normal protocol, and speaks volumes about the dysfunctional way decisions were made.

There was now an air of panic, fury and impotence at the White House. To lose one potential chief of staff may be regarded as a misfortune; to lose two looks like carelessness, as Oscar Wilde might have said, were he reporting Washington politics at the end of 2018. Someone, anyone, surely would want the job. This spoke to the darkening clouds that were gathering over the Trump administration, with a mass of legal problems beginning to close in on the President – and the knowledge that it was likely to get a lot worse.

And this wasn't just an issue relating to finding an appropriately qualified chief of staff. A super-smart lawyer friend of mine, who had worked in the private sector and on Capitol Hill on a Judiciary Committee inquiry, was returning to the private sector and was seeing advertised any number of jobs in the executive office of the White House. These are jobs that in normal times would never need to be promoted. There would be a long queue of the most capable people with shimmering CVs fighting to get the chance to burnish their credentials with a spell at the White House. But it no longer works that way. There is a sense that what you are getting involved with will be chaotic; that given the President's multiple legal difficulties you might find yourself needing to retain outside counsel, which is cripplingly expensive; and finally, how many people have emerged from their time at the Trump White House with their reputation enhanced?

In this climate, the White House hurriedly put out a statement saying that Mick Mulvaney, the Director of the Office of Budget and Management, would also take on the acting role of Chief of Staff. The prospect of Mulvaney taking on the post permanently took a hit when footage emerged of him during the 2016 election campaign describing Donald Trump as a 'terrible human being'. Mulvaney would claim that he and Trump joked about it – but it is hard to believe the President was laughing when he watched it. It all looked a bit scrappy, gave the impression that his appointment had been a scramble, and conveyed the image of a White House at the mercy of events, not in control of them. Exactly the sort of thing a strong chief of staff is meant to forestall. But an acting chief of staff? The one job that is meant to convey strength and stability and it is an 'acting' role? How does that work? If you are trying to say to Washington and the rest of the world that the second most powerful person in the administration is there in an acting capacity, you are sending a very mixed message.

The approach of Mulvaney also seems to represent a third way in doing the job. Mulvaney, like Kelly, wanted to impose some order and structure in the executive branch that he is presiding over – but unlike Kelly he was not trying to constrain the President. He is firmly signed up to the 'let Trump be Trump' school of management. Mulvaney is happy for the President to go his own way. That has pleased the President. He is also not going around – as Kelly did – telling everyone how much he hates and detests the job. And that has pleased the staff.

John Kelly would give an interview soon after he left the White House. He said it was a 'bone crushing hard job'. And he set the bar in a fascinating way on how his tenure should be measured. He said he should be judged by what the President did *not* do. In other words, don't look to the legislation that he helped push over the line. Look instead at what he stopped an impulsive and reckless president from doing. The chief of staff not as facilitator, but as safety net.

# Chapter 3

# The Cabinet Room

Probably the most famous cabinet ever assembled by an American president was the so-called 'team of rivals' that Abraham Lincoln brought together in 1861. Much is made, and rightly, of the extreme polarisation in US politics today, and the fiercely partisan nature of debate. But America in the 1860s – though it had the enviable benefit of no Twitter or Facebook – was on the point of genuine disintegration; it was a Divided States of America, with the South seeking to secede from the North over the issue of the abolition of slavery. And the country was about to plunge into the Civil War, which would claim the lives of three-quarters of a million men out of a population of 35 million. Lincoln, the self-educated lawyer from Kentucky, who was not much versed in the ways of Washington, needed the 'brightest and the best'; he needed people who could hold America together at this moment of maximum peril for the nation. The first shots in the civil war would be fired more or less as soon as Lincoln assumed the presidency.

Lincoln went about his task by bringing in people who wouldn't just be 'yes men' – compliant ciphers who would do his bidding – but strong-minded politicians in their own right, with their own bases of power. It was an effective ploy, as the historian Doris Kearns Goodwin emphasised in her influential 2005 book *Team of Rivals*, subtitled 'The Political Genius of Abraham Lincoln'. Those who had fought him for the 1860 Republican presidential nomination – New York senator William H. Seward, Ohio governor Salmon P. Chase, and Missouri's distinguished elder statesman Edward Bates – found themselves appointed to the highest positions in the land. Despite their difference – and the bitter rivalry – they gradually warmed to Lincoln during those fraught Civil War years. That is, with the exception of Chase, who was never reconciled to his defeat and still thirsted for the presidency. He would continue to plot incessantly against America's 16th president. But Lincoln indulged him, on the principle expressed most eloquently by President Lyndon B. Johnson, a hundred years later, when he said of his troublesome FBI director, J. Edgar Hoover, that it was better to have him in the tent pissing out, than outside the tent pissing in. Chase, though, did eventually quit in 1864, only for Lincoln – stunningly – to appoint him as Chief Justice of the Supreme Court.

By now, compatibility was a second order concern for Lincoln. After the ravages of the Civil War, there could only be one purpose, one goal – and that was to staunch the bleeding and restore the Union. And on that basis, there was common endeavour from these disparate men. Lincoln was the first among equals, yes. But he wanted big figures, who felt free to challenge him. And he knew they would. Lincoln worked to the time-honoured political axiom that you hold your friends close, and your enemies closer.

It is probably fair to say that is not the overriding philosophical underpinning of today's president, or the guiding principle behind his cabinet appointments.

Donald Trump just has to take a few steps from the Oval Office, through the door into the outer oval office and straight into the cabinet room. The large oval table – a gift from Richard Nixon in 1970 – seats 20, and each cabinet secretary sits in a strictly appointed place, according to the date the department was established. The President sits at the middle of the table with his back to the Rose Garden. And lest anyone should be in any doubt which is the President's chair, his has a higher back and arms than anyone else's. To his right sits the highest ranking of the department heads, the Secretary of State; to his left sits the Secretary of Defense. Opposite him is the Vice-President – and Mike Pence is flanked by the Treasury Secretary and the Attorney General.

All cabinet meetings are held there, although there are records of interesting 'awaydays'. In 1844 the 10th US president, John Tyler, invited members of his cabinet aboard a new warship called the *Princeton* for a cruise on the Potomac, the river that runs through Washington and leads out into the Chesapeake Bay. The ship had a 12-inch cannon aboard, which someone had seen fit to call the Peacemaker. And throughout this happy little voyage, the big gun was fired ceremoniously to the delight of onlookers lining the banks of the river. Drink was consumed, and there was an atmosphere of celebration. After several hours, and several toasts, the captain of the ship, one Robert F. Stockton, was persuaded to fire the cannon one last time – only for the gun to explode, sending white hot metal scattering across the deck and killing eight people including two cabinet members,

Secretary of State Abel Upshur and Navy Secretary Thomas Gilmer. Tyler, who was below deck at the time, was unhurt. Well, that's one way to create the need for a cabinet reshuffle.

No cabinet in any administration stays the same for long, but in Donald Trump's the turnover of people from the top table has been quite something. The revolving door has needed grease applied regularly. In the room each cabinet chair bears a brass plate with name, position and dates of service. When a cabinet member departs, the tradition is that their cabinet chair is bought by the staff and presented to them as a gift. In which case, since Donald Trump's election, cabinet chair makers and the brass plaque manufacturers of Washington DC must be enjoying something of a boom.

Just how far the Trump administration would be from the Lincoln model became clear when the President brought his cabinet together for the first time. The cameras were brought in to witness the opening round table discussion. It was a first to be able to record at such length the inner workings of the cabinet of the 45th president.

This was the room which had been the nerve centre for fraught discussion led by Franklin Delano Roosevelt over whether the then isolationist US should join the war against Nazi Germany after Pearl Harbor, and later the brinkmanship during the Cuban missile crisis as John F. Kennedy was engaged in the most dangerous poker game with his Soviet counterpart Nikolai Kruschev. Forty years later George W. Bush brought his key national security advisors together there on 12 September 2001, to declare that freedom and democracy were under attack. Look back over the momentous periods of US history, and all the president's men would have been sat around the table, with the key advisors sitting on the room's outer edges, while looking down from the walls were the portraits of predecessors who had wrestled in their own era with the nation's destiny, and who would be a source of silent reassurance (or discomfort) for those who succeeded them.

In June 2017, five months after his inauguration, Donald Trump was eventually able to bring his completed cabinet together for the first time, after his nominees had finally navigated their way through the rocks and rapids of tricky confirmation hearings. What unfolded was less 'team of rivals' than the 'squad of sycophants'. The meeting seemed to be an exercise in smarm. What follows is an only slightly edited version of what was said. It starts with the President giving a *tour d'horizon*, praising his cabinet – but most of all lavishing praise on himself. It is then the turn of his newly appointed cabinet secretaries. It is probably best to skip this next bit if you have a delicate stomach or are prone to queasiness. I have quoted it at length – though not exhaustively – because it is telling as an insight into the demeanour of his senior staff, and revealing too in how unabashed the President is to be bathed in praise and adoration.

DONALD TRUMP: This is our first Cabinet meeting with the entire Cabinet present. The confirmation process has been record-setting long – and I mean record-setting long – with some of the finest people in our country being delayed and delayed and delayed.

It is an incredible, talented group of people in this room: generals, governors, congressmen, entrepreneurs, business leaders and many, many others. I chose each person at this table and I chose them not only because of their remarkable experience and success, but because they've all been united by one shared goal, what they want to do, one very simple, but very beautiful, goal: serving and defending our beloved nation.

I will say that never has there been a president – with few exceptions; in the case of FDR, he had a major depression to handle – who's passed more legislation, who's done more things than what we've done, between the executive orders and the job-killing regulations that have been terminated. Many bills; I guess over 34 bills that Congress signed.

So, we're here to change Washington, return power to the people. We're here to give people a great shot at a great, great job, and even opening small businesses and employing other people. I look forward to hearing all of the reports from the different people in the room today.

We have done, as I said, about as much as anybody ever in a short period of time in a presidency. That's despite a tremendous opposition from the other side. We have done something that's very special. And you see it in the economy numbers, because the economic numbers have been incredible.

So, I think what we'll do – most of you know most of the people around the room, but I'm going to start with our – our Vice-President. Where is our Vice-President? [Inaudible] [Laughter] There he is.

And I'll maybe start with Mike.

MIKE PENCE (Vice-President): Thank you, Mr President. And just the greatest privilege of my life is to serve as the – as vice-president to the president who's keeping his word to the American people and assembling a team that's bringing real change, real prosperity, real strength back to our nation.

TRUMP: Thank you, Mike.

JEFF SESSIONS (Attorney General): Mr President, it's great to be here and celebrate this group. We are receiving, as you know – I'm not sure the rest of you fully understand – the support of law enforcement all over America.

They have been very frustrated. They are so thrilled that we have a new idea that we're going to support them and work together to properly, lawfully fight the rising crime that we are seeing. And it's an honour to be able to serve you in that regard [interrupted by Trump saying 'That – that's great'].

TRUMP: Thank you.

ALEX ACOSTA (Labour department): Mr President, I am privileged to be here. Deeply honoured, and I want to thank you for being – your commitment to the American workers.

TRUMP: Thank you and congratulations.

RICK PERRY (Energy): My hat's off to you for taking that stance [withdrawing from Paris climate change deal] and presenting a clear message around the world that America's going to continue to lead in the area of energy.

TRUMP: Thank you, Rick.

NIKKI HALEY (UN Ambassador): Thank you, Mr President. It's a new day at the United Nations. You know, we now have a very strong voice ... And so, I think the international community knows we're back.

TRUMP: Thank you, Nikki. That's terrific.

MICK MULVANEY (Director of Office of Management and Budget): With your direction, we're able to focus on the forgotten man and woman, who are the folks who are paying those taxes. So I appreciate your support and direction in pulling that budget together.

TRUMP: Thank you, Mick.

BETSY DEVOS (Education): Mr President, it's a privilege to serve, to serve the students of this country, and to work to ensure that every child has an equal opportunity to get a great education, and therefore a great future.

TRUMP: Thank you, Betsy.

TOM PRICE (Health and Human Services): Mr President, what an incredible honour it is to lead the Department of Health and Human Services at this pivotal time under your leadership. I can't thank you enough for the privileges you've given me and the leadership that you've shown.

TRUMP: Thank you.

RYAN ZINKE (Interior): Mr President, it's an honour to be your steward of our public lands and the generator of energy dominance. I am deeply honoured. And I am committed and optimistic that we can be both great stewards and be the world's largest producer of energy.

TRUMP: And we can do both. Thank you very much.

REX TILLERSON (Secretary of State): Mr President, thank you for the honour to serve the country. It's a great privilege you've given me.

JIM MATTIS (Defense): Mr President, it's an honour to represent the men and women of the Department of Defense. And we are grateful for the sacrifices our people are making in order to strengthen our military so our diplomats always negotiate from a position of strength. Thank you.

TRUMP: Thank you.

WILBUR ROSS (Commerce): Mr President, thank you for the opportunity to help fix the trade deficit and other things. The other countries are gradually getting used to the idea that the free rides are somewhat over with.

TRUMP: Thank you, Wilbur.

ELAINE CHAO (Transport): Mr President, thank you so much for coming over to the Department of Transportation. Hundreds and hundreds of people were just so thrilled, hanging out, watching. I want to thank you for getting this country moving again, and also working again.

TRUMP: Thank you. Thank you very much.

MIKE POMPEO (CIA chief): Mr President, it's an honour to serve as your CIA director. It's an incredible privilege to lead the men and women who are providing intelligence so that we can do the national security mission.

And in the finest traditions of the CIA, I'm not going to share a damn thing in front of the media. [Laughter]

DAVID SHULKIN (Veterans Affairs): Mr President, thank you for your support and commitment to honouring our responsibility to America's veterans. I know that this is personally very important to you. I have the great honour of being able to represent the 21 million American veterans that have done such great things for this country and I've worked every day to make sure that we're honouring that responsibility. Thank you.

TRUMP: Thank you very much.

STEVE MNUCHIN: Thank you, Mr President. It was a great honour travelling with you around the country for the last year and an even greater honour to be here serving on your cabinet. On behalf of everybody at the Treasury, I can assure you we are focused on creating sustained economic growth, sweeping tax reform, and fighting terrorism with sanctions and all other programmes within our control.

BEN CARSON (Housing and Urban Development): Mr President, it's been a great honour to – to work with you. Thank you for your strong support of HUD and for all the others around this table that I've worked with. We're making tremendous progress at converting to a business model. Already seeing tremendous savings there.

REINCE PRIEBUS (Chief of Staff): On behalf of the entire senior staff around you, Mr President, we thank you for the opportunity and the blessing that you've given us to serve your agenda and the American people.

And we're going to continue to work very hard every day to accomplish those goals.

TRUMP: Thank you, very much. Thank you. Thank you all very much. Thank you. Thank you, everybody. Thank you very much.

Well, Socratic dialogue it wasn't. It seemed to be an exercise in fawning, as one after another they seemed to enter into an encomium bidding war. I see your 'honoured' and raise you a 'greatest privilege'. Aah, but I see your 'greatest privilege' and raise you a 'blessing'. And Donald Trump sat in his slightly taller chair than everyone else, a self-satisfied smile on his face as he listened to the reports, head nodding knowingly, feeling very much taller than everyone else. This was less first among equals than first among minnows.

Certainly none of the interventions had quite the impact of the Treasury Secretary, William Windom at the end of the nineteenth century, as he spoke on a subject dear to this president's heart, trade: 'As a poison in the blood permeates arteries, veins, nerves, brain and heart, and speedily brings paralysis or death, so does a debased or fluctuating currency permeate all arteries of trade, paralyze all kinds of business and brings disaster to all classes of people.' After that elegantly crafted peroration Windom sat down, lit a cigar, took a sip of water – and suffered a fatal heart attack.

Nothing as dramatic has befallen any of Donald Trump's cabinet – but many nevertheless have found their careers cut short prematurely. The current trade representative, Robert Lighthizer, made the joke in that round-table presidential love-in, that he was late for work because he'd got stuck in the swamp. Of all the insurgent messages that Donald Trump unleashed during the 2016 presidential election, the one that perhaps struck a chord with most people across the political divide was his promise to 'drain the swamp'.

The self-serving, self-perpetuating élites of Washington DC would get what was coming to them, according to the candidate. Their swanky lunches in expensive eateries, paid for by ubiquitous lobbyists, would be over. The fact-finding trips abroad, the best corporate hospitality money could buy, the black Lincoln town cars with blacked-out windows ferrying them around, the revolving door between government and fabulously paid jobs in corporate-land would all become a thing of the past. Now there was a new sheriff in town who was going to bring a new ethical code. No longer would money buy influence. And the people that Donald Trump had chosen to be in his cabinet would be the servants of the people, not of well-heeled, tan-leather-upholstered, made-to-measure suited, coiffed special interest groups. Corruption had met its nemesis; it would be relentlessly rooted out, and those guilty of such malfeasance would be unceremoniously and brutally put to the sword. Or at least that was the theory. The reality turned out to be somewhat different.

From that group of people, who sat together for the first cabinet meeting in June 2017, it is remarkable how many have either been forced out or quit, and how many others have big, murky ethical clouds hanging over them. If this was a new dawn for ethical government, it didn't really look like it. And how many who stood their ground against the President, because they disagreed with this or that aspect of policy, either quit or were pushed out.

Scott Pruitt, who'd been put in charge of the Environment Protection Agency, was very firmly a Donald Trump favourite. They spoke the same language. He shared all the president's instincts on the climate – broadly speaking, that climate change was a 'hoax' – and he set about his mission with gusto. He had come from Oklahoma, where he served as that state's attorney general. While in that role he was one of the principal architects of the legal battle against Obama's climate change policies, repeatedly suing the agency that he would soon head. He described himself in his biography for that job as 'a leading advocate against the EPA's activist agenda'. So when he was appointed its new leader, many staffers thought the President had put in a fox to run the chicken coop.

And so it turned out. He took a scythe to many of the environmental regulations that Barack Obama had introduced – on car emission standards, or industrial pollutants. Environmental scientists in his department who took a differing view were ostracised – or fired. Along with Trump, whose own view was that 'global warming was created by and for the Chinese', Pruitt oversaw the efforts to dismantle systematically the major climate regulations. Trump announced at the beginning of June 2017 that the US would withdraw from the Paris climate accords. Pruitt followed that up a few months later with a pledge that America would withdraw from the Clean Power Plan, a regulatory structure introduced by Barack Obama to limit greenhouse gas emissions on a state-by-state basis.

The Obama-run EPA estimated the Clean Power Plan could prevent 2,700 to 6,600 premature deaths and 140,000 to 150,000 asthma attacks in children. But when Pruitt was challenged about the health consequences of doing away with the Clean Power Plan, he argued that the policy was bureaucratic overreach.

There was no doubting Pruitt's efficiency in driving through the Trump agenda – remember Donald Trump during the presidential election campaign had pledged to get coal miners mining again, blast furnaces blasting again, and pipelines built to assist the growth of the US economy. The regulatory shackles were going to be unlocked, and in Scott Pruitt, Donald Trump had his man with a set of keys to do that.

There was also no doubting he liked to live high on the taxpayer's dime. By the time he eventually stepped down/was fired, there were multiple ethics investigations into his behaviour – from within his own department, and from Congress as well. Some of the issues were banal, but hilarious: he enlisted his security detail to run a series of personal errands, including driving him around to find bottles of a lotion that he particularly liked, which were only to be found in Ritz-Carlton hotel bedrooms. Or – my other favourite – Millan Hupp, a Pruitt staffer, would tell congressional investigators that she had to reach out to the Trump International Hotel in Washington after Pruitt said he thought there was 'an old mattress that he could purchase' from the President's hotel. Really? He wanted a mattress on the cheap?

His response to these claims came in an usual response. He attached to his financial disclosure form a broad paragraph with this sentence. "To the extent that I am aware of specific allegations, I dispute the facts asserted and accordingly am not aware of reportable gifts." And then he said if fresh disclosures were made, he would address them as and when they came.

Then there were the really quite big ethical skirmishes: insisting on taking private jets or military aircraft, or at the very least flying first class. He justified that by saying it was for security purposes, naturally – citing the 'toxic environment' in politics and implying he was less likely to face threats if he was in a nice, plump, comfy first-class seat. EPA memos obtained by CNN said that if Pruitt flew economy, the occasional 'lashing out from passengers' could 'endanger his life'. (NOTE TO SELF: next time the BBC tell me I have to fly economy, I will use the Pruitt 'life in danger' defence.)

But this was the least of it. When he was in Washington he stayed at the home of a lobbyist for a peppercorn rent. Pruitt lived for about six months in a Capitol Hill condominium owned by a health care lobbyist whose husband had lobbied his own department, the EPA. He paid a fraction of the market rate. Ridiculously, this came to light after a former deputy chief of staff told congressional investigators the energy lobbyist, J. Steven Hart, called Pruitt's chief of staff to complain that Pruitt was behind on rent, and the couple eventually evicted Pruitt by changing the code on the locks. Again Pruitt does not deny any of this. His spokesman merely said that there was no link between any policy decision he made and the price he paid – and who he paid – for his housing. Well that's good then.

I could honestly take up the rest of the chapter with Pruitt excesses – the $42,000 of unauthorised expenditure to install a soundproof telephone booth in his office; the EPA staff who were tasked with persuading a fast food chain, Chick-fil-A, to allow his wife to become a franchise owner. His demand that he be given a 24/7 security detail, even though his post was not normally deemed high risk – he even insisted they use their sirens and flashing lights when moving around, irrespective of whether he was on government business or not. He was also alleged by House of Representatives Democrats to have run a number of different email accounts and calendars so that he could schedule meetings in secret, without their existence ever appearing on official records. Likewise, he was reported to have used a number of different phones so there were no call records of who he'd spoken to. Now if memory serves me correctly, Republicans made quite a big fuss about Hillary Clinton using a private email server when she was Secretary of State. Pots and kettles? Stones and glass houses?

What was astonishing about Scott Pruitt was not that he resigned/was fired, but that he was able to last as long as he did – particularly given the President's swamp draining promise. Week after week new stories would emerge about questionable behaviour, bringing unwelcome attention. And week after week the President chose to turn a blind eye. But Trump was torn – he knew that these daily headlines were damaging, but he didn't want to give a 'scalp' to the media, and he thought Pruitt was one of the administration's most effective operators. Another theory that I heard advanced about what finally tipped Trump over the edge in deciding to get rid of him was annoyance at just how much attention he was getting; just how much ink was being spilled on Scott Pruitt. The limelight could only belong to one person.

Over the years I have reported on any number of political resignations. There have been the letters that were slightly pitiful when a politician has fallen short, and has been caught in a humiliating scandal. There are the letters spitting anger and rage, that are all but wrapped round a brick and hurled through the window of the president or prime minister with a molotov cocktail attached. Scott Pruitt's will earn its place in the annals – for its total lack of contrition, and the grovelling 'I love you so much, Donald' tone. It really is something:

Mr President, it has been an honor to serve you in the Cabinet as Administrator of the EPA. Truly, your confidence in me has blessed me personally and enabled me to advance your agenda beyond what anyone anticipated at the beginning of your Administration. Your courage, steadfastness and resolute commitment to get results for the American people, both with regard to improved environmental outcomes as well as historical regulatory reform, is in fact occurring at an unprecedented pace and I thank you for the opportunity to serve you and the American people in helping achieve those ends.

That is why it is hard for me to advise you I am stepping down as Administrator of the EPA effective as of July 6. It is extremely difficult for me to cease serving you in this role first because I count it a blessing to be serving you in any capacity, but also, because of the transformative work that is occurring. However, the unrelenting attacks on me personally, my family, are unprecedented and have taken a sizable toll on all of us.

My desire in service to you has always been to bless you as you make important decisions for the American people. I believe you are serving as President today because of God's providence. I believe that same providence brought me into your service. I pray as I have served you that I have blessed you and enabled you to effectively lead the American people. Thank you again Mr President for the honour of serving you and I wish you Godspeed in all that you put your hand to.

Your Faithful Friend,
Scott Pruitt

Pruitt wasn't the only one to find that his moral compass was struggling to locate magnetic north. The health and human services secretary, Tom Price, was forced out after it emerged that he'd spent – well, strictly speaking, the taxpayer had spent – a fortune on travel for him to swan around on private jets. An investigation by the Office of the Inspector General found that he improperly used federal funds for his travel to the tune of three hundred and forty one thousand dollars. Price's coat was already hanging by a wobbly peg, after repeated efforts to repeal and replace the signature Obama era policy – the Affordable Care Act – had foundered and flopped. That didn't impress the President, but it wasn't fatal. His penchant for Gulfstreams, though, proved to be. Just before his departure, he apologised for taking the flights and offered to reimburse the Treasury for the relevant costs. The former Georgia congressman wrote a letter of apology in which he noted, 'All of my political career I've fought for taxpayers. It is clear to me that in this case, I was not sensitive enough to my concern for the taxpayer.' I wonder which bit of hiring private jets he thought *would* be sensitive enough for taxpayers. Anyway, it was too late, and after 231 days in the role he was gone. The President said he didn't like the 'optics'.

Then there was the Veterans Affairs Secretary, David Shulkin. He was the only Trump nominee to be unanimously confirmed. He was that rarest of birds: someone who had served in the Obama White House yet was enough in favour to be offered a berth in the Trump cabinet. Rumours of a toxic atmosphere within his department started to circulate, and there were policy disagreements with Trump nominees over the extent to which he was privatising the VA, the sprawling and vast federal department that provides healthcare to those who serve and have served in the military. Trump surrogates felt he should be going much further.

But it wasn't policy that did for him, it was money. And a nice trip to Europe for him and his wife. The report of the department's internal inspector was damning. He had ordered a subordinate to handle personal travel plans for him and his wife during an official trip to Europe. While there, he was found to have improperly accepted tickets for Wimbledon as a gift during the trip. Among other 'serious derelictions', the report also accused Shulkin's chief of staff of potential criminal conduct by making false statements and altering a document so that the Veterans Affairs Department could 'improperly' pay for Shulkin's wife to travel to Europe with him, at a cost to taxpayers of $4,312. Shulkin always maintained that there was 'nothing inappropriate' about what he did, and that he had paid for the Wimbledon tickets himself.

But the eventual report (which Mr Shulkin described as inaccurate and biased) was less supportive of Mr Shulkin. It found that one of his staff had 'effectively acted as a personal travel concierge' to Shulkin and his wife for the trip to Copenhagen and London. Meanwhile Shulkin and the VA made misstatements to the media about aspects of the trip, the report says, with Shulkin inaccurately claiming to a reporter that he had bought the tickets for the tennis tournament himself. The VA Secretary would discover his services were no longer required when the President tweeted that he had been fired. He wouldn't be the last to suffer that fate.

Others in his cabinet have got themselves into similar scrapes. Ben Carson, who ran against Trump for the Republican nomination, and was appointed housing and urban development secretary, got into trouble after it appeared he was rather too interested in his own housing, and in particular the development of his office. A $31,000 mahogany dining room table and chairs was ordered as part of a refurbishment of his office suite. When this became public, Carson said he was not aware of how expensive the dining room set was and requested that the order be cancelled. He insisted it was nothing to do with him, and that the order for the furniture had been placed by subordinates. Emails unearthed using freedom of information legislation proved otherwise.

Mr Carson's wife, Candy, played a central role in coordinating the redecoration of the office – even down to scheduling an appointment with interior decorators, reviewing photo boards of furniture choices and pressuring staff members to find more money for furnishings, according to the emails. This was all going on as the Trump administration proposed extensive cuts to his department's budget. The trove of emails also revealed that senior HUD officials were scrambling to work out ways to reconcile Mrs Carson's demands for the major upgrade to the office suite with federal laws that prohibit expenditure of more than $5,000 on office furniture without congressional approval. Carson, who in his previous life had been a brain surgeon, had given the White

House a mighty headache, but he was not required to walk the plank over this.

Nor was Ryan Zinke, the Interior Secretary. Zinke, who hailed from Montana and had once been a Navy SEAL, arrived for work on his first day on horseback, complete with cowboy hat. But when he wasn't riding horses, he too had a bit of a thing about getting around on private planes. Thousands of dollars were spent on charter flights. He used his political clout to censor politically unhelpful work. So a report on climate change by the independent body which runs America's wonderful national parks, the National Park Service, was censored because it reached conclusions at variance with the views of the administration. He is alleged to have blocked a casino project on a Native American reservation that was ready to be given the go-ahead, after visits from a potential competitor's lobbyists who ran their own casino 12 or so miles away. And a property deal was also under investigation that he stood to benefit from. Zinke's answer to these multiple investigations being carried out by his department's Inspector General was novel. The *Washington Post* reported that he sought to fire the incumbent, and replace him with someone more emollient, who had been a political appointee by the Trump administration, rather than a career public servant. And to the specific charges, Zinke said he wasn't going to spend thousands of dollars 'defending himself and his family against false allegations.'

Zinke was gone by the end of 2018, as a slew of ethics investigations gathered pace and his presence in the administration became a growing embarrassment. In early 2019, with all those ethics questions over his head, it was announced that he was teaming up with Corey Lewandowski, Trump's former campaign manager and still a regular visitor to the White House, in a Washington lobbying firm – exactly the sort of revolving door practice that the President had promised to end.

Even one of the most senior members of the Trump cabinet would find himself in hot water. The Treasury Secretary, Steve Mnuchin – yes, you've guessed it – would get into trouble for the whole private jet thing. Although his case has a couple of interesting twists. While in office, Mnuchin, the super-wealthy former Goldman Sachs financier, got married to the Scottish model and actress, Louise Linton. She is 18 years his junior, and confessed in a glossy magazine interview that their personalities are polar opposites (which sort of begs the famous Mrs Merton question, 'What first attracted you to the multi-millionaire Steve Mnuchin?').

It was reported that he had requested a military jet to fly him and his new bride to their European honeymoon over the summer, a revelation that raised a whole series of questions about the wealthy couple's use of government aircraft. Mnuchin would confirm that his staff had explored the idea as a way of ensuring that he had access to secure communications and information while he travelled abroad. He would say "I never asked the government to pay for my personal travel.' And claimed the story was misreported.

This came after an even more extraordinary episode when he flew with Louise Linton on a private government jet to visit Fort Knox in Kentucky. On her Instagram account, Ms Linton posted a photo of her walking down the steps from the blue and white government plane, tagging all the different haute couture designers she was wearing – a Valentino this, a Hermes that, a Tom Ford something else. When a member of the public upbraided her for this, with the comment 'Glad we could pay for your little getaway', the Treasury Secretary's wife gave the woman both barrels:

'Adorable! Do you think the US govt paid for our honeymoon or personal travel?! Lololol. Have you given more to the economy than me and my husband? Either as an individual earner in taxes OR in self-sacrifice to your country? I'm pretty sure we paid more taxes toward our day "trip" than you did. Pretty sure the amount we sacrifice per year is a lot more than you'd be willing to sacrifice if the choice was yours.'

And then, with a patronising, supercilious, lip-curled flourish, she added this:

'You're adorably out of touch ... Thanks for the passive aggressive nasty comment. Your kids look very cute. Your life looks cute.'

Inside Fort Knox, the happy couple would pose holding a newly minted sheet of uncut bank notes, with his signature on each dollar bill. For the photo she wore elbow length black leather gloves, and pouted at the camera. People joked that they looked either like a gangster and his moll, or a Bond villain and accomplice. But where they really flew too close to the sun was, well, where they really flew too close to the sun. The day they chose to fly to Fort Knox on 15 November 2017 was special in one other respect. It was – coincidentally – the same day that certain parts of America would witness a rare total eclipse of the sun. And – guess what? – where they were going in Kentucky was on the line of totality. So the obvious conclusion was drawn – what a perfect day to be flying to Kentucky in a private jet and to witness, at 36,000 feet, the sun being blotted out by the moon. Mnuchin strenuously denied that this had played any part in his decision to go that day.

There are a number of things remarkable about these collective lapses or near lapses into what might be termed 'sleazy' behaviour. The first and most obvious is just how many cabinet members were caught up in any number of questionable episodes, over such a short period of time. This isn't a catalogue of scandal that unfolded over the eight years of a two-term president. This is inside the first couple of years.

One other thing about the Trump team was just how incredibly wealthy it was. It was flush with billionaires, multi-millionaires – oh, and a smattering of generals. It was the richest group ever assembled. The joke was you either needed to have bread or braid to get into a Trump cabinet. Presumably the military men were the poorest of those who sat round the famous table, but it should be recorded that none of them was caught up in any of these scandals. One of the great advantages of a cabinet not drawn from the legislature is that you can appoint people who are genuine experts in their own field and who aren't desperately trying to learn the subject on the job.

The other big plus is that there aren't the same pressures as in, say, the British system, to hold regular reshuffles, so that the young tyros get their chance to shine – the parliamentary under-secretary who wants to be a minister of state, before getting a promotion to secretary of state and a seat at the cabinet. In the British system this is about party management and discipline. If you're the prime minister you reward with promotion those backbenchers who stay in line, are hardworking and stay out of trouble; your power of patronage means you can block and marginalise those who are nuisances, lazy and cause you headaches. In the British system you are also seeking to balance the different factions within the governing party. Look at Theresa May and the desperate efforts she made to keep some kind of balance between Euro-sceptics and 'Remainers' during the tortuous Brexit process. Even a prime minister like the 'Iron Lady', Margaret Thatcher – who certainly didn't have the authority issues that Theresa May had – nevertheless had to manage the party's rival wings. She was never able to purge completely the 'wets' from her cabinet, much though she might have liked to.

The US president has no such concerns. He can pick the brightest and the best; those whose experience in business, academia or public service makes them the obvious choice to oversee one of the great government departments. With some in Donald Trump's cabinet you could see exactly why they had been chosen. James Mattis was a four-star Marine Corps general, who had been head of Central Command under the Obama administration; he was a pillar of the defence establishment. (What also endeared him to Donald Trump was his nickname: he was known as Jim 'Mad Dog' Mattis – Trump would relish introducing him at rallies, hamming up the 'mad dog' bit for all it was worth.)

His Commerce Secretary, Wilbur Ross, had been known as the 'king of bankruptcy' before being brought into the administration. He was like the Richard Gere character in *Pretty Woman* – though not quite as good-looking. He bought distressed and failing companies, broke them up and sold them on for a profit, making himself a billionaire in the process. You could see why the President appointed Ross, even though, when he had to make his personal financial disclosures, he was not worth the $2.5 billion that he had previously claimed, and that had earned him a place on *Forbes* Magazine's billionaires list. Poor old Ross was only worth $700 million. A pauper really. Although during the government shutdown at the end of 2018 and the beginning of 2019, when federal workers went six weeks without pay, he didn't exactly show his most empathetic side when he questioned why these people needed to queue at food banks for handouts. Cake anyone?

But some of the others, well, you just had to scratch your head. Betsy DeVos from Michigan had been a major Republican Party donor, and you certainly didn't need to worry about her name being erased from the *Forbes* billionaires list. Her husband is listed as America's 88th richest man. They sit comfortably among America's super-wealthy. The extent of their wealth became something of a national joke during the summer of 2018 when vandals set adrift from its mooring on Lake Erie the family's 163-foot yacht, the *SeaQuest,* worth $40 million. Sympathy was tempered when it was reported that the family owned nine other vessels.

In her time in Michigan she had been a firm advocate for charter schools, home-schooling and vouchers so that parents can send their children to private schools. But during her confirmation hearings she revealed that neither she nor her children had ever set foot in a state school as students. And her actual knowledge of how state schools operated, how teachers worked and pupils lived was – let us put it kindly – not exactly top of the class. Her confirmation as secretary of education made history: she was the first to be appointed by the casting vote of the Vice-President, Mike Pence (the VP can only cast a tie-breaking vote in the Senate, but is otherwise ineligible to vote). On a visit to America's biggest school district in New York, DeVos made a deliberate point of *not* visiting any state schools. This led to what in normal circumstances would have been a career ending car crash of an interview for the programme *60 Minutes*. Here is a sample from it:

Had the public schools in her home state of Michigan improved? she was asked. 'I don't know.' Were the number of sexual assaults equivalent to the number of false accusations? 'I don't know. I don't know.' Why was she known as the most hated cabinet secretary? 'I'm not so sure exactly.' Had she visited bad schools? 'I have not. I have not. I have not intentionally visited schools that are underperforming.'

'Maybe you should,' said the interviewer.

'Maybe I should, yes.'

Two years in, Betsy DeVos was still a firm favourite of the President. But what about those he wearied of, those who had not committed any ethical transgression, but had simply fallen out of favour with this capricious leader?

The treatment meted out to Trump's first Secretary of State, Rex Tillerson, was extraordinary. Serving for just a year, Tillerson became one of the shortest serving US foreign ministers ever. Thickset and white-haired, when he took up the post he was lauded by establishment Republicans as someone who would be one of the 'grown-ups' in the room. If anything was likely to get under the President's thin skin it would be the suggestion that there would be a group of men who would act as wise counsel to stop him careering off the rails – the nurses and matrons for a wayward toddler, if you like. But Tillerson, with his distinguished career as a corporate titan – he had for more than a decade been chairman and chief executive of Exxon, one of America's most important and significant global companies – was seen as a 'big beast' who would be able to stand his ground with Donald Trump, and wouldn't be cowed.

That was one part of it, but that business background, a history of running a global company, a career spent closing deals in the Middle East and Russia – these were seen as invaluable attributes. And he was commended to Trump by any number of former senior administration officials – the likes of former Secretary of State Condoleezza Rice and former defence secretary and CIA director Robert Gates championed his cause with Donald Trump. But very quickly problems began to emerge. What was clear was that neither man trusted the other. And that is simply an untenable position.

Ambassadors would write cables back to their governments based on conversations they had had with Rex Tillerson, stating what the US position would be on this or that issue – only to find it directly contradicted by the White House. So along Massachusetts Avenue in north-west Washington, where all the embassies are housed, diplomats started to pose the question: what's the point of talking to him if he doesn't know the President's mind and the President doesn't care what he thinks? There were any number of flashpoints. It was clear Tillerson wanted to keep the US in the climate change agreement, but Trump wanted out. Trump prevailed. Likewise on the Iran nuclear deal, where scant attention was paid to Tillerson's concerns about the dangers of US withdrawal, and the universal acceptance that Iran was in compliance with the terms of the treaty. Again Trump prevailed.

One of the most jarring disagreements was on what US policy would be towards the massively wealthy Gulf state of Qatar, also the site of the Al Udeid airbase – home to ten thousand US and US-led anti-ISIS forces. But Mr Trump called Qatar a 'funder of terrorism at a very high level'. And he said that within minutes of the State Department questioning whether the Saudis were using the terrorism charge as cover for 'long-simmering grievances' between the Arab nations. So, to the world it looked as though Rex Tillerson's State Department was lining up behind Qatar; while at the White House they were falling in behind the house of Saud. It would be a central source of tension between President and Secretary of State. Tillerson found himself in the middle of a power battle for control of Middle East policy with Donald Trump's son-in-law, Jared Kushner – who was furiously advocating for the President to make Riyadh the first foreign stop of his presidency. Kushner prevailed.

What didn't help Tillerson was his broadly antipathetic view towards the staff he worked with at Foggy Bottom (a name that always sounds as though it should be the punchline of a joke), the district of Washington where the State Department is housed. He thought it was bloated and inefficient; they thought he didn't understand what they did, and even if he did, he didn't much care for their work. Under his watch, 60 per cent of the department's top-ranking career diplomats quit, with new applications falling by a half, according to figures put out by the American Foreign Service Association. The place had hollowed out. Key diplomatic missions had no head; some staff were acting five grades *above* their pay grade. Juniors were making policy. And when Tillerson wanted to bring people in, he was often blocked by the White House. On a presidential trip to Asia, staff were talking to journalists on the plane about what their Far East policy should be. They were making it up as they went along.

One friend of mine, who was headhunted for a very senior position, had endless meetings, and was told he was exactly what they wanted, only for the whole process to just fizzle out. It wasn't that anyone else was appointed to the post; the job just remained vacant. Another hole in America's diplomatic armoury.

But what really did for Tillerson was a report that emerged on the US network NBC of a meeting that took place at the Pentagon in October, 2017. He had apparently called Trump 'a moron'. Actually, what he is believed to have said was that Trump was 'a fucking moron'. Not good. This story emerged on the day when the President was flying to Las Vegas to offer comfort to the families of those who had been killed and injured in America's worst mass shooting incident, when a gunman, holed up in the Mandalay Bay Hotel, had opened fire on thousands of people who had gathered for an outdoor country music festival below.

Before the President departed from Washington word had gone out from the White House that Tillerson needed to go out and clear up the mess. So Tillerson, who was not exactly media friendly, reluctantly came before the cameras. He insisted he enjoyed a close relationship with Trump and called him 'smart'. Yes, but what about you calling him a moron? 'I'm not going to deal with petty stuff like that,' Tillerson said from the State Department Treaty Room. 'I'm just not going to be part of this effort to divide this administration.' Umm. That is what we call in the business a non-denial denial. And everyone recognised it for what it was.

Now one immutable law about surviving in Trump's administration is that no one shall get between the President and a headline. As Donald Trump boarded Air Force One at McCarran Airport in Nevada, the TVs were switched on – and the headlines were not 'Donald Trump consoles victims of worst mass shooting'. They were 'Tillerson refuses to deny calling Trump a "moron"'. Really not good. The President was volcanic. Tillerson was the headline and for all the worst possible reasons. And all the way back from Las Vegas to Washington, Donald Trump fumed.

If this incident sealed his fate, the dénouement would come a few months later. Tillerson had been on a long and exhausting trip to Africa, and was on the last wearying leg home. Tillerson was neither user friendly, nor media savvy and not *au fait* with newfangled twenty-first-century things like social media. All of which was a bit of a problem. Because as his staff turned on their phones as they landed, they all very quickly became aware of a presidential tweet, and one of them would have to be tasked with breaking the news to the Secretary of State. The tweet read:

Mike Pompeo, Director of the CIA, will become our new Secretary of State. He will do a fantastic job! Thank you to Rex Tillerson for his service! Gina Haspel will become the new Director of the CIA, and the first woman so chosen. Congratulations to all!

Well, strictly speaking, congratulations to all except Rex Tillerson, who had just been fired in the most brutal way imaginable. The President hadn't even bothered to pick up the phone to tell him in person before announcing it on Twitter.

This one-time giant of corporate America, who had been begged to come out of retirement to serve his country, had just been given the most unceremonious heave-ho. Humiliation doesn't begin to describe it. It's hard to avoid the conclusion that the one-time host of *The Apprentice* – with its famous catchline: 'You're fired' – finds it easier to get rid of someone in a confected boardroom, under television lights, than he does in person. In the brutal world of politics, he repeatedly showed himself to be a coward – either doing the firing via Twitter or handing the gun to his chief of staff, so he could be the one to carry out the execution.

Tillerson returned to the State Department and bade his staff a tearful farewell, with a thinly coded attack on Donald Trump, who wasn't mentioned by name. 'This can be a mean-spirited town,' he said, 'but you don't have to participate in it.' And he spoke about the importance of treating people with respect. 'Each of us get to choose the person we want to be, and the way we want to be treated, and the way we will treat others.'

But as if all this wasn't bad enough, there was worse. The chief of staff, John Kelly, gave an off-the-record briefing to journalists – which inevitably found its way into the public domain. He spoke about how he had tried to warn Tillerson on the Africa trip that he might be about to receive bad news from the President. Kelly told us that at the time he called, Tillerson was suffering from a bad stomach bug from his journeying through Africa and 'was on the crapper' as he broke the news. So not just humiliated but embarrassed as well.

After a long silence, Tillerson would eventually pull the curtains back a touch on what life had been like in

Trumpworld. 'What was challenging for me coming from the disciplined, highly process-oriented ExxonMobil corporation,' Tillerson told the CBS network months after his firing, 'was to go to work for a man who is pretty undisciplined, doesn't like to read, doesn't read briefing reports, doesn't like to get into the details of a lot of things, but rather just says, "This is what I believe."' And he went on to say that this was a man who acted on his instincts, which looks like impulsiveness. But perhaps the most damning thing he had to say about working with Donald Trump was the extraordinary lack of respect he had for the law. 'So often the President would say, "Here's what I want to do, and here's how I want to do it,"' he told the *Houston Chronicle*, 'and I would have to say to him, "Mr President, I understand what you want to do, but you can't do it that way. It violates the law."'

Remarkably, even though months had passed from his firing, Tillerson's comments could not go unanswered. Any criticism of the President brings a big, swinging counter-punch – and it came literally within hours of the former Secretary of State's comments being made public. On Twitter – and with even more gusto than is normal – Trump said that Tillerson had been as 'dumb as a rock', he didn't have the mental capacity required and he was 'lazy as hell'. Yes, the same man who, when he was appointed, Trump had been praised for his 'tenacity, broad experience and deep understanding of geopolitics'.

Going back to the 'love-in' that took place round the cabinet table that first time it was assembled, the remarkable thing is just how few are left unscathed. A record number have been forced to quit, some have been fired, while some survive despite the ethical cloud that hangs over them. The turnover is unprecedented and life expectancy is short.

The only person at that first meeting to leave the cabinet with head held high was Nikki Haley, the US Ambassador to the United Nations. Unlike Tillerson, who never seemed to learn to speak the language of Trump, what Nikki Haley could do was translate Trumpian dialogue and turn it into a form of words that those around her on the East River in New York would find more palatable. At times she would distance herself from the President. Most notably when the White House said she had been 'confused' when she said the administration was getting ready to impose fresh sanctions against Russia. 'With respect,' she witheringly fired back, 'I don't get confused.'

But most of the time she was able to put a more human face on some of the 'America First' rhetoric that was anathema to the internationalists at the United Nations. She was also totally street smart. She understood Washington politics in a way that Tillerson never did; she knew how far she could push it; and she knew how to fight America's corner at the United Nations. So it was a bit of a bombshell when she came into the West Wing undetected and told Donald Trump she wanted to resign. Officials were blindsided. But this was no disorderly departure. This had more of an old-fashioned feel to it. Both sat in the Oval Office as the President lavished praise on her: 'She's done a fantastic job and we've done a fantastic job together. We've solved a lot of problems and we're in the process of solving a lot of problems,' he told reporters. While she thanked the President for the opportunity to serve, Haley, the former governor of South Carolina, who has political ambitions of her own, added that she would not be running against the President in 2020. I suspect that had she not said that, the farewell would have been nothing like as cordial.

Donald Trump had something else to say on Nikki Haley's planned departure. Paying tribute to her spell as the United States' public face to the world, and one of the key jobs in the administration, he said that she had made it 'a more glamorous position'. Obviously being good-looking and 'glamorous' should be a key part of the 'job spec' for the UN job, so it was really not much of a surprise at the close of 2018 that the person nominated to succeed her was a woman called Heather Nauert. She was, on the face of it, your stereotypical 'glamorous' blonde ex-Fox News presenter, but she was undoubtedly smart and mastered the brief quickly. She had one other huge asset going for her. She very quickly earned the trust of the President. She came to the job with no diplomatic or policy making experience, nor having ever held elected office, but she was the President's pick to be in charge of US foreign policy at the United Nations.

There is another wrinkle in this appointment. During the November 2018 midterm elections Republicans found themselves doing terribly among educated women voters – and that cost them a number of seats in the House. But in making the announcement that Ms Nauert was his choice to be at the UN, he also said he was downgrading the job, so it would no longer be cabinet level. What a combination: upgrading the importance of glamour; downgrading the status of the job. I think a political strategist might comment that the optics of that, given Republican Party difficulties, left a little to be desired. Before Ms Nauert's nomination got very far she withdrew her name from consideration.

The eagle-eyed among you will have noticed that I have gone around the cabinet table in this chapter and barely mentioned Jefferson Beauregard Sessions III. The story of Jeff Sessions and his tenure at the Justice Department as Attorney General is such an epic tale and rollercoaster ride that it really deserves a whole chapter to itself. His brief, tumultuous tenure came to an end after the November 2018 midterm elections.

The last departure of 2018 was of the Defense Secretary, Jim Mattis (his tenure too will be covered in more detail in a later chapter). His exit from government would also mark the passing of the last of the so-called grown-ups from the administration. Just a few days before Christmas 2018 he had woken to a Trump tweet that did not please him. Not one little bit. For a start it was on a matter of defence policy – his purlieu; second, it hadn't been discussed with anyone; third, Mattis believed it was fundamentally wrong; and fourth, this wasn't just Trump sounding off. He meant it. The offending tweet was that America was pulling its troops out of Syria because the war against ISIS had been won. 'We have defeated ISIS in Syria, my only reason for being there during the Trump Presidency.' In other words, the President woke up one morning and, without telling anyone, decided to pull American troops from Syria, and reduce America's commitment to Afghanistan. Worse, it looked like the person who had persuaded him of the wisdom of this course of action was not anyone in the administration, but the President of Turkey, Recip Tayep Erdogan.

It was a decision that begged myriad questions to do with where this left America's allies, and where this left the Kurds, who had been instrumental (and American backed) in the fight; to do with whether defeat had really been achieved, to do with consultation, to do with wider geopolitics – but for Jim Mattis it begged the very personal question – and one he had been wrestling with for some time: could he any longer serve under this president? It had always been a delicate balance. His sense of public service, patriotism and love of the armed forces – and his importance as a counterweight to the President's more impulsive and impetuous pronouncements – had hitherto tipped the scales in favour of him staying. But if his advice and the counsel of the generals in the Pentagon was to be routinely ignored, then there was only one conclusion to be reached. He had to quit.

His resignation letter (quoted in full in a later chapter) was as far as you could get from the one delivered by Scott Pruitt. It amounted to a thinly veiled repudiation of Donald Trump's defence and foreign policy, and it made clear how much the two men did not see eye to eye. 'Because you have the right to have a Secretary of Defense whose views are better aligned with yours on these and other subjects,' Mattis wrote, 'I believe it is right for me to step down from my position.' Mattis said he would leave at the end of February 2019. But Trump wasn't having someone else dictating the terms. So at a cabinet meeting a week or so after the shock resignation the President announced that he was bringing forward Mattis's departure date. Why? Because it allowed Trump to claim that he'd brought Mattis's career to an end. In the President's mind Mattis didn't quit. He was fired.

The astonishing attrition rate brought an interesting change in man management from the President. He dispensed with the whole business of actually appointing successors who would have to go through the cumbersome confirmation process, as part of Congressional oversight. He just appointed cabinet ministers on an 'acting' basis. There was another calculation in this. Once a cabinet member has been approved by Congress, they have a degree of independence. They have the approval of lawmakers. They don't just have their job thanks to the patronage of the president. But this way? In an acting capacity? All fealty is then owed to the President – and displease him and you are gone.

The other exceptional thing about all this is that in any other administration a cabinet that had suffered so many casualties and calamities, resignations and rebuffs, where so many people had crossed a line, or been incompetent, or committed such a collective mass of ethical transgressions, or all of the above, it would have all but brought down a president. But in today's Washington, it seems, a senior member of the administration getting into trouble is almost a second order event. Most Americans, I suspect, would barely remember the names of these characters because they came and went so quickly. And with a president who never lets the limelight move away from him, these people who enter the administration with such high hopes never had the opportunity to imprint themselves on the American consciousness. And so another cabinet member goes. Shrug. Another scandal erupts. Whatever. Another private plane is leased. And?

These things are passing with barely a flicker, in a world where the new normal seems to change so fast. And as for the man who promised to come and sort out the drainage problem in the swamp? Well, the swamp looks more swampy than it's ever been.

# CHAPTER 4

# The Briefing Room

If you stand in Lafayette Park, opposite the White House, and look straight at the elegant building in front of you – the tall imposing mansion bit on the left is the East Wing. And then look to the right, and it is the lower rise West Wing, with an immaculately turned out Marine Corps guard on duty whenever the president is in his office. Linking the two is a single-storey building. That is where the Briefing Room is found, along with the offices of a number of the more junior communications people working for the president.

From the Oval Office to the Briefing Room is around 27 steps. I should quickly add that they are 27 steps President Trump has never taken to answer questions from reporters. Unlike his predecessors, who would frequently come to brief, he has only once come onto 'our territory' in the White House. A deliberate statement? Almost certainly. We come to him. He doesn't come to us. This is a president who obsesses about his press coverage, like few others. He is not the first to feel that he gets a raw deal, but few in history have had such a burning sense of injustice about media coverage as

Donald Trump. With a Democratic Party unsure of what it stands for, and unclear about what it wants to be in Trump's America, he sees the media as the enemy. Indeed, it is a good deal more acrimonious than that. Twenty-seven paces from the Oval to the Briefing Room. But a million miles apart in so many other respects.

The Briefing Room as it has now evolved was opened by George W. Bush in 2007, and is named after James S. Brady, the press secretary under Ronald Reagan, who was shot and paralysed in the assassination attempt on the President's life in 1981. There is a series of windowless offices and booths in the basement, with a lively population of rodents (cue whatever rat joke you like), and a grotty kitchen – though it has a very smart coffee machine provided by the actor Tom Hanks, who recognised how exhausting it was going to be covering this President and sent it as a present to the White House Correspondents' Association. The room itself is seven rows of blue seats, seven across. Seats are strictly allocated – TV networks and news agencies at the front. Important newspapers and cable news channels after that. Until you get to the back row, where you will find the *Guardian* and the BBC. Actually, we have to share our seat with a new online, pro-Trump cable channel – it is not an arrangement where we get one buttock each on the seat. We get alternate days. But seeing as the briefing has become a thing of obsolescence under this administration it really doesn't matter.

Just how seismic and epic the change would be with the transition from the 44th to the 45th president became apparent on the first full day the new administration was in office. So let's start at the very beginning.

President Trump's inauguration would take place on 20 January 2017. A Friday. A helicopter flew the Obamas away from the Capitol after the ceremony, and the Trump team moved in later that day. On the Saturday the President went to the CIA headquarters at Langley, Virginia, where he made a highly political speech, which seemed to suggest he was yet to make the transition from campaigning to governing. And it gave a clue also of what was to come in his relationship with the media. In his speech to the nation's intelligence community, he said that the suggestion that he had been critical of the intelligence services over which he now presided had been more fake news, a confection got up by journalists. Presumably he'd forgotten his tweet from a few days earlier when he blamed the spies for leaking information about him, and in reference to their behaviour asked, 'Are we living in Nazi Germany?' He must have thought these intelligence officers weren't – well – terribly intelligent.

But let's leave that to one side – that was small beer. I had gone to the White House to do a live report on the President's first full day in office, with my assessment of how it had gone. Outside the Briefing Room, a sign had been put up saying there would be a press conference in a couple of hours' time. Briefings on a Saturday evening just don't happen. Or when they do, they are to announce that something of global significance has just happened. So, I called the office and said I wouldn't be coming back, but would wait until the briefing.

There weren't that many people in the room when Sean Spicer, the President's first press secretary, came to the podium. The networks don't have that much news on Saturday evenings, and the schedule tends to be overtaken by college football – a huge thing in America. And a lot of people were home seeing their families for the first time in ages after the hectic build-up to the inauguration.

At the end of the Obama era the daily press briefings were being conducted by Josh Earnest. He is smart, charming, clean cut, with college boy good looks, very polite and extremely articulate. And his briefings could be slightly interminable. Not dull, that would be the wrong description. But some-times, befitting his name, a little earnest. He would allow the different TV correspondents to repeat more or less the same questions that had already been asked, so that on the evening newscast the NBC correspondent, say, could be seen asking the key question to the press secretary, instead of – and heaven forbid – having to rely on the question the person from ABC had asked. For the most part it was all quite convivial. He respected the press; the press respected him.

No longer. Sean Spicer came into the Briefing Room that evening like an angry swarm of hornets. Josh Earnest he isn't. Slightly thicker set and shorter, with suits that initially looked a size too small, but later seemed a size too big – and he'd often look rather sweaty under the TV lights. What now unfolded was less a briefing, more a rant. He would take no questions. This was a conversation in which only one person would speak. Him. And it was to berate sections of the media for their 'deliberately false reporting'. What had riled the President – and you felt that Spicer was merely reading out the newly installed President's words – was the suggestion that Obama had had more people than he did at his first inauguration. And so Spicer laid it out unequivocally: 'This was the largest audience to ever witness an inauguration – period – both in person and around the globe.'

The whole thing lasted barely five minutes. But it clearly indicated we were in a new age with the White House – and it would be a new and challenging era for reporting. The facts were quite simple to determine. You just compared and contrasted the two photographs taken from the Washington Monument at the time when the inaugural addresses were being delivered on the steps of the Capitol. And what those two photographs showed was that the largest audience to ever witness an inauguration ... had come to see Obama. Period.

But Donald Trump wouldn't have it. Even though there was a brilliant attacking defence that he could have made – that his supporters were less well off, were too busy eking out a living to put a meal on the table for their kids and weren't the well-heeled, educated, liberal middle classes who lived around Washington and who could afford the luxury of taking the day off – the message from the President was that his staff had to continue to maintain this falsehood. Attack. Attack. Attack. And no one does that better than Kellyanne Conway, senior advisor to the President, who would go on television the next day to deny that she was propagating a lie. No, heaven forefend, Spicer was using 'alternative facts', she told the bemused interviewer. In other words: a falsehood.

Our challenge as journalists was how to report this. I think a very short time ago we would have fallen into an easy and lazy template: the White House says this, the Democrats say that – only time will tell who's proved to be right. Jon Sopel. BBC News. Washington. But in this context that seemed mealy-mouthed and inadequate. This new era was going to call for a new style of reporting: aggressive impartiality. If one person says 2+2=4, but someone else says 2+2=6, we can't just say, 'Time will tell who is right.' So, after refreshingly little discussion from my senior colleagues in the BBC, we just called it. We said what the White House had claimed about the numbers attending the inauguration wasn't true.

Across Washington and around the world, media organisations were wrestling with the same issue: How far to go? When is it appropriate to say that the President has been untruthful? When is it correct to say he misspoke? When do you cut through all the flannel, and just simply say he is lying? It wouldn't be the last skirmish. Some of them became a lot bloodier.

All 45 presidents who have occupied the White House from George Washington onwards have felt at various times a burning resentment about the press, even if then they didn't have to deal with the relentlessness of the 24/7 news cycle. The symptoms then were identical to those felt today – that they are not getting a fair shake; that policies are wilfully misrepresented; their words are taken out of context; their enemies are given a so much easier ride. And you can go back to the age of the founding fathers and find that even Thomas Jefferson was mithering about his press coverage. In 1807 he wrote to a newspaper complaining: 'Nothing can now be believed which is seen in a newspaper. Truth itself becomes suspicious by being put into that polluted vehicle of falsehood and error.'

And journalists could play rough. When John Quincy Adams went swimming in the nude in the Potomac River, it's reported that Washington's first woman reporter stole his clothes and would not give them back until the President answered her questions. More recently, Lyndon B. Johnson famously (and somewhat ruefully) said, 'If one morning I walked on top of the water across the Potomac River, the headline that afternoon would read, "President Can't Swim".'

Reporters dedicated to covering the White House 'beat' are really something that only started in the twentieth century. Until then the focus had been on covering Congress – where the laws were made. And if the president happened to be on Capitol Hill, that is when you would cover him. Other presidents had had a haphazard relationship with the press, but it really started to formalise with Theodore Roosevelt. Roosevelt who had a knack, a theatrical gift, if you like, for shaping the news and getting it covered in the way that he wanted. He cultivated reporters. And, unimaginable today, Roosevelt loved to take trips across the nation, disappearing for weeks at a time. Sometimes he would go off into the American wilderness and be incommunicado. Other times he would set off on the burgeoning network of railways and would take reporters with him. And with the growth of the newspaper industry, and increased literacy ... Roosevelt saw a new way to get his message across, with intimate, off-the-record briefings. David Greenberg, the author of *Republic of Spin*, tells how he would gather in his office a handful of his favourite reporters. They were at times derisively called the 'fair haired'.

A barber would be giving him a 'wet shave', and he'd be lecturing the newsmen about politics, policy and gossip, as they struggled to get a question in. One of the great muckraking reporters of the day was a man called Lincoln Steffans. And he would wait until the straight-edged razor skimmed Roosevelt's lower lip, and he would then try to fire off his questions. If Roosevelt became animated in trying to answer him, the barber would say, 'Steady, Mr President.'

Today there are millions of people following Donald Trump on Twitter, and it's been remarked that here perhaps for the first time is a president who is able to communicate directly with the electorate without it being mediated by the media. But that is to ignore America's post-recession and wartime leader, Franklin Delano Roosevelt (a distant cousin of Teddy), and his 'fireside chats'.

From March 1933 to June 1944, Roosevelt addressed the American people in about thirty speeches broadcast via radio. In this pre-television age, some 90 per cent of Americans had a 'radio set'. He spoke on a variety of topics covering everything from banking to unemployment, to fighting fascism in Europe. Millions of people found comfort and renewed confidence in these speeches, which became known as the 'fireside chats'. The name stuck, even though FDR was nowhere near a fireplace as he was delivering them. The phrase seemed to evoke perfectly the comforting intent behind Roosevelt's words; the informal, conversational tone was no accident. Roosevelt took care to use the simplest possible language, concrete examples, easy to grasp analogies, so as to be clearly understood by the largest number of Americans.

In 1934, the second year of Franklin Delano Roosevelt's first term, the West Wing was completely redesigned and the press room rebuilt. It had desks, typewriters and telephone links to telegraph companies. Areas were set aside for correspondents to play cards and chess in between filing their stories. It was at this time that a wealthy benefactor paid for an indoor swimming pool to be built where the Briefing Room is today, so that FDR, who had contracted polio in the 1920s, would be able to exercise in private.

After the Second World War, news organisations were dedicating more and more staff to cover the White House beat, and moving resources away from Congress. The television age had arrived, and the president, whoever he was – and however comfortable/uncomfortable he was in front of the camera – had to learn to live with this intrusive lens on his doings.

By 1950, the then president Harry Truman had a problem. There were simply too many reporters, too many TV cameras and all the attendant paraphernalia, too many foreign reporters, to hold news conferences in his office. One writer noted that on the days when the press would gather, the Oval Office resembled a Times Square subway platform during rush hour.

So Truman decided that the fourth estate had to be moved. He plumped for the Indian Treaty Room, in what is now called the Eisenhower Executive Office Building, the imposing office block just next door to the White House, occupying the corner plot on 17th and Pennsylvania Avenue.

By the 1960s, the press room in the EEOB was badly in need of repair, but it would take about a decade for the White House to get round to doing anything about it. Presidents Kennedy and Lyndon B. Johnson, meantime, were enjoying the pool. Kennedy, who suffered from a chronic back complaint, relaxed there to ease the pain. His entourage, his assistants irrespective of rank, were invited to join him as he exercised at lunchtime.

With LBJ it was a different story. LBJ was an intimidating figure to say the very least, but *Town & Country* magazine noted in a January 2017 article that his staff 'would find any credible excuse to scatter whenever LBJ expressed a desire to take a swim, for not only would he swim in and lounge around in the pool completely naked, but he would insist that others do the same. In a scene that is most unsettling to imagine, he once cajoled the preacher Billy Graham to join him in one of his skinny-dipping sessions. (They prayed together in the water.)'

It is not without irony that the person who drained the pool and set in train the creation of the Briefing Room on top of it was Richard Nixon – his preferred method of relaxation was bowling, not swimming. It was ironic, because the only person who has had a more toxic and dysfunctional relationship than Donald Trump with the media is Nixon. And when you read some of the things that Nixon did, you start to think that maybe Donald Trump is a bit of a pussycat. But it is worth spending a little time looking at Nixon's relationship with the media – because so much of it is a prelude to what has happened since Donald Trump moved into the White House. It is as though the 45th president has picked up the baton from the 37th. The echoes of history are unmistakable.

Nixon had a famously antagonistic relationship with the media that went back to his days in Congress. Convinced that the media had contributed to his narrow loss to John F. Kennedy in the 1960 presidential election (he was badly worsted in the first of the televised debates when he appeared sweaty and with a five o'clock shadow against the suave, handsome and supremely telegenic JFK), and having lost a 1962 election for governor in California, Nixon opened a notorious news conference with this statement of pure self-pity. 'Now that all the members of the press are so delighted that I have lost, I'd like to make a statement of my own.' He then launched into a rambling assault on the media. On another occasion he said to the journalists, 'Don't get the impression I'm angry. You can only be angry with those you respect ...'

Yes, he was thin-skinned, but what set him off was his belief that on major questions of policy, a liberal/left media was out to sabotage his efforts. At the time the biggest question tearing at America's fabric was the Vietnam War, and he was busy trying to sell a policy that was the 'Vietnamisation' of the conflict – in other words the training up of South Vietnamese forces to take on the Vietcong. So, Richard Nixon took to doing what his predecessor LBJ had done – using the televised address to address the American people. Frequently.

The networks balked at giving the President so many free, unfettered opportunities in primetime and took to putting on panels of experts immediately afterwards, to mark, if you like, the President's work. This drove Nixon nuts. He would deliver a live, primetime televised address – only to see its contents filleted afterwards by those smug, wise-owl commentators he saw as seeking to undermine his presidency. Nixon wasn't going to tolerate this. The Vice-President, Spiro Agnew, was sent out to bat, and the US networks were told by Nixon that it was in their interests to make sure they broadcast it live. They did, and in his speech to a Republican audience in Des Moines, Iowa, Agnew railed at the executives and reporters in charge of the editorial decisions as a 'tiny, enclosed fraternity of privileged men elected by no one'. And with this speech came a campaign to encourage voters to complain to the Federal Communications Commission (FCC) and the networks. That autumn, the administration circulated memorandums outlining how best to attack the networks by using the FCC, the Internal Revenue Service and the Justice Department for political ends, including challenging the operating licences of individual stations.

But if Nixon at best mistrusted, and, at worst, hated the networks, he put a lot of effort into fostering closer relationships with local TV stations – something again that finds an echo today. Donald Trump goes out of his way to cultivate good relationships with the often privately owned local stations, such as the Sinclair Broadcast Group. Owned by a massively wealthy conservative family, Sinclair has 173 stations in 81 broadcast markets stretching from coast to coast, with TV stations just about everywhere in between – at a time when local news outlets outscore the national ones both in overall viewership and trust. There was a decidedly odd and widely ridiculed video that Sinclair put out, with each of its anchors reading an identical script, critiquing the state of modern journalism. It could have been written by Donald Trump, echoing his talking points almost exactly.

For Nixon, to some extent the bullying worked. The networks became a little fearful. But for the most part he kept his vendettas private. Not for him the daily denunciations of the press being 'the enemy of the people', that are a feature of the current president. He schemed and planned his revenge. But it was only after his demise that some of the more extraordinary planned acts of revenge became public. Remember the broadcasting space of the 1960s and 1970s was a lot smaller than it is today. And with fewer broadcasters getting enormous audience share, the news anchors of the nightly broadcasts were huge stars – much more than is the case today when audiences are so much more fragmented. But Nixon did go after one of the biggest names of them all, Dan Rather. Along with Tom Brocaw at NBC and Peter Jennings at ABC, Rather was one of the big three in American broadcasting. But his tough, uncompromising reporting on Nixon in the lead-up to Watergate led to fury in the White House, so the President tried to organise covertly a 'write in' campaign to have him sacked from the network. Word went out to loyal Republicans that they should contact the network to demand that he be fired. It came to nothing.

But if that smacks of clumsiness, there were more sinister efforts to silence his critics. In his book *Poisoning the Press* Mark Feldstein wrote: 'Nixon's administration wiretapped journalists, put them on enemies lists, audited their tax returns, censored their newspapers, and moved to revoke their broadcasting licenses.' Indeed, there was one reporter who Nixon loathed above all others – Jack Anderson. He had been reporting on Nixon for twenty years, and had turned up all manner of unhelpful, muckraking facts about the President. He was now a syndicated columnist reaching millions of people across the US. So what did Nixon do? He commissioned 'the plumbers' – the name given to the operatives responsible for the break-in at the Watergate – to 'take him out'; in other words, have him killed. The 'hit' was never carried out.

Donald Trump may have had his run-ins with us – and there are certainly a large number of journalists who will not be featuring on his Christmas card list (it might be easier to approach it the other way round, and count the few who *will* be getting the Trump family card) – but he hasn't yet resorted to ordering a 'hit' on anyone in particular. Or at least we don't think he has! But he has conducted a systematic hit on the media, whose effects should not be underestimated. Theodore Roosevelt used to talk about the president having a 'bully pulpit', from which he could dictate the terms of the national debate, browbeat those who stood against him, and advance his own agenda. In today's America Trump is using that bully pulpit to pummel the media unashamedly.

Indeed, after the 2018 midterm elections when the Democratic Party regained control of the House of Representatives – and therefore control of all the key committees – one of the first things the new leadership announced they were going to look into was whether the President misused the power of his office by targeting media opponents. The President has repeatedly taken to Twitter to attack one of America's most successful and innovative companies, Amazon. It seemed he thought Amazon should be paying the US Postal Service far more for its parcel delivery service, even though it was a contract between the two bodies that they had freely entered into. So what is it about the CEO of Amazon that Donald Trump dislikes? Simply the fact that Jeff Bezos is also the owner of the *Washington Post*, a newspaper that has produced exclusive after exclusive on the less savoury aspects of this administration.

At the beginning of 2019 the *National Enquirer* magazine had a salacious story about Bezos and his mistress. Days before publication, the Amazon owner and America's richest man announced that he was separating from his wife. The magazine boasted that this had been the tabloid's most extensive and expensive investigation ever. They had text messages, photos. It looked to be a classic tabloid sting. But Bezos – a man who doesn't ever have need to say 'I wonder whether I can afford this' – launched his own counter-investigation into how the publisher had got hold of personal text messages and photos. That alarmed the parent company of the *Enquirer* so much that they threated Bezos with even greater humiliation. A lawyer from AMI wrote to threaten the billionaire that they would publish 'dick pix' in their possession (the legal phrasing, describing the state of the Bezos manhood, was quite something).

But Bezos didn't blink. In a lengthy blog post he turned the tables on the *National Enquirer* to reveal what he said were AMI's attempts to use blackmail and extortion. The unsavoury methods of this celebrity mag were laid bare. This is all remarkable enough, but there was another level of murkiness. The owner of the *National Enquirer* is one David Pecker, and longstanding close personal friend of Donald Trump, who had already carried out 'special ops' to protect the President. (It was Pecker who had paid $150,000 for the story of the former *Playboy* model, Karen McDougal, who wanted to go public with her claims that she and Mr Trump had had a longstanding affair. Pecker bought the exclusive rights to the story; in return McDougal had to sign a non-disclosure agreement, preventing her from telling anyone else. But Pecker never published the story – a practice known as 'catch and kill'.) This now begged a very big question – was this a simple tabloid story, or was this a targeted 'hit' on a Trump enemy? Whichever, it was a lesson that you don't take on the world's richest man lightly. Bezos had come out on top. Or as the *New York Post* headlined it, with admirable brevity, 'Bezos exposes Pecker.'

Another issue that the President involved himself in was the planned merger between the telecommunications company AT&T and media giant Time Warner. Trump made clear that he wanted to block the deal because it would raise prices for households and stifle competition. A court rejected that, but Donald Trump wouldn't let it go, saying that the proposed deal would lead to 'too much concentration of power in the hands of too few'. Of course, the fact that Time Warner is the parent company of his broadcasting nemesis, CNN, had nothing to do with it. House Democrats promised their first investigation into Trump following the November 2018 elections would be into whether the President used 'the instruments of state power to punish the press'.

There is one other news organisation that the President obsesses about, though he might try to pretend otherwise –

and that is the *New York Times*, or the 'failing' *New York Times* as he would have it. I am never sure whether it's a newspaper he loves to hate, or one that he hates to love. But it's his hometown paper, and it is clear he craves their acceptance. It is also clear that it's the newspaper he monitors most closely. There have been tweets where he has disparaged the paper's indefatigable White House correspondent, Maggie Haberman – calling her third rate. Yet, when a documentary was made about the *NYT*, who was it who we saw ringing up Haberman to discuss coverage, but the President. When I now read her articles and see the line 'sources close to the president', I am pretty certain the 'source' is a white guy in his seventies with an orange tinge to his skin and an extravagantly coiffured hairstyle.

It was an encounter that took place at the beginning of 2019 that was most interesting, in what it revealed about Trump's attitude to the press in general and the *New York Times* in particular. He had invited the paper's publisher, A.G. Sultzberger, to the White House for an off-the-record dinner. Sultzberger declined, saying he wanted it to be on the record and he wanted to bring along Haberman and another top *Times* reporter, Peter Baker. Trump acquiesced. The two journalists went along too, and conducted a pretty conventional news interview with the President; but afterwards Sultzberger engaged the President on his anti-press rhetoric and its consequences. 'We've seen around the world an unprecedented rise in attacks on journalists, threats to journalists, censorship of journalists, jailing of journalists and murders of journalists,' the *New York Times* publisher told him. His language was creating a climate in which dictators and tyrants were able to employ the President's words in suppressing a free press, he went on.

What is striking as you read the transcript of their conversation is the extent to which the President really seems to listen, asking questions about what he's being told by Sultzberger. He does not dismiss it out of hand, as might have been expected. Nor, it should be added, does he promise to curb his 'fake news' and 'enemies of the people' chants at rallies, but there emerges from the exchanges a hint of a reflective president.

At the first rally he held after this conversation, it made no difference. The attack on the media was as full-throated and uncompromising as ever. It was in El Paso in Texas, where the President was whipping up support for his border wall with Mexico. Except, on this occasion, at least one member in the audience took Donald Trump's anti-media rhetoric to heart, and attacked one of the cameramen in the press area. It was a BBC cameraman, Ron Skeans, whom I work with every day at the White House. He was attacked from behind and was sent flying. So obvious was it that the President interrupted his speech to check whether Ron was OK. He wasn't hurt, thankfully – but as A.G. Sultzberger had been trying to impress on the President, words have consequences.

During the conversation with Sultzberger at the White House, Trump invariably turns the conversation back to his own treatment, and his deep sense of grievance that he is treated unfairly, meanly even. Of the press in general, he complains, 'What amazes me, because I have great respect for the press, it amazes me that I can be treated so badly and I won. And we're doing well. You know, it is pretty hard to believe actually.'

But when it comes to talking about how the *New York Times* covers him you can just see it's personal. It clearly hurts, and it is almost like a child endlessly and tearfully seeking the approval of a strict parent. Though Sultzberger points out that it is the newspaper's job to hold to account whoever the occupant of the White House is, the President isn't buying it. 'I just think, honestly, I'm enti— I came from New York, I love New York, I'll be back there someday, and I do, I love the place. And I sort of am entitled to a good story ... I came from Jamaica, Queens, Jamaica Estates and I became President of the United States. I'm sort of entitled to a great story from my – just one – from my newspaper.'

There is one other room that I contemplated writing a chapter about, and that is the private dining room in the West Wing. It wasn't much used by Obama, but has become the place where this president likes to 'hang'. It is the room where he has made the most alterations. He has installed a fancy chandelier, but his pride and joy is the 60-inch, flat screen TV that he has installed above the fireplace in the room, just a couple of offices along from the Oval Office.

At the beginning of 2019 there was an extraordinary leak of his daily schedules. What they showed, if you were being unkind, is that this president does next to no work. If you were being generous, you would say he allows himself to benefit from plenty of unstructured thinking time. 'Executive time' is the euphemism that is used. And a lot of each day is ring-fenced executive time. If anyone doubts this, just after the leak of these schedules there was a faintly hilarious episode where one of the cable news anchors accused Trump of being the laziest president ever. Within 45 seconds of the presenter saying this, Trump went onto Twitter to say, 'No president ever worked harder than me.' He hadn't thought this through. If the intention had been to convince us that he doesn't sit about watching television, hadn't he proved the complete opposite? This downtime is invariably spent in the private dining room watching the television and tweeting. Piles of newspapers, cuttings and files sit on the table. He records huge amounts of material too, so he can critique who's doing well and slap down anyone performing badly. And he likes to watch himself. A lot.

Donald Trump has a profound belief that the most effective communicator in his administration is Donald Trump; that the best strategist in his administration is Donald Trump; that the only person who can be trusted to get his message across is Donald Trump, and the only person who really knows how to play the media game is – darn, you guessed it – Donald Trump. And like so much that Donald Trump believes, there is more than a grain of truth to it – and a hot air balloon's worth of warm air.

After all, he has been in the self-promotion and branding game all his life. Prior to his entering politics people remember him for two things. OK, maybe three. First, he was a wealthy property developer in New York. Secondly, he was the long-time presenter of *The Apprentice*. And the third thing was his lifestyle, as the swaggering man about town – according to his own carefully cultivated lore he was the man women wanted, and the man that men wanted to be. Veterans of New York news media still laugh at how Trump would call them up, pretending to be a publicist named John Barron, or sometimes John Miller, in order to offer titbits of Trump's glamorous personal life – the leggy models who were on his arm, which actresses were pursuing him, the A-list celebrities all begging to hang out with him. All aimed at creating one image: Donald Trump as a master of the universe.

He could be brilliant. And he could be his own worst enemy. For brilliance, read this, in September 2018. It was the height of the drama about getting Brett Kavanaugh appointed to the Supreme Court, despite a series of sexual assault claims against him – and it was to be the most electric day in Washington, with him giving evidence, and his accuser Christine Blasey Ford also before the Senate Judiciary Committee. On that same Friday, meanwhile, Trump was due to see his deputy attorney general, Rod Rosenstein, who was overseeing the Mueller investigation, amid speculation that the President was about to fire him. But Trump announced the Rosenstein meeting would be postponed. I am sure it was instinctive rather than strategic, but he was like a TV exec who just knew you don't win a ratings battle if you schedule your two top dramas against each other on the same day. The show starring Rod Rosenstein and the President would have to wait for another day.

But there were times when we were left wondering whether the President had the faintest idea what he was doing. I remember sitting in the Rose Garden on a beautiful end of summer, start of autumn day, and the President had called us together to celebrate his renegotiation of the NAFTA trade deal. It was a big success story. A big deal. Something you would guess the communications team in the White House hoped would be running as the lead story on cable and the nightly news shows that evening. But Donald Trump allowed himself to be side-tracked by another far less positive story, which he could have easily stonewalled.

Often it has seemed that the one thing this president can't abide is the notion that he is *not* the centre of the conversation. Not the headline on the nightly news. It often seems that on quiet news days he will simply create a story out of thin air. A propos of nothing a tweet will appear, waging war on someone or something. And like taking a match to tinder dry grass – whoosh – you have created a fire. He boasted at one point how he could often be the subject of four different front-page stories in the *New York Times* or *Wall Street Journal* – not distinguishing whether the story was good or bad for him. It is as though he lives by the maxim attributed to P.T. Barnum: there is no such thing as bad publicity.

That is not how the rest of the communications shop at the White House saw it. Can you imagine how exasperating it must be to create a press strategy, only to have your principal actor shred it on a whim as he relies on his own gut instincts to wing it, whatever the consequences. At various times efforts have been made to tamp down the open hostility that the President shows to the press. A friend of mine was approached to become White House communications director. He has an impeccable record of public service, and sits at the highest level of the private sector. He is a loyal Republican and a proud patriot. He met members of the family, and the most senior White House officials. But astonishingly for this devoted citizen, nearly all the advice he received was to give it a wide berth. The job was undoable. The President would not listen to advice. He would go his own way, and all your job would consist of was to be like the street cleaners who follow the horses once the State Coach and the Sovereign's escort have passed down Whitehall for the State Opening of Parliament – aka shit shoveller.

It was exasperation with the way his press secretary, Sean Spicer, was performing at his daily news conferences in the Briefing Room that led to an early intervention from the President. After Spicer's initial appearance in the Briefing

Room and then his subsequent encounters, he very quickly became a figure of parody, lampooned mercilessly on shows such as *Saturday Night Live* – where the character of Spicer was played brilliantly – and witheringly – by, wait for it, a woman. A woman! Melissa McCarthy as Spicer was genius. A genius piece of casting; a genius piece of acting. Trump hated that almost as much as he hated the way he was portrayed by Alec Baldwin. And the President came to a conclusion: if your press secretary isn't cutting it, do it yourself.

So one morning, when the White House was just confirming the name of its pick to be labour secretary, it was also announced that his name would be unveiled in a presidential news conference. That was highly unusual. A presidential news conference to name the labour secretary? No way. There was more to this than met the eye. What had purported to be a news conference held in the East Room, with its crystal chandeliers, gold damask curtains and parquet floor, in fact turned out to be a cage fight, with Donald Trump using his mixed martial arts skills to kick, punch and smack round the chops anyone who irritated him. As it happens, that turned out to be pretty much everyone.

If this was a news conference designed largely to show the utter contempt in which he held the media, it was very effective. We were out of control. We were fake news. 'The press has become so dishonest that if we don't talk about it, we are doing a tremendous disservice to the American people. Tremendous disservice,' Trump said. 'We have to talk to find out what's going on, because the press honestly is out of control. The level of dishonesty is out of control.

'I turn on the TV, open the newspapers and I see stories of chaos. Chaos,' he said. 'Yet it is the exact opposite. This administration is running like a fine-tuned machine.' I was 'another beauty' for being from the BBC. At a news conference where he repeatedly accused the media of dishonesty he told reporters that his election victory had been the biggest in terms of electoral college votes since Ronald Reagan. At which point a reporter stands up and says Barack Obama won by a wider margin. So the President counters: 'I was talking about Republican victories.' So the reporter fires back – but George H.W. Bush had a far bigger victory. And the President, completely unruffled at having delivered fake news himself, just blamed others and said that was what he had been told.

This in a microcosm became the template for the relationship. Broadly speaking the President would make the accusations of 'fake news' – not because something that had been written or broadcast was untrue, but because it was something he didn't like and didn't fit with his narrative; though he would utter repeated falsehoods that could be demonstrated to be untrue.

There is such a thing as objective truth and there are such things as verifiable facts. And very often it seemed the President traded in neither. There are those who say the President knows exactly what he is doing, and is deliberately trying to confuse and sow doubt. Others who insist that it is part of his psychological make-up – when he says it, he believes it to be true – and woe betide anyone who says the emperor has no clothes. What is his own reality, what is delusion is beyond my pay grade to pronounce on. But it must be particularly uncomfortable for the staff who have to go out and defend or explain entirely manufactured statistics, and claims that are not in any way tethered to reality.

There has been some amazingly good, detailed, thorough, no-stone-left-unturned journalism in the Trump era; stunning reports where newspapers have clearly committed massive resources to an investigation that would take months to come to fruition. Stories where the journalists concerned would wonder pre-publication whether this will be the one. This will be the one to bring down a president. This will be their Pulitzer prize-winning, name forever carved on journalistic escutcheon, Woodward and Bernstein moment. And then with fanfare and a thud the story lands – and is gone again in a matter of hours.

The *New York Times* unveiled an absolute blockbuster of an investigation into the Trump family's complex tax arrangements. When published in the newspaper it covered 18 pages. The detail was phenomenal, making it clear that Donald Trump inherited far more money and far earlier than he had ever acknowledged. The report suggested he was a millionaire aged eight – and by the time he graduated from college he was receiving $1 million a year from his father. The *Times* alleged that the way these gifts were structured was improper and potentially illegal.

Again, in normal political times these revelations could have been expected to lead the news for weeks, bringing demands for congressional investigations, and shrill demands for the President to come clean about his finances, sparking a flurry of follow-ups from rival publications desperate to get on. I won't say this story didn't cause a ripple in the pond – it did – but it didn't really cause waves. It came. And it went. And Donald Trump was left with barely a mark on him. Again.

Part of this can be explained by the fact that Donald Trump came to Washington as a political outsider, which means that he is given far more latitude than would be afforded a 'conventional' politician who had risen up through the ranks of either Congress or a governor's mansion. Bit of a dodgy track record with women? 'Sure, we knew that. He was a wealthy playboy.' Cut a few corners with his taxes? 'Tell me something I don't know.' Says things that are politically incorrect? 'Good on him – wish I could get away with that.' These are views I heard again and again as I travelled around the United States during his election campaign.

And now that he is their president, his supporters don't expect anything different. As I say, that is part of it. The other part of it is the assiduous way he has sought to sow doubt about the trustworthiness of the media. Go to a Trump rally – and he loves nothing more than being on the road, reconnecting with his fanbase – and one of the staples of these events is the attack on the media. We will be standing on a raised platform towards the back of the auditorium, and you just know that, sooner or later, the President will have the audience turn towards us – and he will go on one of his favourite riffs: that there is no group of people more dishonest; that we are 'fake news'; that we are the enemies of the people; that we are liars who shouldn't be believed. And the atmosphere is ugly. We are jeered and booed, insulted and spat at.

No matter what the weather and what the circumstances, the attacks continue. No matter that some have expressed concern that this is inciting violence. Even after five staff working for one of America's oldest newspapers – four of them journalists – were gunned down in the offices of the *Capital Gazette* in Annapolis, Maryland, and the President ordered flags to be lowered to half-mast at the White House, at his next rally he carried on his verbal onslaught about journalists and journalism. It was the same after a Saudi journalist working for the *Washington Post* was butchered in his country's consulate in Istanbul. The President condemned his murder in unequivocal terms, and said it was particularly awful that it was a journalist – but then at his next rally went on the attack about fake news.

And the President has been absolutely consistent and relentless in his attacks. He has refused to attend the White House Correspondents Association annual black-tie dinner. He thought it would be hypocritical. His Twitter account has a more or less daily blast at the shortcomings of the media – the only exception being Fox News, which holds a particular place of affection and respect in the President's heart. For every one interview a rival network gets with him, Fox probably gets ten. The Rupert Murdoch-owned network is his go-to choice.

One of the persistent questions that arise about virtually every aspect of the Trump presidency – and forgive me if I come back to a question I have already posed elsewhere in these pages – is how much of what he does is driven by instinct, how much is deliberate strategy; how much is impulse and how much is this a chess grandmaster planning several moves ahead. On most things you feel that the President has a sixth sense, just an incredible political gut sense of which way the wind is blowing. He's a man who likes to throw things up in the air and see how they land. And, yes, dealing with the consequences of things that go wrong. Some of his biggest decisions – like the sacking of the FBI director, James Comey – backfired massively. Some of his greatest gambles – like meeting Kim Jong-un – were made when it was impossible to know what the consequences would be.

But in his attacks on the media there seems to be deliberate strategy. One of the people who has interviewed him a couple of times since he became president – and is not from Fox – is Lesley Stahl. She is a presenter of the best news programme on American television, *60 Minutes*. She recounted a conversation she had with Trump when no cameras were present. 'At one point, he started to attack the press,' Stahl told an audience. 'There were no cameras in there.'

'I said, "You know, this is getting tired. Why are you doing it over and over? It's boring and it's time to end that. You know, you've won ... why do you keep hammering at this?"' Stahl recalled.

'And he said: "You know why I do it? I do it to discredit you all and demean you all so that when you write negative stories about me no one will believe you."'

There you have it in a nutshell. This is a president who wants the American people to believe what he says, and disregard the rest. He said it best himself when he was at the White House with a group of veterans, and he told them: 'What you're seeing and what you're reading is not what's happening.' In other words, reality is what I say it is.

And is it having an effect? Hell, yes. Polling by the CBS Network over the summer of 2018 found that 91 per cent of people who identified themselves as 'strong Trump supporters' trusted him to provide accurate information; only 11 per cent said the same about the news media. If this doesn't send a shiver down the spines of media moguls and editorial directors, it ought to. This isn't just one poll, I should add – all polls are reporting similar findings. There was a Gallup Poll that came out which was also striking. When people were asked why they didn't trust the media, about 45 per cent referred to things like inaccuracy, bias, 'fake news' and 'alternative facts' – in other words, the language used by Donald Trump had passed into the mainstream. What the public was parroting were Trump talking points.

With the media under sustained onslaught from the President, mistrusted by growing sections of the public; technological change transforming what we consume and how we consume it; old-fashioned newspaper circulation in terminal decline, broadcast news bulletins watched by fewer young people and increasingly becoming the preserve of the elderly – is this the worst time ever to be a journalist? Has there been a more desperate era to be in this business? If you have shares in a news organisation, is it time to diversify your portfolio?

Nope. Journalism is thriving in the Trump era. The appetite for news about the goings-on of this administration has been off the scale. Outlets that were flagging before Donald Trump moved into the White House are now booming; newspapers that were struggling are starting to turn in big profits. And, dare I say it, I suspect had Hillary Clinton won the presidency – or one of the other Republican hopefuls – I wouldn't have been commissioned by this fine and discerning publisher to write one book, let alone three. (Like London buses, there's another one coming along after this.)

CNN – an absolute punchbag for Donald Trump – has been reporting record profits. The 'failing' *New York Times* is piling on digital subscribers – yes, partly because the product has got a lot better, but also because the more the President attacks the famous title, the more people feel they need to subscribe. And, of course, Twitter, which was in danger of being totally eclipsed by other social media platforms prior to the 2016 election, has been given a new lease of life by the 45th president and his hyperactive thumbs. I went to a baseball game at the fabulously old-school Wrigley Field in Chicago, and as I sat watching the Cubs with a senior executive from one of the country's major media groups, he was bemoaning the fact that his company had not cashed in as well as other news organisations on the fascination and fixation with Trump. He wanted to know who I thought were the sharpest White House correspondents with the best contacts books and who they should sign.

The problem comes when that shifts a few degrees north. When reporting fairly becomes secondary to delivering an anti-Trump message that will act as clickbait, that will sell a few more newspapers or push up viewing figures – in other words, monetising either the pro- or anti-Trump sentiment. In a deeply polarised America it often seems that the broadcast media has decided it has to take sides too. The American media landscape has changed since Donald Trump became president. At the Palace of Westminster you always know where you are by the colour of the carpet beneath you – red, you're in the House of Lords; green, you're in the Commons. Switch to Fox and you know you're in Trump country; turn over to MSNBC or CNN and you are on the other side of the divide. Some will argue that it was always like that, but under Trump it has become much more exaggerated. And the short period either side of the midterm elections of 2018 epitomised it perfectly.

In the run-up to the elections, news emerged that a 'caravan' was forming of immigrants from Central America who planned to march hundreds of miles to the US border. This ragtag bunch of women, children and young men contained some who would seek to enter for asylum, and no doubt many who would enter the country illegally. The President seized on this as an opportunity to burnish his credentials as someone who would be tough on immigration. It was an 'invasion', he declared, and everywhere he went he spoke about this invasion. He deployed the army – thousands of soldiers were sent to the border. America was on a war footing. A bigger force than was then present in Syria and Afghanistan combined would defend the territorial integrity of the US against this 'caravan' hundreds of miles away.

I was at an airport early one morning, and was watching the headlines on Fox. 'According to reports 100 members of ISIS are part of the caravan in Guatemala.' What? A neat 100. Not 99 or 101. And reports from whom? With what attempts to verify this claim? They'd flown from Raqqa to Guatemala, we were asked to believe. The network would also report that many of the marchers were riddled with disease, which they would bring into the US, and that the caravan was funded by George Soros – the ultimate bogeyman for the right. It was nonsense and fear mongering, with a light dusting of anti-Semitism. No evidence was ever offered for any of this. And the moment that the midterms were over, the President dropped all mention of this moment of national peril. It was hard to resist the conclusion that thousands of troops were deployed not to save the nation but to shore up the Republican vote.

The run-up to the midterms also saw a home-grown terrorist sending pipe bombs to a number of prominent Democrats – the Obamas, the Clintons, the actor Robert de Niro (who's been an outspoken critic of Donald Trump), George Soros (obviously) and Joe Biden. You would think something like this would just bring condemnation without equivocation from across the political board. Not in divided America. Some Fox commentators thought it was a Democrat plot: how convenient to have prominent Democrats attacked just before the elections, to win them sympathy. Even the President spoke about 'the bomb thing' as though it was something other than what it seemed. Eventually the man arrested in Florida was shown to be a fanatical Trump supporter who was a regular at Trump rallies. Another conspiracy had sprung a rather big leak.

The other thing that happened just days before the midterm elections was the murder of eleven Jewish worshippers at a synagogue in Pittsburgh by a heavily armed white supremacist. The Shabbat killings just added to this profound sense of unease about the direction in which America was heading. But on Monday morning on MSNBC, one of the main presenters of the breakfast show, Mika Brzezinski, opened the peak hour with a long peroration about how the President was an inveterate liar. There was no attempt to report facts. It was an entirely one-sided monologue. So I switched channels and turned over to CNN, and they had as their lead item a down-the-line interview with the Rabbi from the Pittsburgh synagogue.

In those circumstances I play a stupid game as a former news anchor – and try to second guess or imagine what my first question would be. It was obvious, to me. It would have been a version of how are you doing/how is the community coping/has the reality sunk in? Not very original – but you just want to open up the conversation. Instead, that morning the news presenter started with 'Who do you blame?' The obvious riposte to that is 'the gunman'. But that's not what lay behind the question. That wasn't the headline the CNN guy was after – he wanted the rabbi to blame the President; to say that his divisive rhetoric had brought this surge in hate crimes. It was the tenor of all discussion throughout the day on CNN.

Did the President have the right to feel that he wasn't getting a fair shake in the wake of this? Probably. And then came the midterms themselves and, the day afterwards, another extraordinary presidential news conference. But before we come to that, let me just deal with something terribly prosaic: how journalists like me are able to enter the White House.

I still find it amazing that we have such access to the centre of power. Actually, access is the wrong word; maybe proximity is better. You can't just wander into the Oval Office, but you are free to open the blue sliding door that separates the Briefing Room from the White House proper to speak to the team in 'lower press' – and it's amazing who you can bump into. I spent a decade working in the lobby at Westminster, and it would be just unthinkable to be able to wander in and out of the famous black door at 10 Downing Street with impunity.

If you have a 'hard pass' like I do you can come and go from the White House estate at will, once you have been through the security post on Pennsylvania Avenue. Needless to say, to become the recipient of one of these hard passes you have to go through a bit of a security rigmarole. The Secret Service will do background checks, you will be finger-printed – and woe betide you if you lose the pass.

Anyway, back to the news conference after the midterms. The President at first seemed extremely weary. He had declared the results nearly perfect, but seemed to be tired and scratchy. He perked up when it came to questions. And he took questions for the best part of an hour and a half. From American journalists and from foreign ones; some friendly but many hostile. And say what you like about this president, you could hardly accuse him of being remote. True, he may have scarcely entered the Briefing Room, but in the Oval Office, in the East Room, on the South Lawn pathway from the White House leading to Marine One, at the back of the plane on Air Force One the President is hugely accessible.

But then came an encounter with Jim Acosta, the chief White House correspondent for CNN. Acosta is suave, a bit of a Clooney lookalike, personally delightful, and has a big ego (I don't say that as a criticism – if having a big ego was a disqualifier I'm not sure how many of us would still have a job). But he has been guilty of grandstanding on any number of occasions, and does kind of project himself as the conscience of the White House Correspondents Association. The lonely fighter of the President's intemperate language. The spear carrier for the rights of a free press. He famously walked out of the Briefing Room when Sarah Sanders refused to condemn the President for using the phrase 'enemy of the people' to describe the press. Though was it ever realistic to expect the President's press secretary to condemn her boss? If she did that she would no longer be able to serve the President. What she said was that the President chooses his own words, which seemed an elegant way for Ms Sanders to skirt the issue. But Acosta wouldn't let it go. When she would go no further he walked out. Now isn't that the very definition of grandstanding?

It was a similar story when the President called him to ask a question. Even though there is bad blood between them, Trump still pointed to the CNN man; and he was one of the first to be called. But Acosta didn't want to ask a question, he wanted to conduct an interview with the President. He asked three separate questions on different topics, and an exasperated Trump told him to shut up and give the microphone to someone else. Rudely. There was a bit of a tussle for the microphone with an intern, but it was entirely legitimate for the President to want to let other reporters have the opportunity to ask their questions.

It was a piece of theatre that actually suited both men. To Trump's supporters this would show the rudeness and impossibility of the 'fake news' media and vindicate their president's caustic approach towards them; to Acosta it burnished his and CNN's credentials as the people who would speak truth to power – and stick it to Trump. And for Acosta, who had a book to write, the exchange would have probably added significantly to the advance he would be able to demand. Brand Acosta had had a good day. So too had Donald Trump.

But Trump wasn't presidential in the way he treated Acosta; and Acosta wasn't respectful in the way he spoke to the President – and this is not a lame 'we've all got to be polite' because of the augustness of the office. The whole thing just felt like journalism as provocation. The President was doing what we all ask him to do – making himself available to answer our questions. We might not like the answers he gives, but it's his prerogative to answer as he sees fit – since when do we get to write his script? And for 90 minutes the President took on all comers. The stars from the networks and national press, local newspapers, international publications.

But then the next day the White House managed to turn their win into a loss. The Secret Service revoked Acosta's pass to the White House estate – no doubt at the President's insistence – thus making it much more difficult for him to do his job. The claim from the press secretary was that Acosta had 'laid hands' on the intern, and to further her case she posted a doctored video that had originally appeared on a right-wing, conspiracy theory-soaked website. The video was the very definition of 'fake news'.

This action sparked a predictable furore over free speech and the rights of journalists enshrined by the First Amendment of the US Constitution. The President warned that there were other rude correspondents he would also like to have banned. It sent a chill through the journalistic community, a community not hitherto noted for its ability to take collective action. But over this *all* the major news organisations – including Fox News – spoke with one voice, agreeing on legal action against the 'weaponisation' of a 'hard pass'. CNN would argue that the actions pursued by the White House would 'threaten all journalists and news organisations'. Relations between the press and the President took another downward turn.

And the President's mood would not improve when the White House had eventually to surrender. It lost in court, and despite its claim that it would carry on the legal fight, the battle ended with a whimper not a bang. An ill-considered ban, which looked tough at the outset, had foundered on its first real contact with the US legal system. It was the President 0, CNN 1. And can you imagine how much that must have hurt.

But that is to see things as the President sees things, where everything is a zero-sum game; where there are only winners and losers. Worryingly for the long-term health of journalism, too much of the media sees it that way too, as though we are somehow part of the resistance. Marty Baron, the editor of the *Washington Post*, has been a powerful voice on the dangers. He has made clear to his newsroom that however Donald Trump may treat us, we must not retaliate. Journalism must rise above this. He is not our foe. We are there to hold him to account. Fairly and honestly. Toughly and accurately. Critically yet dispassionately. Let the Democratic Party or dissident Republicans or whoever is seeking elected office be the enemy. Journalism is not the enemy of the people; nor should it be the enemy of the President.

# CHAPTER 5

# The Residence

The East Wing is the grand mansion of Washington. If the West Wing is where the dirty business of making the sausages is done, the East Wing is where they are put on finely polished silver platters and served with cocktail sticks, and handed out by immaculately turned-out liveried staff. It is where the state banquets are held; it is where the President conducts public ceremonies – the handing out of medals to worthy recipients; the venue of news conferences when a visiting prime minister, president or member of royalty is in town. It is the public and ceremonial face of the presidency. It is also where the Residence is.

It is also the domain of the First Lady. This is where she has her office and staff. And the First Lady (capital F, capital L) is an official position within the government, fully funded by the US taxpayer. My first experience of the profound difference between the British and US systems came on my first visit to the White House, back in 1998. Tony Blair was prime minister and Bill Clinton was laying out the red carpet, giving him a state visit (even though, of course, the British prime minister is not the head of state – the Queen is).

There was a press briefing where the US journalists wanted to know what the First Lady would be wearing at the banquet that evening. Hillary Clinton's press person started going through the list: shoes by this one; dress by such and such designer; make-up by Mme Macquillage and hair by Monsieur le Scissors, etc. Then one of the US journalists asked what Cherie Blair would be wearing – and up popped the Downing Street press woman, a take-no-hostages, feisty Scot called Maggie Cleaver who sadly died a few years ago: 'First I haven't the faintest idea, and second I wouldn't dream of asking her.' Adding for good measure, 'She's a private person.' The US journalists looked astonished, with puzzled, 'but what have we done wrong' expressions on their faces. In Britain there isn't even a title – consort to the prime minister? Wife/husband of? Although things have moved a touch nearer to the American system in the intervening 20 or so years – while the PM's partner is given some support, it is still nothing like the role played by the First Lady.

The basement and ground floor of the Residence are the public areas; the top two floors of the East Wing are not quite the flat above the shop, as Margaret Thatcher used to describe her somewhat cramped quarters at the top of 10 Downing Street – but they are places you go only at the invitation of the first family. If you ever attend a White House function there is always a secret service officer on duty to check you don't by mistake – or design – wander up the staircase to the private quarters. And unlike the Downing Street flat there is nothing poky about the top two floors of the Residence.

For those most esteemed visitors on whom you want to bestow a special welcome there is the Queens' Bedroom, part of a suite of rooms that also includes the Queens' Sitting Room and the Queens' Bathroom. Any number of European royals have spent the night there. Queen Elizabeth first stayed when she came to Washington in 1957 to visit President Eisenhower, and was a frequent visitor after that, returning to Washington for the US Bicentennial in 1976; she made a state visit at the invitation of George H.W. Bush; and came again when his son was president.

Then there is the Lincoln Bedroom, which as the name does not suggest, is somewhere Abraham Lincoln never slept. But he did work there, and the décor has a mid-nineteenth-century, chintzy feel to it. Big heavy furniture, and a famous bed with giant rosewood headboard, make for the most cracking overnight invitation a President can offer up to friends and political supporters by way of reward. They will be entertained in the Yellow Oval Room, a grand drawing room that has been used down the ages for the visits of presidents and kings and queens. It opens out onto the Truman Balcony on the south side of the building, with wonderful views across to the Washington Monument and down to the Potomac. President Truman's demand for the addition of this balcony set off an enormous furore at the time about whether its construction was in keeping with the neo-classical design of the rest of the White House.

This floor also has a kitchen and dining room, where the president and first lady can try to maintain an air of normality: of doing the things that other normal humans do, like cooking their own food and eating it. The Clintons turned it into a family kitchen – installing a TV too, naturally – and by all accounts this is where Bill would sit with the White House butlers and watch the basketball. Barack Obama and Michelle would have as many family dinners together as possible with their girls.

On the top floor is another suite of bedrooms, which each president and first lady have put their mark on – starting with the solarium built by President Taft. The top-floor sitting room was turned into a gym by the Clintons, and was keenly used by George W. Bush when he moved in. There is a games room and a music room too – plus many more bedroom suites. One of the touches that Donald Trump has added, according to his former aide, Omarosa Manigault Newman, is a sunbed – which would explain his frequently tanned appearance, but with white eyes where he would have been wearing protective glasses. I took one photograph on my smart-phone of the President at a news conference in the Rose Garden, and later I thought there must have been something wrong with the camera. He was, well, an irradiated shade of electric orange, while the people he was thronged by were of totally normal colouring. Sarah Sanders would seek to explain away that deeply tanned appearance by putting it down to his good genes. Hmm.

The lower floors of the White House are the ones which the public can tour. Unlike 10 Downing Street, which no member of the public would ever be able to visit – unless they knew someone working in the building who could show them around – the White House is the 'people's house', with tours organised when the president and first lady are away.

In the days when relations with the press were rather better than they are now, I was invited to the last two Obama Christmas parties at the White House before he left office.

I am sure that among the events organised by the Social Secretary – the other key person who has their office in the East Wing – the evenings of receptions for the media (one night for print, the other for broadcasters) are ranked as two of the least important. But these evenings are special. Really special. For a start the house is decorated exquisitely. It is as if Walt Disney himself has intervened and brought a touch of his magic kingdom to the humdrum world of politics. Beautiful trees and decorations adorn the rooms, the champagne flows. It is as if fairy dust has been sprinkled around the place. Marine bands play in different rooms – a jazz ensemble here, a string quartet there, some rock and roll somewhere else. Representatives from all the branches of the armed forces are in their immaculate dress uniforms to guide you around and make your evening more special. And you are free to wander the lower two floors of the White House, as if your most special friend in the world has lucked out on the best wedding venue there is; into the plate room, where there are samples of the dinner services that each president has had designed to mark their period in office; and there's the library, the red room, the blue room and the green room.

In the mansion's two biggest rooms, the East Room and the State Dining Room, there are tables groaning with the most delicious food – oysters, lobster, shrimp, filet mignon, lamb chops, wonderful salads, and endless little delicate pastries, cooked by the White House chefs. In the corner of the State Dining Room stands a huge 3D gingerbread sculpture of the White House itself. And along the corridors you pass the portraits hanging from the walls of previous presidents. John F. Kennedy, with arms crossed looking down thoughtfully. Lincoln, legs crossed, right hand on his chin. Bill Clinton, staring ahead purposefully, one hand in pocket, the other hand resting on a table. You had to pinch yourself that this was really happening and that you were really there.

Then the dénouement of the evening. Your time with the President and the First Lady. This is not some haphazard encounter where you bump into each other in a corridor. No, it is much more like what I remember from being a child and queuing at the local department store to see Santa. As you arrive at the White House you are given a colour coded ticket, and when it is time for your colour you form an orderly queue and are taken downstairs into the Map Room. One military officer checks you and your partner's names. Another confiscates your drinks – do you really want to be photographed between the First Lady and President with a half-empty glass of fizz in your hand? A third military person puts you into the holding position – and then your names are called out. It is all done with enormous grace and charm, and designed to put you at maximum ease, even though you are inwardly panicking that some piece of the spinach tart might have lodged itself stubbornly and prominently between your front teeth.

You walk into the Diplomatic Reception Room, where Barack and Michelle are waiting for you. You shake hands, and the more bold – and less British – sneak a hug and a kiss as well. There is a brief bit of chit-chat with your host and hostess, you stand in front of the fireplace, with a portrait of George Washington above the marble mantelpiece, lush Christmas trees on either side of you – and you put on your best smile. Three camera flashes later, you are on your way out – and the next couple are on their way in. This practice was carried on by the Bushes and the Clintons, but did not carry on with Donald Trump. Though who can blame him, frankly? Standing in the same spot for the best part of three hours, with a fixed smile on your face as your tormentors – the serried ranks of the White House press corps – pass through. Exhausting. Who needs it?

That night when my wife, Linda, and I finally left the White House we were on a high. We were probably a little bit tipsy, we had almost certainly eaten too much, we had met the most wonderful people, who had all been charming and welcoming. And we got into the taxi to go home discussing whether that was the best party we had ever been to and whether there could be a more perfect evening. But then we got home, only to discover that our stupid (or maybe not so stupid) dog had managed to climb onto the dining room table, and had wolfed down a whole packet of Fortnum and Mason mince pies – full of raisins and sultanas, that can be deadly for dogs. So, an emergency dash to the Friendship Animal Hospital and stomach pump later – and my pocket $1,000 lighter – the glow of our first White House party with the President was beginning to lose some of its lustre.

Today's White House has altered and changed bit by bit over the years, but the major work of reshaping it was carried out nearly sixty years ago under the watchful and interior design conscious eye of Jacqueline Kennedy, wife of John F. Kennedy. She was only 32 years old when she became First Lady, and did not seek the political limelight. Having spent a year abroad studying French literature and then worked briefly for *Vogue*, she was chic and poised – and so when she moved into the White House with her young family, she set about its restoration and transformation. Period antiques would be placed strategically around the place, the world's leading musicians would be brought in to enliven fancy White House dinners. It was the greatest transformation of the building since the attempt made by the British in 1814 during the Revolutionary Wars. They tried to burn the place down.

In 1962 she hosted an extraordinary TV documentary where, with her slightly whispery drawl, she took viewers on a tour of the White House, whose changes she was overseeing. In some of it she speaks directly to camera; in other sections she is interviewed by one of the great American war correspondents, Charles Collingwood. She is asked to justify the expenditure – and explains that until she moved in her predecessors were free to sell or get rid of any furniture or artefacts they didn't like. But a new law passed by Congress that she had championed would mean everything in the White House would be part of the government art collection. Her sense of history, her poise, her detailed knowledge of antiques (and maybe her striking beauty too) had Americans transfixed. The documentary won her an Emmy award. Just as her husband was the first president of the television age, so she matched him with her ease in front of the camera. She was smart, self-confident, a modern woman in an era of change.

She was undoubtedly one of the most significant and well-known first ladies to be in the White House. But what is the role? What do you have to do? What marks out a significant first lady from an also ran? It's not as if there is a strict definition of the duties and responsibilities. There are no fixed key performance indicators set by the American people for what they want from their first lady. And they don't run on an agenda in the way the president does. It is very much up to the individual to set their own goals and priorities.

It's then up to the American people to decide whether they like what they see.

Maybe the words that chimed most closely with Melania Trump when she moved into the White House were those spoken by America's first presidential wife, Martha Washington, back in the late 1800s. She famously said the position of first lady can sometimes feel akin to that of a state prisoner. Mrs Trump has said the most difficult part she has found about the role is the loss of privacy, the feeling (not imagined) that you are always under a microscope. 'I cannot move freely any more,' she told ABC News. 'Before I could easily move, like, in a minute I could go somewhere. Now it's a bigger production. You need to, wherever you go it's a big, big production.' When asked whether she felt like a prisoner, she said she didn't – before quickly adding, 'This will not last forever.'

Jackie Kennedy can be considered a significant first lady because of the profile that she brought to the job, and the part she played in modernising the way the White House operated and ran, and in particular opening it up to the public. But though she did help on the margins, and did get involved with some national security issues, she chose very much *not* to be a frontline combatant in the political battle. She certainly wasn't an Eleanor Roosevelt.

The First Lady to FDR was political down to her finger-tips, and was probably the first First Lady to use her role to champion causes dear to her heart. She fought alongside her husband for the New Deal, the sweeping range of policies designed to lift the US out of poverty after the great depression. She championed civil rights – once risking arrest in 1938 when she travelled to Birmingham, Alabama, and flouted that state's segregation laws by shunning the 'whites only' section en route and sitting directly behind an African American associate. She would go on to be appointed to the board of the National Association for the Advancement of the Coloured Person (NAACP) – a body whose work carries on to this day.

She championed women's rights too in a pre-feminist age. Reporting the White House when FDR won the presidency was very much a 'men only' profession. So she organised a number of 'ladies only' press conferences – and that had the effect of forcing newspaper editors into hiring more women reporters. It also endeared her to many female voters – and helped her husband win votes in his re-election battles. And she wrote a daily newspaper column, in which she tackled the most controversial issues of the day. It ran from 1936 right through until 1962. The only four days she missed of 'My Day', as the column was called, were in 1945 after her husband died.

Hillary Clinton as First Lady was in that mould, but nothing like as successful, even though she was a brilliant lawyer, and one of the most accomplished first ladies in American history. Deeply immersed in the detail of policy, and one of her husband's most trusted advisors, she was put in charge of the hottest of hot potatoes in American politics – healthcare reform. It is the most deeply polarising of subjects, and boy did she polarise opinion: about healthcare and about her. A divisiveness that would ultimately cost her, and mean she wouldn't become the woman to shatter that glass ceiling and become the first female president.

The more successful approach is the one adopted by a number of other first ladies – which is to use your privileged position to support causes that are vitally important social issues, but which will not leave you fried on the live rail of US politics. Barbara Bush, wife of the 41st president, was a determined champion of the importance of literacy; Michelle Obama – another high-achieving lawyer – would be a fierce advocate for healthy lifestyles to tackle the epidemic of obesity among children in the US. What was interesting about her initiatives was the extent of coordination there was with what her husband was doing. It was East Wing and West Wing working in tandem. So while he was returning to the divisive subject of healthcare reform, via the Affordable Care Act, she was also championing a health issue, but not in a way that would leave her scarred like Hillary Clinton.

And then there are the slightly quirky issues that have been advanced by first ladies. Lady Bird Johnson, wife of Lyndon B. Johnson, thought that America's great natural beauty was being sullied by the endless advertising hoardings that were becoming ubiquitous on America's highways and interstates. She worked tirelessly for the protection of wild flowers, and demanded that more be planted. Ultimately, she would spearhead legislation that would become the Highway Beautification Act – instead of billboards there would be flowers. Well, some flowers – and still very many billboards. This was a hobby horse. She rode it successfully onto the statute book.

And then there have been the first ladies who by their own candour and openness have shone a light on subjects that polite society tended to ignore. Betty Ford, wife of Gerald Ford, successor to the disgraced Richard Nixon, would arguably have more of an impact on American life than her husband in his slightly less than 900 days as president. She spoke about mental health and the benefits of psychiatric treatment. She spoke about women's rights and a woman's right to choose on the issue of abortion. Weeks after she became First Lady she had a mastectomy to treat her breast cancer. Afterwards she decided to speak openly about it – still something of a taboo at the time. In 1975 she won *Time* magazine's coveted person of the year nomination. Gerald Ford, after just two and a half years in the job, trying to re-establish respect and confidence in the presidency, would lose in his 1976 bid to win re-election. In that campaign, Betty's approval ratings stood at a stunning 75 per cent. 'I would give my life to have Jerry have my poll numbers,' she commented.

So what of Melania Trump? How does she see the role? What sort of first lady does she hope to be? The flippant answer from a number of separate accounts is that she never wanted to be First Lady, or not according to the writer Michael Wolff, whose account of life on the campaign and in the first months of the Trump presidency is the result of extraordinary – and probably misguided – access granted to him by a chaotic team where no one seemed to be in charge. *Fire and Fury* is a riveting read, even if at times he seems to have embellished the odd story. Wolff claims that Melania Trump burst into tears when it became clear on that night in November that her husband was on course to victory. It is an account, I should add, that she disputes. According to Wolff she had only gone along with Trump's bid to win the presidency because she was certain he was going to lose. She hated the limelight, and just wanted to go back to her – relatively – anonymous life in New York. She feared, too, what extensive media exposure would do to her young son, Barron. He would be the first young boy in the White House since the Kennedy era. There were a number of others around Trump who had also never believed he was going to win.

In that sense this is a story of life imitating art. It is the unlikely plot of the brilliant Mel Brooks film, *The Producers,* in which a washed-up producer and a dodgy accountant raise a load of money to put on the most sick and tasteless musical ever (who can forget the cast singing 'Springtime for Hitler'?) in the hope that it would fold after the first night, so they would be able to keep all the money. Except the audience loved all the outrageous comments, and the provocative nastiness of it all. The worse it got, the more people cheered. Melania Trump had apparently made a similar bet with herself.

There was little from her pre-White House life to point to what sort of figure she would cut in the role. She is every bit as unique a first lady as her husband is a president. In the public eye perhaps the most notable/notorious thing she did was a magazine photoshoot in which she posed naked on a fur rug inside Donald Trump's private Boeing 727 jet, that has the word TRUMP emblazoned along the fuselage. I've looked and can see no record of that having been done by anyone else who has gone on to become first lady.

The spread for *GQ* magazine from 2000 was done when the Slovenian-born model Melania Knauss (as she was then) was Trump's girlfriend. The headline for the piece was the not ever so bashful: 'Sex at 30,000 feet. Melania Knauss earns her air miles.' In one photo she stands on the wing of the plane wearing a skimpy red bikini, silver revolver in her hand, aimed back at the camera; in another she sits on the plane's white leather sofa, her breasts about to spill out, while in front of her is a studded, leather attaché case over-flowing with jewels that are also spilling out, her gold toe and fingernail polish matching the Trump plane's fittings. She is also photographed in the cockpit wearing a sort of loosely linked, silver chain vest that leaves little to the imagination. It is brash, it says loads of money. It is gilt heavy and guilt free – hallmarks that some have suggested have become a moniker for this presidency.

One could say 'So what?' Nasty perhaps. Unnecessary even to raise, given that what models do is pose for photos. And if you are on a fashion shoot, you are going to put yourself in ridiculous positions. But this was not a case of an embarrassing teenage transgression; of Melania Trump trying to airbrush her past when she became First Lady. There was no fumbling attempt to make sure the pictures never saw the light of day. She was in her twenties when the photos were taken, and was proud of them, it seems. Donald Trump, at the time, asked for the photos to be sent to his office. Eighteen years later, when she became First Lady, attention was drawn to the spread, via the White House website. On the personal biography page for Melania Trump it says: 'She has graced the covers of *Vogue, Harper's Bazaar, British GQ, Ocean Drive, Avenue, In Style* and *New York Magazine*.'

These photographs, though, did raise a series of interesting questions about her immigration status when the shoot took place. It was around this time she began to petition the US authorities for the right to reside permanently in the United States, under a programme reserved for people with 'extraordinary ability'. It is a scheme designed for nuclear physicists, Olympic athletes, Oscar-winning actors and the like. People who have demonstrated 'sustained national and international acclaim'.

Now, true, Melania Trump had appeared on a billboard in Times Square advertising Camel cigarettes; and she had also been photographed for the swimsuit edition of *Sports Illustrated*, hugging a six-foot inflatable whale – and all those front covers already mentioned – but estimable though those achievements are, they are not normally considered qualifications for the so-called Einstein visa. The year she was granted her EB-1 visa, only five other people from Slovenia were granted one.

But what that visa gave was the ability to sponsor her parents, Viktor and Amalija Knauss, to come to the US too. In 2007 they listed their address as Mar-a-Lago, Trump's luxury, exclusive and eye-wateringly expensive private members club in Florida, which he has dubbed the 'winter White House'. Mr and Mrs Knauss have now been granted US citizenship, and have moved to live near their daughter, just outside Washington, where she and son Barron spend a lot of time. A representative of Mr and Mrs Knauss made it clear to the press that they received 'no special treatment because of their relationship with the first family', but one cannot help wondering whether the influential property billionaire, Donald Trump, intervene on Melania's behalf to help secure her the visa when they were dating? It would be interesting if he had, because this is the type of 'chain migration' (where one family member's admittance to the US allows several others to come) that he now inveighs against.

In the first six months Melania Trump was a first lady pretty much in name only. She stayed in New York in Trump Tower, and only made occasional visits to Washington. This was done to allow Barron to finish his school year, without the upheaval of moving in between. And at an incredible cost to the US taxpayer in terms of additional security being provided by the US Secret Service. But even at weekends, there were times when it seemed they could have met up, but for whatever reason chose not to. When she and Barron did move into the White House the rhythm of life – if you can use the word 'rhythm' to describe something as cacophonous and arrhythmic as this presidency – had already been established, and Melania found that some of her East Wing staff had been poached to go and work for her stepdaughter, Ivanka – who was the product of Donald Trump's second marriage to Ivana. The two, according to many reports, do not enjoy an easy relationship. Ivanka, as a key advisor to her father, plays a dominant role in the West Wing; Melania is queen of the East. Donald Trump has to navigate his way between the two.

There was a portrayal of Melania Trump in the months after the election that was well wide of the mark. She was variously depicted as a bit dim – the dumb model with the heavy East European accent on the arm of the billionaire; and also as the hapless prisoner, Donald Trump's captive, unable to break free. A Rapunzel figure, whose hair wasn't quite long enough to allow her rescuers to reach her in the isolated tower. The joke that went around was 'Blink twice if you need rescuing, Melania'. It simultaneously poked fun at her position, and also what often appeared to be a lack of facial expression, that people surmised was the result of too much Botox and too many facelifts. #freemelania became a popular hashtag in those early days.

Melania Trump may never have wanted to be first lady – but she is her own woman. And during the most tumultuous period of the campaign when the *Access Hollywood* tape emerged of her husband bragging about what he could do

to women as a result of his fame, she was sent out to rein-
force the Trump defences. She gave an interesting interview
to CNN's star anchor, Anderson Cooper. Of course, she said
the Donald Trump on the tape was not the man she knew.
But she also went on: 'People, they don't really know me,
people think and talk about me, like, "Oh, Melania, oh,
poor Melania." Don't feel sorry for me.'

And she's a fighter. Soon after the presidential election she
sued the *Daily Mail* for defamation over false allegations that
she had acted as a highly paid 'escort' in the 1990s – a case that
she won, and claims the paper withdrew. What was interesting
– and extraordinary given the public position she held – was
not so much the legal grounds for the defamation, but why
they were so injurious to her. According to her attorney, Charles
Harder, the *Mail* article had hurt her chances of establishing
'multi-million dollar business relationships' during the years
when she would be 'one of the most photographed women
in the world'. And in his court filings the lawyer went on:
'The plaintiff had the unique, once in a lifetime opportunity
as an extremely famous and well-known person, as well as a
former professional model, brand spokesperson and successful
businesswoman, to launch a broad-based commercial brand in
multiple product categories, each of which could have garnered
multi-million dollar business relationships for a multi-year
term.' The products could have included clothing, accessories,
jewellery, perfume and hair care.

Remember, this is the First Lady. A person who is a servant
of the American people, with a full retinue of staff, round the
clock secret-service protection, private government jets at her
disposal, all paid for by the taxpayer – but seemingly more
concerned about her money-making opportunities afterwards.

With a hue and cry growing, the lawyer would later seek to clarify his filing, by saying, 'The first lady has no intention of using her position for profit and will not do so. It is not a possibility.' Reporters who suggested otherwise were guilty of 'misinterpreting' the court filing. Goodness. Sorry. How warped a mind must you have to gain the impression from his deposition that she was interested in making money? A second version of the lawsuit removed this controversial wording. There are those who suggest that Donald Trump is obsessed by his own personal branding; this court filing seemed to prove that Melania Trump didn't lag far behind in that department.

And there have been times when she has not been afraid to show her own irritation at the President. The cameras have caught various occasions where a Donald action has been matched by a Melania reaction. A grimace here, a sharp look there. Most memorable for me perhaps was when I was in the Middle East to cover Donald Trump's first over-seas trip. The first couple had arrived in Israel from Saudi Arabia aboard Air Force One. They were greeted at Ben Gurion airport by Benjamin Netanyahu, the Israeli prime minister, and his wife Sarah. The two countries' flags flut-tered, and the band played as they walked along the red carpet. The Netanyahus walked away from the aircraft, hand in hand. Seeing this, Donald Trump, the globetrotting new boy, reached out to grab Melania's hand. She was having none of it. The First Lady pushed his hand away as you might swat an irritating fly. There are several other examples of presidential outreach snubbed.

All first families find themselves living in a goldfish bowl, to a greater or lesser extent. The eyes of America and the world are firmly fixed on them – the Obamas, the Bushes, particularly the Clintons, and so on, back through history. But no president has been married three times before with such a well-documented and colourful playboy past. And the White House has never had a Slovenian born ex-supermodel as its first lady. The fascination about the state of the Trump marriage has fixated the tabloids and broadsheets, TV and radio – and of course the internet.

The two seem to lead very separate lives. By Melania's own account the two are 'very independent'. Speaking to journalists before the election she said, 'We give ourselves and each other space.' The *Washington Post* would report the extent of this separation, subtly, but with a clear message: 'Donald and Melania Trump's remarkably separate daily routines begin with him getting up around 5:30 a.m., watching cable news shows and tweeting. The first lady wakes in her own bedroom a bit later, according to two close friends of the Trumps. She then readies their 12-year-old son for school, including checking to make sure his homework is in his backpack.'

Melania Trump didn't agree to be interviewed for this apparently well sourced piece by the *Post*, written by their best-connected reporters. But the first lady's spokeswoman did offer a generalised statement, saying, 'Aside from the president's solo trips, the family spends most evenings together,' and that Melania 'is focused on being a mom. She's focused on being a wife, and she's focused on her role as first lady. And that's it. The rest is just noise.'

But there has been nothing so noisy as the sagas involving the former porn star Stormy Daniels, and the *Playboy* model Karen McDougal – both of whom claimed they had affairs with Trump; both of whom were paid off prior to the election to buy their silence. Daniels, whose real name is Stephanie Clifford, claimed her one-night stand with Donald Trump took place at a golf tournament in California in 2006. Just before election day in November 2016 she was paid $130,000 in return for her silence.

She signed a non-disclosure agreement that had been facilitated by Trump's Mr Fixit lawyer, a man called Michael Cohen. Now it should be said that Donald Trump has always insisted there was no sexual encounter – which sort of begs the question why then was she paid $130,000? Surely it can't be that easy to get money out of Donald Trump? You just make up some fictitious allegation, and hey presto the money comes rolling in?

Another of Trump's lawyers, the former New York mayor, Rudy Giuliani, would later claim the President authorised the payment to protect the Trump family, and so that it wouldn't cause upset to Melania. He would also claim to know Melania's feelings about the Stormy Daniels claims: 'She believes in her husband. She knows it's not true.' When that was put to the first lady in an ABC interview, it was met with an icy 'I never talked to Mr Giuliani'. Pressed by the interviewer why he might have said it, Mrs Trump replied: 'I don't know. You need to ask him.'

What was striking about this saga was the way the President kept on changing his story. His accounts of what he knew and when are simply irreconcilable. First of all, he said that he knew nothing about the payment. It had been made by Cohen, without his knowledge and without any discussion. The lawyer had paid the money from his own account and had never asked his client for the money back. (Oh, to have a lawyer like that ... one that pre-emptively sorts out your problems, doesn't charge you, and pays for the privilege out of his own bank account without ever asking for reimbursement ... one can but dream.)

On Air Force One as Donald Trump came to the back of the plane to speak to reporters he was asked about this. Trump claimed he had no knowledge of the payment to Daniels. He also stated he did not know Cohen's funding source. Here's the exchange:

REPORTER: Mr President, did you know about the $130,000 payment to Stormy Daniels?

TRUMP: No. No. What else?

REPORTER: Then why did Michael Cohen make those if there was no truth to her allegations?

TRUMP: Well, you'll have to ask Michael Cohen. Michael is my attorney. And you'll have to ask Michael Cohen.

REPORTER: Do you know where he got the money to make that payment?

TRUMP: No, I don't know. No.

That was April 2018. A few days later the FBI raids Cohen's offices and takes away a mass of papers and files, to the absolute fury of the President. Worse would follow when Cohen started to cooperate with the Feds. In Trump's mind Cohen went from hero to zero in the blink of an eye. With Giuliani now installed as personal counsel to the President, the former New York mayor appeared on Fox with

Sean Hannity – an even closer Trump ally. Giuliani suddenly rewrote the President's story with this *coup de foudre*:

> GIULIANI: Having something to do with paying some Stormy Daniels woman $130,000, I mean, which is going to turn out to be perfectly legal. That money was not campaign money, sorry, I'm giving you a fact now that you don't know. It's not campaign money. No campaign finance violation. So—
>
> HANNITY: They funnelled it through a law firm.
>
> GIULIANI: Funnelled it through a law firm, and the President repaid it.
>
> HANNITY: I didn't know he did?
>
> GIULIANI: Yes.

This is now a complete and total contradiction of what the President said on Air Force One when he claimed he knew nothing about the payment. Not only did he know, he'd repaid Cohen. Giuliani elaborated that the President had paid Cohen back $35,000 per month from his private account.

And now the media was left with an important editorial decision – when do we move from saying that what the President has said is not an untruth … to calling it a lie. This passed that threshold. What he said on Air Force One was a lie. He knew about the payment when he claimed he didn't. He knew about the payment because he'd repaid Cohen what he owed him. He knew why Cohen had paid her the money. But now the President had to offer some clarification, and when it came, there was something slightly unusual about it that made me giggle. The President once again chose his preferred means of communication, Twitter. And I have to say one of the things I *love* about this president is how authentic he is. When he tweets you know it is *him*; you can hear his voice, and you know it comes from the heart. It is so unfiltered, when what we are normally fed by politicians is a diet of carefully prepared and nuanced messages that have been through filters and sieves and drainage systems to take away any sharp edges. It sometimes feels as though we live in an age where the fear of causing offence means we say nothing very much to anybody. With this tweet, though, you just got the tiniest impression it might have been someone else's thumbs on the presidential Blackberry:

Mr Cohen, an attorney, received a monthly retainer, not from the campaign and having nothing to do with the campaign, from which he entered into, through reimbursement, a private contract between two parties, known as a non-disclosure agreement, or NDA. These agreements are very common among celebrities and people of wealth. In this case it is in full force and effect and will be used in Arbitration for damages against Ms Clifford [Stormy Daniels's proper name]. The agreement was used to stop the false and extortionist accusations made by her about an affair, despite already having signed a detailed letter admitting that there was no affair. Prior to its violation by Ms Clifford and her attorney, this was a private agreement. Money from the campaign, or campaign contributions, played no roll [sic] in this transaction.

Methinks a lawyer, with imperfect spelling, might have had a roll, sorry role, in that particular missive. But here's the thing. Blockbuster stories like this one, in a normal political cycle, could be expected to bring down a senior politician. Just consider the ingredients we are dealing with here: a porn star, a president, an alleged sexual encounter, a hush payment just before an election, the President lying on record – and on Air Force One – about the pay-off, allegations from Stormy Daniels that she was threatened by a man in a car park to say nothing 'or else', and the President's (now ex) lawyer in court saying the payment was principally made to influence the election. In December 2018, Cohen was sentenced to three years in prison for this flagrant breach of campaign finance law, and other offences. The submission to the court from federal prosecutors (in other words people employed by the Department of Justice) said that Cohen had acted under the direction of 'individual-1'. Individual-1 is the President. For the first time government employees had stated the President was complicit in breaking the law.

His changing accounts, the conviction of Michael Cohen, and the relentlessness of Stormy Daniels and her pugnacious lawyer were exposing him to some legal and a lot of political jeopardy in the West Wing, and more delicate problems in the East Wing. When Stormy Daniels went on TV to give her compelling account of what had happened on the alleged one-night stand – including salacious details like spanking Mr Trump on the bottom with a rolled-up copy of a magazine that had his face on the cover – the President flew back from his Mar-a-Lago retreat by himself. Melania stayed behind. When the story first broke of the $130,000 payment, she had been due to accompany her husband to the meeting of the global élite in Davos, Switzerland. But she went somewhere else instead. On the night of the State of the Union address – the biggest annual set-piece in the Washington political calendar – she arrived at it separately from her husband. Not only that, what she was wearing (it wouldn't be the only occasion) also astonished spectators. She arrived wearing a white trouser-suit. Now who else do we know who likes to wear a white pant-suit (as Americans call the outfit)? Why, Hillary Clinton, of course. Cue a tsunami of speculation and comment. Was she sending a message? Was this solidarity with a former first lady who'd had to put up with her husband's errant behaviour? Was this a way of reproaching her own husband?

Let's add into this mix the *Playboy* model Karen McDougal who was the subject of the 'catch and kill' operation discussed earlier. She alleged a longstanding affair with Donald Trump (denied by him), not just a one-night stand as Stormy Daniels had claimed.

Her silence was bought, as we have seen, by a close friend of Trump and publisher of the scurrilous *National Enquirer* magazine, David Pecker. Throughout the presidential election campaign it ran a series of salacious stories, deeply damaging to Hillary Clinton – and with only the flimsiest basis in reality. Stories about Trump were entirely positive. Karen McDougal's story was bought up by the *National Enquirer* with the explicit aim that it would never see the light of day. It is chequebook journalism in reverse. You use your money to get the exclusive rights to a story you will never publish, as a favour to a friend in need. She is bought out and signs a tight legal contract; her story is caught and killed. When details of this arrangement were eventually made public,

McDougal would also appear on primetime TV. She told CNN that she wanted to apologise to Melania for the affair. 'What can you say except I'm sorry ... I wouldn't want it done to me.'

When asked about reports of her husband's alleged infidelities, and the strain it put on her marriage, Mrs Trump told ABC: 'It is not concern or focus of mine. I'm a mother and a first lady, and I have more important things to think about and to do. I know people like to speculate about our marriage, and circulate the gossip. But I understand the gossip sells newspapers, magazines getting advertisers. And unfortunately, we live in this kind of world today.' If that sidestepped the question, there was one more exchange that was equally telling. The reporter asks whether she loves her husband. 'Yes, we are fine,' she replies – which is not exactly an answer to the question. And she goes on: 'Yes. It's what media speculate, and it's gossip. It's not always correct stuff.' Not always correct? That's a far cry from 'It's entirely false'.

Let me add a personal memory for what it's worth. At the height of all this, we had met up with a couple of friends who we regularly see for dinner. We had gone a month or two earlier to a rather cool, but down-at-heel Belgian restaurant in trendy H Street, near the Capitol. So, this Saturday in February – just three days before Valentine's Day, we decided we would go more up-market, and book a table at the Trump hotel on Pennsylvania Avenue. It was early evening and the place was quiet. The building used to be the headquarters of the post office, but it had now been transformed into a five-star hotel. There is a stunning atrium where we were having cocktails before going upstairs to the restaurant. And we joked that there was no chance the President was coming in as there was no security anywhere to be seen. And then after about ten minutes a man arrived with a sniffer dog. And then a few more people, this time apparently with all manner of electronic equipment, which was being set up on the staircase that leads to the BLT Restaurant. After 20 minutes the place was crawling with people wearing earpieces and talking into their hands, and then who should walk directly past where we were having drinks but the President and the First Lady. They went up to their table; and a few minutes later we to ours.

We were about two tables and maybe 20 feet apart. And to the casual observer they looked like any other married couple out on a Saturday evening date-night. They were not particularly affectionate – but then who is after years of marriage? They sat chatting quietly and in an apparently friendly and animated way to each other. The scene was entirely normal – except for the handful of armed agents standing, looking out from their table across the restaurant. And the dozens posted elsewhere in the hotel. We learned afterwards that in the kitchen a US Navy steward accompanied by a secret service agent checks and oversees the preparation of the President's food to ensure no one tries to poison him.

At the end of the meal they got up to leave. The President started engaging with other diners – posing for a photograph at one table where a group of young people were celebrating a birthday. A hello here and a handshake there, him dressed in formal dark suit and striped navy tie, her dressed stylishly, as ever. This may have been Saturday, but there was nothing dressed down about them. What was noticeable was the extent to which Melania Trump stood back from all this. By the time they walked down the stairs to leave, a crowd had gathered in the atrium, cheering and waving, a few chanting 'USA'. But Melania now withdrew. The backslapping and hand-shaking could be done by her husband. She seemed to want to have nothing to do with it. This is a private, reserved woman who will only go along with so much.

The media narrative at the time was that they weren't talking to each other. They were. We saw this with our own eyes. I should add that the conversation around *our* table was perfunctory to say the least. We could barely take our eyes off the booth where the first couple were sitting; what they were eating (steak), what he was drinking (Diet Coke), what they were talking about (sadly, no idea). I offer one other observation. I remember coming away from the restaurant thinking that maybe all this stuff about their marriage being in crisis was so much stuff and nonsense. But I have just looked back at the photos I sneaked while they were eating (I know – tacky in the extreme, but I'm a journalist for good-ness' sake, and you wouldn't want my observations without the ability to back them up ...) and it is kind of noticeable that in many of them he sits with his arms very tightly crossed while she is talking. Maybe their evening out together wasn't quite as enjoyable for him as I had first imagined. But if they really weren't talking, or they were hurling plates at one and other – would they have chosen to go out for dinner to a public place? From everything that's been seen in the first two years of this presidency, Melania is not a dutiful 'keeping up appearances' wife.

And I know we journalists can be guilty of over-analysing things. But there are choices that Melania Trump has made as first lady where, if you didn't arch an eyebrow, you would be falling short in your sceptical duties. The question that I posed earlier in the chapter about what sort of first lady she would be is answered by the campaigns she prioritises to support. Melania Trump has chosen to throw her weight behind a campaign called 'Be Best'. What is Be Best? Its focus is to wage a war against cyber-bullying. There were guffaws across the land as people posed the question: who is the biggest cyber bully in America today?

In March 2018, Melania invited senior executives from Twitter, Facebook and other tech companies to the White House to discuss the issue. 'I am well aware that people are sceptical of me discussing this topic,' she said in her opening remarks. 'I have been criticised for my commitment to tackling this issue, and I know that will continue. But it will not stop me from doing what I know is right. We have to find a better way to talk to each other, to disagree with each other, to respect each other.'

Through a series of subtle and not so subtle messages, Melania Trump would use her platform to stand up for what she thought was right – of course – but while simultaneously seeming to rebuke her husband. No overt criticism of him, no public name calling, just leaving it up to others to draw their own conclusions. She will happily say she doesn't always agree with what he posts, but it was up to him to take responsibility for what he did.

Perhaps the most controversial policy (yes, I know that's a high bar) the President pursued was over the vexed issue of immigrants crossing the southern border from Mexico, when the administration showed a harshness that few could believe. Mothers were separated from their children at the border, and the children were incarcerated in cages. It seemed an act of extraordinary callousness. That is remarkable enough. What was truly unforgivable was that the state prised these children away from their mothers with no systems in place to reunite child and mother at a later date. Overnight this civilised, liberal democracy had created hundreds, perhaps thousands of orphans. You can argue the merits and demerits of the policy; you can press the case for the need to tackle illegal immigration; you can suggest that such a draconian measure is necessary to warn off other mothers from seeking to enter the country illegally – but having no mechanisms, no bureaucratic record keeping of who belonged to whom and where these tiny children had been taken? Some people suggested that Trump's America was becoming like Nazi Germany. No, in Nazi Germany, they kept meticulous records. Terrifying, yes. But meticulous.

With a storm raging, and the President being assailed from all sides, what did Melania do? The one-time immigrant went to the border to see the children and the mothers, in what looked like a calculated act of solidarity with them and against the administration her husband headed. She also wore a coat that generated nearly as much comment as the policy itself.

Two quick things about Melania Trump that need restating: she is immensely style conscious; she is also very image conscious, not unlike a number of her predecessors – but none quite had her pedigree as a supermodel. Her first solo trip abroad was to Africa. What was the stand-out moment? When she posed beside the Pyramids at Giza in Egypt, it was as though the First Lady had gone back to her modelling days. It was a carefully contrived backdrop, and she looked like she had come off the set of an Indiana Jones movie. She wore white trousers, a white shirt with a black tie, and a cream jacket with a Panama style hat. When people wrote about her outfit, she asked without irony, why don't people focus on what I say rather than what I wear? Hmm. Where to begin.

The green, parka style coat she wore when she went to the southern border had written, graffiti like, in large letters on the back: 'I really don't care. Do u?' Was it a dig at the press, who, like her husband, she views with disdain? Did it mean nothing? (Hard to believe you would pick that jacket out of the wardrobe without being conscious of the message you wanted to convey.) Or was it, as many Washington insiders surmised, a dig at her husband? Was she saying she didn't care what he thought about her going? She would later claim it was aimed at 'the left-wing media' – but she also made clear her displeasure at the child separation policy. 'It was unacceptable for me to see children and parents separated. It was heart-breaking. And I reacted with my own voice. I went to the border and met with the Border Patrol.'

A timid, lost soul does not go and do this. This was one of the few occasions when public opinion was running so strongly against the President that he changed course. You can be sure his wife's intervention would have played a big part in an uncharacteristic U-turn. Indeed, Chris Christie, the former New Jersey governor – and a close friend of the family – says she is a not to be underestimated player in the White House court. 'She's the most powerful ally you can get if you're attempting to influence Donald Trump,' he says. 'No one influences Donald Trump more than Melania Trump. Nobody.'

And some have underestimated her to their cost. Ask the one-time deputy national security advisor, Mira Ricardel. She fell out with the First Lady on that trip to Africa, over disparaging remarks she was alleged to have made behind the scenes about two of Mrs Trump's staff travelling with her. She queried the way government expenditure was being used. False claims, said the First Lady. Mrs Trump raised the matter when she got back to Washington, but got nowhere. The First Lady was being fobbed off. No one was listening. So, she borrowed from her husband's playbook. She had her communications director, Stephanie Grisham, put this out on Twitter: 'It is the position of the Office of the First Lady that she [Mira Ricardel] no longer deserves the honour of serving in this White House.' Mrs Trump was ignored no longer. Ms Ricardel's boss, the powerful, formidable, not to be trifled with National Security Advisor, John Bolton, went into battle on Ms Ricardel's behalf. To no avail. Ricardel, the long-time political insider, was now an outsider.

Melania Trump may be a political novice, an unwilling recruit to the position of First Lady; she may hate the publicity and the unwanted scrutiny; she may define herself as a mum first and everything else second; she may yearn for her days in New York; and may occasionally despair at her husband's behaviour and some aspects of his policies, but in Washington she had shown she knew what to do in a knife-fight. The most vital survival skill in this cruel town.

# CHAPTER 6

# The Surgery

In the rooms around the White House and in Washington DC where moments of national drama have unfolded, the White House Medical Office has rarely even been a footnote. It has not been a place where historians have sat with pen in hand, poised to inscribe a new chapter in America's national story. Room 91 in the Eisenhower Executive Office Building, next door to the White House, and a doctor's office with two consulting rooms, positioned between the Palm Room and the Map Room in the basement of the East Wing, are hardly places to get the pulse racing (even when the man in the white coat is wearing a stethoscope). If the vice-president is only one heartbeat away from becoming the president, well, crudely speaking, it is the White House physician's job to ensure that the VP never gets any closer than that. Yes – the uncontroversial job of the president's doctor is to keep his patient alive and that heart beating.

The president's physician is a man typically who lives in the shadows. These people are drawn from the military and stand outside the normal White House command structure, where everyone answers to the president's chief of staff. The doctor treating the president is not part of that organogram. He answers to his service superiors. Admiral Ronny Jackson had treated George W. Bush, been the physician to Barack Obama, and in an exceptionally rare piece of continuity the 45th president agreed that he should continue in that role. Under Obama and Bush, Jackson was rarely more than a few feet away from the president, travelling with them around the world, the permanent presence ensuring the Commander in Chief's health. But though never more than a couple of steps away, they were never in the spotlight. They would be anonymous, and unknown to the public, a figure who would be seen in the corner of camera frame emerging from Air Force One, or walking behind the president, as they get into a motorcade.

Occasionally he or she would be seen in a medical white coat, which was a bit more of a giveaway about who they were, but generally they were able to get on the metro at Farragut North, near the White House, and no one would be asking for selfies. That would change, however, with the Donald-Trump-life-is-a-reality-TV-show presidency. And as everyone knows who watches that genre of television, anyone can become an overnight star. Everyone has their fifteen minutes of fame. That is where for a brief second things went dizzyingly right for Dr Jackson, and where soon afterwards things went spectacularly wrong for this lifelong member of the military.

His story is akin to a modern morality tale. He wasn't so much Icarus who flew too close to the sun. Icarus had ignored the remonstrations of his father when he went on his ill-fated flight and saw his wings melt before crashing into the sea. This is more about succumbing to the dangers of flattery, of coming into the orbit of something attractive but which is simultaneously destructive. This was a doctor who would eventually have to swallow a very bitter medicine.

Where presidential physicians have been in the news before, it has tended to be over their role in keeping their patients' medical history secret – something you would normally want from any physician. Doctor/patient confidentiality is of course a bond that should not be broken. But where does the effort to maintain confidentiality tip over into dissembling? Where does saying little become misleading? Often – undoubtedly under political pressure – the doctors would release medical bulletins about the president whose care they were entrusted with that were at best euphemistic and, at worst, downright lies.

After Woodrow Wilson fell ill, his doctor released a vague, optimistic statement saying that he was suffering from 'exhaustion', but it was 'not alarming'. In fact Wilson had collapsed from a serious stroke, and was paralysed. Wilson and his formidable wife Edith ran the government for more than a year while he remained bedridden. There was no real mechanism for removing a president from office if he insisted he was fit to carry on. And it was not terribly surprising, at a time when life expectancy was between 60 and 65, and politicians rarely ascended to the presidency until well into their fifties, that the doctors had a lot to be secretive about.

Franklin Delano Roosevelt projected an image of strength and decisiveness. For the best part of 12 years, the American public had no idea that the New Deal president could barely walk. He had contracted polio comparatively late in life, when he was 39, and was invariably photographed sitting down.

Secret Service agents were tasked with ensuring that no photos emerged revealing the extent of his incapacity. When he had to be filmed walking, he would be wearing leg callipers, he'd have a cane in one hand, and his other would be resting on his son's arm for support. Weakness is never a good look in politics, and so every effort was made to shield the public from the difficulties he was struggling with on a daily basis. But his re-election in 1944 came as he was suffering from congestive heart failure, and even though Ross McIntyre, the White House physician from his first term, was fully cognisant of his condition, he assured worried members of the Democratic Party – and the American public – that the President was in fine health. Not strictly true. He would die three months into his fourth term.

It was a similar story with President Eisenhower. In 1955 he had a heart attack, and though the public was assured that he had made a full recovery, he was discouraged from running for re-election by a prominent cardiologist – advice he chose to bat away. In 1956 he was diagnosed with Crohn's disease, a serious gastrointestinal disorder, which required surgery. Shortly after that, Eisenhower suffered a stroke, but managed to complete his term in office.

And then came the very picture of health and vitality, vim and vigour: John F. Kennedy. Decorated war hero, young, dashing, Hollywood good looks, stunning and stylish wife – and as we would discover long after his death, racked by the most chronic and debilitating back pain, so much so that at times he could barely walk; he was a sufferer from Addison's disease, and had so many pills inside him – uppers, downers, steroids – that if you shook him he would rattle.

Kennedy's assassination in 1963 shook the world. It rocked America to its core, and the reverberations are still felt today. And there would be two important, intertwined side effects whose relevance would prove important in 2016, when Donald Trump assumed the presidency. The first was a sense that while America's written and codified constitution covers nearly everything, it was fuzzy and unclear on questions about the succession in the event of the president's serious illness, sudden death or mental incapacity. The other thing it brought – and this was a culmination of decades of unease – was a demand for greater transparency and much more public disclosure about the health of the president.

JFK's killing that bright November day would four years later result in the ratification of the 25th Amendment to the US Constitution. When Lyndon B. Johnson was sworn in on Air Force One as it stood on the tarmac at Love Field Airport in Dallas, hours after the shooting, his ascension to the presidency meant that – for the 16th time – the country had no vice-president. There was no tested way of dealing with a severe presidential illness, like the one Woodrow Wilson suffered – which in effect, left his wife running the country. LBJ had previously suffered a heart attack, and the next two people in the line of succession were the Speaker of the House – aged 71, and the 86-year-old President of the Senate.

The 25th Amendment also clarified a set of procedures to be followed if the president became, in the judgement of his most senior cabinet colleagues, incapable of executing his duties – whether because of physical frailty, or because of mental incapacity. As Donald Trump fired off endless volleys of irascible tweets, or seemed to ramble incoherently in broadcast interviews – so the stability of the man with his finger on the nuclear button became a subject of serious, if whispered, discussion. And that in turn led to all manner of people revisiting the provisions of the 25th Amendment, in particular Section 4. It states:

Whenever the Vice President and a majority of either the principal officers of the executive departments or of such other body as Congress may by law provide, transmit to the President pro tempore of the Senate and the Speaker of the House of Representatives their written declaration that the President is unable to discharge the powers and duties of his office, the Vice President shall immediately assume the powers and duties of the office as Acting President.

Stripped of legalese, and put simply, the vice-president and cabinet officials decide on the removal of the president. If the majority votes for him being forced out, then a letter is sent to the president pro tempore of the Senate and Speaker of the House, informing them of their vote.

The president could send a counter-letter saying he is fine and capable of performing his duties. That would allow the president to continue in office, unless the vice-president and cabinet send another letter within four days restating their case. Then, the vice-president would become the acting president while it is then sent to Congress to decide.

Both houses of Congress would have to vote within 21 days, and a two-thirds majority from each chamber is required to remove the president from office and fully institute the vice-president as the replacement. If the vote in either chamber falls short, the president resumes his duties. That section of the 25ᵗʰ Amendment remains unused. That said, when George W. Bush had to undergo surgery he used the provisions of the 25ᵗʰ Amendment to put the Vice-President, Dick Cheney, temporarily in charge.

The demand for disclosure and transparency around the president's health was one that grew and grew. Once upon a time, in an age of deference, a gruff 'he's in fine health' from an estimable physician would have been enough to satisfy the American public, but those days have gone. In an information rich age, where panels of 'experts' can sit round the table on cable television pontificating on whatever the latest medical intricacy in the news that day was, that will no longer do.

Just as Americans view the White House as the 'people's house', so they view the health of their president as ultimately a public matter. He is after all 'the people's president'. There is no statute requiring presidents to release their health records, just like they're not required *legally* to release their tax information. But in the modern era, many have done so anyway. So in 1992 came the revelation that Bill Clinton suffered from allergies, had mild hearing loss, and a left knee ligament strain.

If you go onto the White House website and navigate your way to the archive section, you will find a memorandum sent from Dr Jackson (then physician to Barack Obama) to Josh Earnest, the press secretary, in March 2016. It sets out in extraordinary detail the results of the annual physical the President had recently undergone. And this would be released to the press.

Vital Statistics
Age: 54 years, 6 months
Height: 73.5 inches
Weight: 175 pounds
Body Mass Index: 22.8 kg/m2
Resting heart rate: 56
Blood pressure: 110/68 mm Hg
Pulse-oximetry: 98% room air
Temperature: 97.8 degrees

Physical Examination by System
Eyes: Visual fields were normal. Uncorrected bilateral visual acuity was 20/20. Fundoscopic exam was normal bilaterally. No ocular pathology was discovered.

Head/Ears/Nose/Throat: Normal exam of the head, ears, nose, and pharynx.

Neck: Normal thyroid exam. No noted lymphad-enopathy. Auscultation of the carotid arteries normal.

And on and on it went: pulmonary this, cardiac that, neurological, cranial, cerebellar something else. We had his lab test results – his HDL cholesterol, his LDL. You name it, it was all set out. And a conclusion which read: 'All clinical data indicates that the President is currently very healthy and that he will remain so for the duration of his Presidency.'

Two things are immediately striking about this health report: the first is the extraordinary amount of detail the then president was happy for his physician to disclose to the rest of the world about the inner workings of the Obama corpus. The second is that for a man of 54, how extraordinarily healthy Barack Obama was after the strains of nearly eight years in office. But what if the report had been carried out four years earlier, when the President was about to seek a second term, and had perhaps turned up a few 'nasties'? Would the President and his press secretary have been as happy then to disclose Dr Jackson's report, warts (though probably something worse than warts) and all – with all the political consequences that would flow from it?

Or what about when Hillary Clinton collapsed in New York during the campaign in 2016 as she was on her way back from commemorating the victims of 9/11? Then, a doctor released a statement saying the cause had been pneumonia. The candidate had been prescribed Levaquin for treatment. She'd also had a recent sinus infection. But in this case, she had little choice *but* to disclose what had happened. Then 68 years old, the mix of her age and being caught on film keeling over, and eventually caught by her Secret Service detail just before she hit the deck – and then filmed, seemingly semi-conscious, having to be bundled into her limo – was not a good look for a candidate. At any time it would be bad; when she was running against her take-no-hostages opponent, Donald Trump, it was disastrous.

It was inevitable that serious – and legitimate – questions about her health would arise and take centre stage. Throw into that mix a good dollop of misogyny – the idea that women are not really strong enough to be president – and you have a fairly perfect storm. That she disclosed details of her pneumonia and the medication she was taking should not be interpreted as an act of openness. The Clintons' reflex after so many bruising encounters is to be anything but open – just look at how much easier life would have been for her if she'd been more candid, far earlier, about her use of a private email server when she was Secretary of State. The phrase 'Clinton candour' in Washington is viewed as an oxymoron. No, the information her team made public was born out of political necessity; not out of a Damascene conversion to transparency and a commitment to freedom of information.

Donald Trump didn't succumb to the temptation to release his tax returns. That little treasure trove of mystery and speculation he would keep to himself. But he did release a health bulletin from his then New York physician during the presidential election campaign. It really should be read in full, as it was released to the press.

To Whom My Concern:

I have been the personal physician of Mr Donald J. Trump since 1980. His previous physician was my father, Dr Jacob Bornstein. Over the past 39 years, I am pleased to report that Mr Trump has had no significant medical problems. Mr Trump has had a recent complete medical examination that showed only positive results. Actually, his blood pressure, 110/65, and laboratory test results were astonishingly excellent.

Over the past twelve months, he has lost at least fifteen pounds, Mr Trump takes 81 mg of aspirin daily and a low dose of a statin. His PSA test score is 0.15 (very low). His physical strength and stamina are extraordinary.

Mr Trump has suffered no form of cancer, has never had a hip, knee or shoulder replacement or any other orthopaedic surgery. His only surgery was an appendectomy at age ten. His cardiovascular status is excellent. He has no history of ever using alcohol or tobacco products.

If elected, Mr Trump, I can state unequivocally, will be the healthiest individual ever elected to the presidency.

Harold N Bornstein, MD, FACG
Department of Medicine, Section of Gastroenterology
Lenox Hill Hospital, New York, NY

Now let us leave to one side the heading 'To whom my concern' (let's be generous: Dr Bornstein may have been having a particularly busy day, or you just can't get the secretarial staff these days) and let us not detain ourselves on the details of his blood pressure – the results aren't just good. They're not even very good. They are 'astonishingly excellent'. When have you ever seen a doctor write something like that? No, let us focus on the final paragraph; it is the one I like most: 'If elected, Mr Trump, I can state unequivocally, will be the healthiest individual ever elected to the presidency.'

Hmm: who else do we know who has a bit of a penchant for the superlative? Someone whose conversation is peppered with the greatest ever, the best ever, the biggest ever? Could it be that the no doubt respected Dr Bornstein had – how can one put this delicately – a little help with the drafting from the person he was writing about?

Bornstein is a character born to play a role in a Trumpian drama. He is New York through and through. He drives a soft-top sports car, wears open-necked shirts revealing multiple gold chains. Though in advanced middle age, he has straggly blond/grey hair going down to his shoulders, a neatly trim blondish moustache and beard, and wears dark tinted glasses with clear rims. He looks more like a doctor of love than a doctor of medicine. Or maybe someone from a Bee Gees tribute band ('Stayin' Alive' no doubt his encore song).

Bornstein, though undoubtedly flamboyant, would stay out of the limelight beyond supplying that medical bulletin on his patient. That would change after the election. And when he did speak it was nothing short of what you would expect from a Trumpian drama. It cheered up enormously a chill February day. His re-emergence into the public domain came as he claimed that three men saying they represented Trump had entered his office in February 2017, and demanded that he hand over Trump's medical records. The three were said by Bornstein to be Trump's former personal bodyguard who worked briefly at the White House, a Trump Organisation legal officer and a third person, whom the New York physician could only describe as a 'large man'. The doctor told CNN that he was 'robbed' and described it as a raid. He didn't claim to have been held at knifepoint, but someone ought to have prescribed the doctor a salbutamol inhaler, his description was so breathless. The 'raid' occurred two days after he told the *New York Times* that Trump took Propecia, a prostate drug often prescribed for hair loss, something that might be seen as not a massively revealing disclosure, but if it was made without the patient's permission, then it is a breach of confidence.

The White House was not in the mood for any more drama than it was already dealing with, so played down the whole incident: 'As is standard operating procedure, the White House Medical Unit took possession of the President's medical records,' press secretary Sarah Sanders told reporters, and really didn't want to add much more to this unexpected addition to the already congested news cycle.

But Dr Bornstein wasn't done; he had something else to say too. The medical bulletin released before the election had not been written by him after all; it had been dictated by Trump (as everyone suspected). 'He dictated that whole letter. I didn't write that letter,' Bornstein told CNN. He claimed Trump read out the language as Bornstein and his wife were driving across Central Park. 'Trump dictated the letter and I would tell him what he couldn't put in there,' he said.

It is fair to say that Harold N. Bornstein and Ronny Jackson are not cut from the same cloth. Indeed, let me go further – it would be fair to say that their qualifications as doctors would probably be the only thing they have in common. They're not cut from the same anything. Harold N. Bornstein is New York City – if you cut him down the middle you would find a Big Apple core.

Ronny Jackson, on the other hand, grew up in small-town conservative Texas. His two other siblings, Gary and Stacy, still live in Levelland where he went to high school. It is a town of a few thousand people where the main industries are cotton and oil. Jackson is clean cut, with hair neatly side parted and a big white-toothed smile. He stands up straight and looks every bit the man who had spent his life in the armed services. His navy portrait looks like it could have been from any of the past eight decades. He has timeless, chiselled good looks.

After university and medical school in his home state, Jackson joined the navy in 1995 at the Naval Medical Centre in Portsmouth, Virginia, where he completed an internship and would graduate later with honours from the US Navy's undersea medical officer programme in Connecticut. With a focus on the special needs of submariners and divers, Jackson's next stop would be the Naval Diving and Salvage

Training Centre in Panama City, Florida, before returning to Portsmouth in 2001, now to train to specialise in emergency medicine. He finished top of his class.

And with that accolade came deployment to Iraq as part of Operation Iraqi Freedom. He joined the 2nd Marines, Combat Logistics Regiment, to work with the Surgical Shock Trauma Platoon. This was the toughest, most demanding work. He was now the emergency medical doctor in charge of resuscitative medicine for a forward deployed unit in Taqaddum. His stint in western Iraq came during some of the worst months of the conflict, with Americans killed and maimed on a daily basis by roadside bombs, insurgent attacks and snipers.

The awards and accolades were now beginning to pile up. He has the Defense Superior Service Medal, the Legion of Merit, the Navy/Marine Corps Commendation Medal, their Achievement medal – as well as other individual, unit and campaign awards. And then there are the qualifications. He is designated as a diving and undersea medical officer, naval parachutist, fleet marine force qualified warfare officer. And on and on the list of achievements go. What all of this adds up to is a highly distinguished armed forces medic, meaning a sizeable chunk of the left breast of his uniform is taken up with medals and ribbons.

In 2006, while still in Iraq, Dr Jackson was selected as a White House physician, first working for George W. Bush, then Barack Obama – during whose presidency he was appointed to the most senior job as physician to the president and Director of the White House Medical Unit (WHMU). Obama would say of him, 'Ronny's positive impact cannot be overstated. He is a tremendous asset to the entire White House Team.' It is one of the few judgements that Donald Trump shared. The number of senior people who stayed on in the White House after the change of administration can be counted on one hand. Admiral Jackson, as he had now become, would be one of them.

And the WHMU is not a one man and his dog operation. As with everything to do with the presidency, if you're going to do it, you do it big. The office of the medical director is in the basement of the Residence, away from the hubbub and rabbit warren of corridors that is the West Wing. White House staff – not just the president – are treated there. Even we journalists get treated there if something bad happens to us while on the grounds. One of my White House colleagues, Jon Decker, then working for Reuters TV, was attacked by Barney, the Scottish terrier that belonged to President George W. Bush. He was given antibiotics and a tetanus booster by the then White House physician. But the unit is capable of doing far more than bandaging a journalist's bleeding hand.

Along with the facility in the adjacent Eisenhower Executive Office Building, the doctors and nurses are capable of dealing with medical emergencies and trauma cases. There is a crash cart in the East Wing, and they are equipped to carry out sophisticated surgery in extremis. There is 24-hour care, with at least one physician on duty at all times. Anyone joining the team has to undergo a full year of trauma care training. And though the numbers vary, Ronny Jackson would have had anything between 20 and 25 doctors and nurses working under him.

Another important aspect of the job is preparing for when the president is travelling abroad. So when the advance team of secret service personnel travel to recce a presidential trip, a number of the medics will go to set up in advance. They will establish at each location temporary emergency medical facilities – this will consist of an eight-person intensive care and surgical team, with a makeshift operating theatre at each stop. Ideally the trip is planned so that the president is never more than 20 minutes away from a level one trauma centre. But in some cases the WHMU staff will carry operating theatre equipment with them in backpacks so that emergency care can be provided on site. Likewise, look at any presidential motorcade and there will be an ambulance in it. Interestingly, the physician and nurse who accompany the president wherever they go will be positioned close enough in the motorcade to respond to an emergency, but far enough away to make it unlikely for them to be tangled up in any disastrous event.

And we haven't even discussed Air Force One yet. It's not like being on a conventional commercial flight, where the cabin crew has access to a bag of medication held in one of the overhead bins. Air Force One comes equipped with a full surgical suite, operating table, two beds, resuscitation equipment, different medical monitors and a fully equipped pharmacy – and of course wherever the president flies, the head of the WHMU goes too.

And just as he did for Barack Obama, it was Ronny Jackson's job to organise the full medical examination for Donald Trump at the Walter Reed Army Medical Center in Bethesda, just on the north tip of Washington. For Jackson this came layered with an additional degree of complexity. Was he to do the standard set of tests that he had performed when Barack Obama was president, or would he address the concerns that had been mooted about the 45th president's mental health?

The world would soon find out. Not for Donald Trump an email written by the White House physician to the White House press secretary to be released to the White House correspondents. No. Instead, Daniel would be sent into the lion's den and give a full, on-the-record, on-camera briefing that would be broadcast live across America about the state of the President's health.

The 16th of January 2018 would be a day few would forget. We're used to seeing key White House staff come to the podium – the National Security Advisor, the head of the economic council, the chief of staff once or twice. But never before had the president's physician done this. And leave aside the content of the briefing – which I will come to shortly – there was one other extraordinary aspect of all this. It was one of the longest briefings that any of us had sat through. It went on and on. And on. And it was clear this was deliberate strategy. The White House didn't want anyone to be able to say that their questions had not been answered, that the esteemed doctor had been curt or cagey, circumspect or evasive. Admiral Ronny Jackson, in his full military uniform, had come to parlay.

He went through the President's vitals at length, which I will spare you the full details of, but here is an important flavour of what was read out to us in the Briefing Room:

Age: 71 years and 7 months at the time of the exam.
Height: 75 inches.
Weight: 239 pounds.
Resting heart rate: 68.
Blood pressure: 122/74.
Pulse oximetry: 99 percent on room air.
Temperature was 98.4.

Physical examination, by system, to include any studies that were done, by system:

Eyes: The President's uncorrected physical acuity is 20/30 bilaterally with corrected visual acuity of 20/20 bilaterally. His visual fields were normal. Funduscopic exam was normal bilaterally. His intraocular pressures were normal, and no ocular pathology was discovered.

Head, ears, nose, and throat: Normal exam of the head, ears, nose, mouth, and throat.

Dental exam: He has healthy teeth and gums. There were no other dental findings.

Neck: Normal thyroid exam. No noted lymphadenopathy. Auscultation of his carotid arteries was normal.

Pulmonary exam: His lungs were clear to auscultation. A screening low-dose CT of the chest demonstrated no pulmonary pathology.

Cardiac exam: Heart exam was normal. Regular rhythm. No murmurs or other abnormal heart sounds were noted. His ECG, or commonly EKG, was normal.

And then Doctor Jackson offered this conclusion:

In summary: The President's overall health is excellent. His cardiac performance during his physical exam was very good. He continues to enjoy the significant long-term cardiac and overall health benefits that come from a lifetime of abstinence from tobacco and alcohol.

We discussed diet, exercise, and weight-loss. He would benefit from a diet that is lower in fat and carbohydrates, and from a routine exercise regimen. He has a history of elevated cholesterol and is currently in a low dose of Crestor.

In order to further reduce his cholesterol level and further decrease his cardiac risk, we will increase the dose of this particular medication. The President is currently up to date on all recommended preventive medicine and screening tests and exams.

All clinical data indicates that the President is currently very healthy and that he will remain so for the duration of his presidency.

Even this brief outline begged a lot of questions, and hands were shooting up from reporters in the Briefing Room. But Dr Jackson would show that as well as being able to use a stethoscope he knew how to deploy a sense of humour too. 'With that, I'll take some questions. Before we get started, let me just make one comment. I would just like to point out for all of you here in this room – many of you which know me – just, if something should happen to you over the next few months and you should fall ill at some point, that most likely I will be the one called to come to take care of you [laughter]. So when you ask your questions, please keep that in mind [more laughter].'

As the questions came thick and fast, it became apparent that maybe the President's physician had more in common with Harold Bornstein than we had all thought. Certainly some of the answers had a certain Bornsteinian flourish.

His heart: 'I think he had great findings across the board, but the one that stands out more than anything to me is his cardiac health. His cardiac health is excellent. And so I think, with all the other things in place – he doesn't have, really, a family history of premature cardiac disease, he doesn't smoke, he doesn't have diabetes … so I think those things, in combination with the excellent cardiac results that we got from the exercise stress test, I think, are very reassuring.' And he went on to assert that 'he will remain fit for duty for the remainder of this term and even for the remainder of another term, if he's elected.'

Then there was his stamina. According to Dr Jackson he has it by the bucket load. He didn't do enough exercise, but, 'despite that, one of the things, being with the President on a day-to-day basis, that has been impressive to me is he has a lot of energy … And the days – we'd get these 14-, 16-hour days, and the staff is just spent after a while. And you're just like, man, when are we going to the hotel? When are we going down? Because you have all the issues of different time zones and things of that nature, too. And I'll tell you, out of everybody there, the President had more stamina and more energy than just about anybody there.'

And of the Trump genes, the report was again glowing: 'It is called genetics …' Jackson said. 'Some people have just great genes. I told the President that if he had a healthier diet over the last 20 years, he might live to be 200 years old.'

Yes, there were things the doctor wanted to change. He wants the President to exercise more and eat better. He wants the gym that is in the residence to be used rather than just gather dust. He is going to involve the First Lady in persuading her husband to change his ways. He needs to lose weight – probably around a stone. But a year on from the debrief on the medical it was questionable how much progress was being made on the exercise front. After the death of the 41st president George H.W. Bush in November 2018, his son George W. Bush came to stay across the street at the administration guest house, Blair House, ahead of the lying in state at the Rotunda and then the state funeral. From West Wing door to Blair house is probably a distance of around 200 yards – or to put it in golfing terms that Donald Trump would find familiar, it is probably a full four-iron shot, but not much more. But on this fine, bright day, the President chose the motorcade over his feet. A dozen vehicles or so made up the convoy, with the last vehicle leaving the White House after the President in the Beast had already arrived and got out.

It is a well-known fact that the President sits in the West Wing while these sessions in the Briefing Room unfold, watching avidly and critically from the private dining room. Every now and then the sliding door between the Briefing Room and the press office will open and a note is handed to whoever is at the podium. Unless it is a piece of urgent breaking news you can be sure this is a little handwritten instruction from the President, demanding that this or that point be made. There was no need to pass anything on to Admiral Jackson. He was knocking it out of the park, as far as the President was concerned.

And there was one other issue in this briefing that was tackled head on – and that was the state of Donald Trump's mind. Dr Jackson revealed that he had carried out a neurological exam, with examination of the cranial nerves, cerebellar function, deep tendon reflexes, motor function, and sensory system – which were all normal. In addition, he carried out a cognitive screening exam using something called the Montreal Cognitive Assessment. According to Dr Jackson, the President got top marks with a score of 30 out of 30.

Dr Jackson made clear that he had never had any doubts about the President's cognitive abilities. 'I didn't think it was clinically indicated because I've spent almost every day in the President's presence since January 20 – or, you know, last year, when he got into office. And I've seen him every day … We have conversations about many things, most don't revolve around medical issues at all. But I've gotten to know him pretty well and I had absolutely no concerns about his cognitive ability or his neurological functions.'

All of which begged a very obvious question – why carry out such a test if you think there is no medical justification for it? Because, Dr Jackson explained, the President had insisted on it. Donald Trump, in a memorable series of tweets had described himself as a 'very stable genius'. In fact, these tweets are too good not to quote in full.

'… Actually, throughout my life, my two greatest assets have been mental stability and being, like, really smart. Crooked Hillary Clinton also played these cards very hard and, as everyone knows, went down in flames. I went from VERY successful businessman, to top T.V. Star … to President of the United States (on my first try). I think that would qualify as not smart, but genius … and a very stable genius at that!'

But with his mental faculties being called into question the President recognised this was an issue that needed dealing with. And while Dr Jackson neither called the President a genius, nor stable – he managed effectively to put the whole issue of whether the 45th president was mentally impaired, unable to carry out the functions of his office properly, to bed. Among the Trump haters you could almost sense the sadness and disappointment – the air had been let out of their most promising balloon. You could perhaps question

Harold Bornstein, but Rear-Admiral Ronny Jackson – the man who had treated George W. Bush and Barack Obama before with distinction? The trauma specialist who had served his nation, seeing service on the front line in Iraq with the marines? Not a chance.

The news headlines that evening online and on TV and radio, and in the newspapers the next morning, were as good as the President could have hoped for. 'White House doctor: Trump "has absolutely no cognitive or mental issues",' said Vox. The CNN headline was 'Dr Jackson's glowing bill of health for Trump'. NBC had 'White House doctor declares Trump mentally "very sharp" and in "excellent health"'. For *Time* magazine it was 'The White House Doctor Called President Trump's Health "Excellent"'.

It was mission accomplished, job done. And shares in Dr Jackson were soaring through the White House roof. The President as part of his daily briefing has the headlines cut out of newspapers and presented to him in a folder. It was hard not to picture him purring with rare delight at the newspaper coverage he was receiving, like a proud actor reading his reviews after the press night, where the critics declare him the next Olivier.

However, the sugar rush brought about by good headlines doesn't last long in the White House. The next battle, the next media onslaught, the next presidential counter-attack is never far away. The Jackson cameo in the story of this presidency was soon starting to fade.

But then came a tweet from the President a couple of months later that would cause a serious outbreak of acute jaw drop syndrome among the Washington political class and journalists alike, which Dr Jackson really should have spent more time finding a treatment for. There had been a lot of it about. Donald Trump's tweet was brief and to the point: 'I am pleased to announce that I intend to nominate highly respected Admiral Ronny L. Jackson, MD, as the new Secretary of Veterans Affairs ...'

Woah. Back up. The VA? Are you kidding? To call this a bit of a step up in the managerial and political experience of this physician would be to put it at its very mildest. In the White House he managed a team of around 30 doctors and nurses, tops. The Veterans Affairs department employs, well roughly 12,000 times that number. The VA has 370,000 staff and has an annual budget of $180 billion. It is a sprawling behemoth, with the second biggest federal budget – only the Department of Defense receives more taxpayer dollars.

The VA's motto is 'To care for him who shall have borne the battle and for his widow and his orphan.' In a country with no national health service, this is the nearest thing to it. There are VA hospitals and health centres across the country whose mission is to provide healthcare for servicemen and women, military veterans and their families. It covers millions of people, has a noble ambition but has been badly managed for years, is racked by scandal – and is one of the hottest of hot potatoes in Washington.

Donald Trump had homed in on the subject with laser-like precision during the election campaign. 'We will take care of our great veterans like they have never been taken care of before,' he told the Republican National Convention, in 2016. Once in the White House he claimed that his administration was following through on that promise. David Shulkin – whose firing from the VA I wrote about earlier – was ostensibly forced out after an official investigation found that he had not declared corporate gifts, and taking his wife with him on a taxpayer funded trip to Europe. There was, though, another more compelling theory about what really lay behind his dismissal.

Shulkin knew his subject, having been the number two in the VA during the final years of the Obama administration. And before that he had become a seasoned and respected hospital administrator, having run New York's Mount Sinai Beth Israel Medical Centre. But the ideological hawks around Donald Trump – and in particular, a couple of wealthy right-wing conservatives – had been making disobliging noises in the President's ear. They were annoyed at Shulkin's resistance to the privatisation agenda that free-market think tanks and Republican donors (with interests in providing healthcare themselves) had been pushing for years.

Maybe Donald Trump had calculated that by appointing Jackson he would have a more malleable and accommodating VA Secretary. Maybe he genuinely thought it was a small step from running a team of 30 to a team of 370,000. Maybe not that much thought was given to it, except for the fact that the President wanted to reward a man who had done him a massive favour with the briefing he gave the press.

An important thing to understand is that there could be precious little interaction between the political staff at the White House and those who are part of the military command structure, such as Jackson. As a physician he did not report to the President's chief of staff, nor was he answerable to the White House lawyer; he reported to his military superiors at the little-known White House Military Office – and although the two different teams saw each other daily, would eat lunch in the same canteen and travelled the world together when the President was on the move, they didn't really interact much. That is why it was such a leap for Jackson to transfer into such a politically exposed position, having only ever known the armed forces chain of command. And building a set of relationships in the political domain, it was recognised, would be important, crucial even to navigating a path to his nomination.

Standard operating procedure when you are seeking to make an appointment like this is that you do full and thorough background checks on the candidate. The only cabinet level job that doesn't require a congressional confirmation hearing is the Chief of Staff. Anyone else has to go through the rigours of detailed questioning before committees, and the *de rigueur* solicitous schmoozing of the senators and House of Representatives members who will decide the nominee's fate. So, the White House – typically – wants to know what skeletons there may be in closets. Has the nominee ever employed an illegal immigrant as a maid or gardener? Have they ever had any disciplinary run-ins at work? Are there people out there who have scores to settle? In other words, is there anything that might derail the process?

In fairness, the White House might have thought such investigation superfluous. Jackson already enjoyed the highest security clearance as the personal physician to the President. And who else in the White House, apart from the First Lady, is going to have such an intimate and personal relationship with him? He is one of the few people entitled to go from his surgery in the East Wing up the staircase that leads to the President's private quarters, without being escorted by a secret service agent.

Not much was done. After the tweet announcing that Dr Jackson would be the nominee, the bureaucracy kicked in – a

timetable for hearings; meetings scheduled with key stake-
holders; appointments for the doctor to widen his political
network.

But then things started to go awry. A few barely percep-
tible murmurs at first, that got louder and would eventually
become a deafening clamour. If the White House wasn't going
to do background checks on their candidate, then the Senate
and House committees would.

All the people who worked for the Rear-Admiral were also
drawn from the US military, so if they had concerns they
had – until the moment of his nomination – either to keep
their counsel, or watch as their complaints were swept under
the carpet. But a little-known Democratic Party senator on
the Veterans Affairs committee, Jon Tester, was contacted by
a number of either current or former staff who had served
under Jackson.

Senator Tester painted a devastating picture: it seems he was
known as the 'Candy Man'. 'On overseas trips, the admiral
would go down the aisleway of the airplane and say, "All
right, who wants to go to sleep?" And hand out the prescription drugs like they were candy and put them to sleep, and
then give them the drugs to wake them back up again,' he
said, claiming this was the evidence from 20 or more people
who had contacted him. 'This doctor has a problem because
he hands out prescriptions like candy. In fact, in the White
House they call him the Candy Man.' The drugs he was
talking about were Ambien, a popular sleeping pill; and the
'uppers' were Provigil, a drug to increase wakefulness. Staff
members on presidential trips would be given these in plastic
bags when they boarded Air Force One. The picture conveyed
was that this was as routine and unremarkable as the hot

face towel and the printed menu being handed out by the cabin crew with whatever was for dinner on the flight.

It was alleged that Dr Jackson didn't keep proper records of what drugs had been handed out and to whom. And in some cases, it wasn't just sleeping tablets that were dished out, but highly addictive and powerful opioids, such as Percocet. Co-workers would allege that he privately kept large quantities of these controlled substances in his office.

Senator Tester also cited allegations that Jackson was drunk on duty during his time working for the administration of the former president, Barack Obama. A summary report handed out by Democrats on the committee claimed that on a number of occasions according to co-workers Jackson was drunk while on call – at times when he was expected to be able to report to duty at a moment's notice in case the President had a health issue. At least once, Jackson couldn't be reached, the senators reported, because he was 'passed out drunk in his hotel room'. These co-workers told senators that Jackson got drunk at a Secret Service going-away party and wrecked a government vehicle. Although those claims have now been thrown into doubt, with both the White House and the Secret Service denying them.

The clean-cut, impeccably turned-out, charming Doctor Jackson was picking up a number of ugly scuff marks, as he found himself in a spotlight he could never have imagined, or planned for. Then came the bullying claims. He used his senior officer rank to push around those beneath him. They also portrayed Jackson as power-hungry. In the summary, co-workers are quoted as saying that he was 'abusive', 'explosive', 'dishonest' and 'vindictive'. He allegedly had 'screaming fits' or 'tantrums' and was 'intolerable' as he gained power in the White House Medical Unit. On overseas trips staff were ordered to leave a bottle of rum and a bottle of Diet Coke in his room, it was claimed.

But even the most cursory enquiries by the political side of the White House would have revealed that the nomination of Dr Jackson was going to hit the buffers. The White House Medical Unit had been investigated before. Years before Donald Trump became president, the working atmosphere had become so contentious within the unit that the Navy's inspector general stepped in. His judgement in 2012 was that the environment was 'toxic' and that one or both of the top two doctors, including Dr Jackson, should go. But no action was taken.

In light of all these disclosures, the Senate committee deferred the hearing to look at Dr Jackson's nomination for the Veterans Affairs Department, and the White House went into damage limitation mode, trying to shore up the President's ill-advised nomination.

But then the inevitable happened. I was in the East Room of the White House for the news conference to mark the state visit of Emmanuel Macron. Ronny Jackson was still the *plat du jour* for the journalists attending. President Trump had two messages about him. One was that Jackson was a top guy, fantastic doctor, man of unimpeachable integrity, how unfair it was that his family was being put through this, and he backed him totally to become VA Secretary. The other was – the game's up. Move out of the way. You are roadkill. Yes, I hear you say, aren't those contradictory messages? Well, indeed they are, but that is broadly what the President had to say.

'He's an admiral, he's a great leader, and they question him for every little thing,' said Trump, suggesting that what these Democratic senators on Capitol Hill were doing was nothing more than muck-raking. But then he carried on at this packed news conference: 'I told Admiral Jackson just a little while ago, what do you need this for?' recounting his conversation with the White House physician. 'This is a vicious group of people, they malign ... what do you need it for?' And just in case Dr Jackson hadn't got the message loud and clear, the President went on: 'I don't want to put a man through a process like this. It's too ugly and too disgusting ... If I were him, I wouldn't do it.'

His nomination was now on life-support. Shares in Ronny Jackson were diving just as fast as they had risen. And though this was never publicly admitted, there were other anxieties about the VA nominee. There had been concern among some White House staff about Jackson having to give evidence before a Senate committee. Specifically, would the evidence he had given to the press on the state of the President's health withstand proper scrutiny? In particular, the worry that Dr Jackson had borrowed too heavily from another doctor, *Candide*'s Dr Pangloss – with his ever optimistic and rosy-eyed view of the world. When Jackson reported that Trump was six feet three inches tall and weighed 239 pounds, that is – miraculously – one pound under the weight where you would be declared obese. And six foot three? He's tall, but the president is not six three; nowhere near. As one commentator noted, if you are a super-fit and toned quarter-back for a pro NFL team you might have that height and weight – but this is a 71-year-old man who lives on Big Macs, fries and pizzas – and takes no exercise.

After the Trump/Macron news conference, word went out that Jackson wanted to soldier on. He was not giving up. For a couple of days, the White House tried to circle the wagons and protect their man. But as anyone with any political nous knew, this was a forlorn operation. This nomination was clinically dead. It was time to pull the plug, as Jackson himself eventually recognised.

He issued a furious statement, denouncing the allegations of improper behaviour that had been levelled against him. They were 'completely false and fabricated', he declared. 'If they had any merit, I would not have been selected, promoted and entrusted to serve in such a sensitive and important role as physician to three presidents over the past 12 years,' Jackson said. 'Going into this process, I expected tough questions about how to best care for our veterans, but I did not expect to have to dignify baseless and anonymous attacks on my character and integrity.' Jackson explained that he had decided to withdraw because the allegations against him had 'become a distraction' for Trump and his agenda.

The allegations were never proved and never tested. That said, an awful lot of people who had worked with him contacted the Senate committee to raise their concerns. And maybe one looks at this whole episode and thinks this is the congressional confirmation process working in exactly the way that it should. A man against whom question marks had been raised is not confirmed to a job.

But Ronny Jackson – surely – should have never ever been considered for the post. He had zero qualifications for it. Yet, off the back of one televised news conference where he flattered the President, Donald Trump wanted to reward his new flavour of the month with a job that was way beyond his skill set. His name was thrown out into the public domain without even the most cursory of enquiries about his suitability by the White House, or about his background. In a private organisation this would be seen as a failure of duty of care towards an employee. There had been warning signs aplenty which had been carelessly ignored.

And so it came to pass that a man who had been a physician to three presidents, had served his country – and survived – in the toughest of war zones, was now torn to shreds under the unsparing and withering fire from senators and the media. And when the going got tough, the White House did what it deemed it had to do, politically – it cut the naval officer adrift.

Dr Robert G. Darling, a former White House physician to President Bill Clinton and a retired emergency medicine doctor in the navy, said, 'This is a guy who served this country, who is in this job pretty reluctantly, and now he's getting hung out to dry.'

The one thing you didn't get is a *mea culpa* from Donald Trump. There was no misjudgement on his part. It was the media who were to blame, egged on by irresponsible Democratic senators who wanted to score political points. They were the ones who had hurt Dr Jackson.

By the time the news conference with Monsieur Macron had ended you just felt that the admiral, who had never sought the role of VA Secretary, was left swinging in the wind. His name and public reputation irreparably tarnished. His family watching powerless as a husband and father was put through the political mincer. He had entered the Trump planetary orbit a hero and got burned up leaving it. A cautionary tale, indeed.

In early 2019 the President announced that Jackson would make a return – of sorts. His title would be Assistant to the President and Chief Medical Advisor. In that position, Jackson would no longer provide medical care at the White House but instead would provide 'technical policy advice' on public health issues within the administration, according to an administration official. Meanwhile the Department of Defense was continuing its ethical investigation into Mr Jackson's treatment of colleagues and whether he dispensed medicines improperly.

In February 2019 a new doctor conducted the President's annual physical. The only change from the previous year: Donald Trump had put on four pounds in weight and was therefore technically obese. No news conference was held. Just a one-page summary released, as quietly as possible.

# CHAPTER 7

# The Office of the Vice-President

Let's make a distinction at the outset of this chapter between the office of the vice-president, and the vice-president's office. The vice-president's office is situated on the same floor of the West Wing as the president's. While the Oval Office is on the south-east corner of the building, the VP's office is on the west side. He also has a suite of grand offices next door at the Eisenhower Executive Office Building, entered via room 274 (just in case you ever find yourself wandering the corridors there), which houses his handpicked team of policy advisors, press officers and legislative assistants.

The office of the vice-president is harder – and more interesting – to define. John Adams, America's first ever vice-president (to George Washington), bemoaned the post as 'the most insignificant office that ever the invention of man contrived'. John Nance Garner is probably not someone you have heard of, unless you are a student of these things. This Democratic Party politician from Texas was elected to the US House of Representatives in 1902 and was there for thirty years. After this long stint in the House he challenged for the Democratic Party nomination for president, but was beaten by Franklin Delano Roosevelt. He would become FDR's vice-president – and he summed up the augustness and majesty of this lofty position that he held by saying the office was 'not worth a barrel of warm spit'. Actually he said it was not worth a pitcher of warm piss, but that was not something you could say in polite society, so the quote got sanitised. Spit apparently more respectful than urine.

Or let's put it in the context of a television programme and a film. Is the office of the vice-president 'Veep' – or is it 'Vice'? And if you're not familiar with either, *Veep* is the satire created by Armando Iannucci, in which the actress Julia Louis-Dreyfus is Vice-President of the United States, Selina Meyer, and desperate to make her mark and an impact. Except she finds the job one long exercise in frustration, humiliation and impotence – as she is routinely overruled, demeaned and marginalised by a White House that sees her for the most part as an irrelevance, except for the occasions when she can be deployed to clear up the most unpleasant messes where there is no glory to be had. In *Vice*, Christian Bale turns in a phenomenal performance as the utterly non-fictional Dick Cheney, the Vice-President to George W. Bush from 2001 to 2009. This portrayal depicts a vice-president as an all-powerful puppet master, in charge of policy, in charge of strategy, in charge of the president.

But are those the two poles on which you assess a vice-president? Even if the reality is *Veep* and not *Vice*, the thing that keeps you going, the reason you get up each morning in the delightful mansion housed inside the Naval Observatory on Massachusetts Avenue, next door to the British Embassy, is that that same morning, the president might not. You are, in that famous phrase, whose provenance is contested, a heartbeat away from the presidency.

According to *Safire's Political Dictionary*, the aphorism 'heartbeat away from the presidency' dates from 1952, when the Democratic nominee, Adlai Stevenson, attacked the Republican VP candidate, a 39-year-old by the name of Richard Nixon, 'who asks you to place him a heartbeat from the presidency'. Fifty years earlier, William McKinley's campaign manager, Mark Hanna, alarmed by the thought of 41-year-old Teddy Roosevelt as nominee for vice-president, is reported to have warned 'that there is only one life between the Vice-President and the Chief Magistracy of the nation'.

And you can be sure, when Donald Trump went knocking on the door of a relatively little-known governor from Indiana to be his running mate, that would have been one of the thoughts that flashed across Mike Pence's mind. At 13 years younger than the man he would be deputy to, it would have been unnatural if he hadn't thought, 'One day it could be me.' And Pence, having lived a life less heavily populated by Big Macs, fries and Diet Coke, would have had more reason than most to think of heartbeats.

Without being too morbid about this, the odds that you'd get at the bookies aren't that bad on the VP succeeding the president – and that is not a comment on the state of Donald Trump's health, or his genes or life expectancy. It is an actuarial point. It is more about being an underwriter than an undertaker. Of the 45 men who have held the post of president of the United States, eight have come to the job as a result of the death of the incumbent: John Tyler,

Millard Fillmore, Andrew Johnson, Chester Arthur, Theodore Roosevelt, Calvin Coolidge, Harry Truman and Lyndon B. Johnson, seeing as you ask. The one other vice-president to make the transition was, of course, Gerald Ford, who stepped up when Richard Nixon was forced to step down.

They are the 'accidental presidents'. A book by a former White House staffer Jared Cohen called *Accidental Presidents: Eight Men Who Changed America* charts the relative success of these men. The book finds that most performed well when given the highest responsibility. One or two were dismal failures. But it is the system of choosing the vice-president that is so bizarre. It is seldom that a running mate is selected on the one basis that truly matters – how would they acquit themselves if faced with the daunting prospect of running the country? Were they temperamentally suited, did they have the policy knowledge, would they carry on from where the president left off? If you look at some of the people who've been asked to be 'on the ticket' it is almost comical to think that they were that one heartbeat away. Sarah Palin, who was John McCain's extraordinary choice of running mate in his unsuccessful fight against Barack Obama in 2008, was immensely entertaining – but a future president? The governor of Alaska was so gaffe prone that the mere mention of her name became a laugh line for American comedians.

Mike Pence is not in the least gaffe prone. Where she was bright, exuberant and colourful, he is drab and slightly grey. And that is exactly what Donald Trump wanted and needed. Remember that when Trump won the Republican nomination it was as much a surprise to Donald Trump as it was to everyone else. He had done on it on gut, determination and by breaking every rule in the conventional campaign book. He had not spent a whole lot of time thinking about who his running mate should be; he hated the idea of having a transition team who would plan his first days in the White House if he won it. Mike Pence was a blurry, indistinct microdot on the edge of a radar screen when the Indiana primary came around in that long and seemingly endless road towards the nomination. He was a Republican governor, of a small Midwest state who seemed to be looking for a horse to back. The two had never met.

Pence had gained a certain prominence – or perhaps that should be notoriety – when as Governor he signed into state law something called the Religious Freedom Restoration Act. It is so innocuous sounding – which right-thinking person would, after all, object to religious freedom? But the legislation was seen by opponents as a new front in the 'culture wars' that have divided America for half a century. The battle between liberal and conservative America; the fight over abortion, homosexuality, the permissive society, racial discrimination, guns etc etc. The religious freedom law would allow businesses to refuse service to the LGBTQ community if the owners felt their religious convictions were being compromised by doing so. So if you were a baker in Indiana and someone came into your shop to order a wedding cake for their gay marriage, under this law it seemed you would have the legal right to refuse. The first actual business to announce that it would be putting this into practice was a family-owned business called Memories Pizza. It put out a statement that while it would continue to serve gay people in its restaurants, it wouldn't cater a gay wedding, as the family thought same-sex marriages to be wrong. When the legislation was passed and the Indiana Governor was asked in an interview on network television whether businesses would now be allowed to discriminate against gay people, Mike Pence repeatedly sidestepped the question, telling the interviewer that he was missing the point – though quite what the point was remained elusive.

The law brought condemnation from corporate America, with Apple and the pharmaceuticals giant Eli Lilly and Walmart leading the way. Mike Pence would later complain that the law was being misunderstood; that it was all a matter of sloppy reporting and wilful misrepresentation – it was a taste of what was to come with the President's regular barrages against fake news and the press being the enemy of the people.

Pence will tell anyone who will listen that he sees himself as a Christian first, a conservative second and a Republican third. This whole episode, however, had raised his national profile, as a solid voice of the evangelical right. It also meant he was the sort of big name endorsement that Republican hopefuls sought. Pence contacted Chris Christie, then the Governor of New Jersey and close confidant of Donald Trump, to see if a meeting could be organised ahead of the Indiana primary. Trump thought the meeting was well worth taking, so he flew with Christie on the Trump plane to Indianapolis. The first meeting was businesslike – the New York showmen discuss the state of the nation and all that was wrong with it with the earnest Governor. Trump was ready to leave and muttered something about there being lots of things that needed to be done back at home. According to Christie, Pence then says to Trump, 'Before you go do you think we could just join hands and say a prayer?' This startles Trump – this is not his MO in Trump Tower meetings or aboard the Trump plane, even in times of serious turbulence. After they left, Trump wanted to know whether Pence always did this. Christie told him he did. Apparently, Trump answered with one word: 'Interesting.'

But the great New York 'art of the deal' maestro had not done enough to get the deal over the line – Pence backed Ted Cruz instead for the Republican nomination – a decision that brought a furious complaint from Trump to Christie: 'Are you kidding me? You take me out to see this guy and then the guy screws me? He stabs me in the back by endorsing Cruz?'

It looked as though that would be enough to ensure that Pence would forever be cast into outer darkness; Trump being a man who has shown that he nurses his grievances attentively. Christie certainly thought so. Which was good news – because when Trump did eventually secure the Republican nomination, the New Jersey Governor felt that the nominee had as good as been promised to him; and that he was going to be the other name on the ticket.

In Christie's version of events Trump had asked Christie; and Christie had said yes. But it would have been a foolish move, given the way politics is conducted in the US. What would have been the net gain to have had the New Jersey Governor as your wing man? Remember that the question Trump needed to ask himself was not whether Christie could one day step up to the plate and take over the presidency. That was the last thing on Trump's mind. It was whether his running mate would bring him extra votes. In that respect Trump played it like every other conventional politician. The VP is there to help you win, not to help you govern.

In Chris Christie you had someone cut from the same cloth as Donald Trump – albeit rather more cloth. They were from neighbouring East Coast states; they were both loud and outgoing; they were pugilists who enjoyed nothing more than a good scrap. They were both better at fighting than praying. But Christie believed that because of Trump's antipathy towards convention and the two of them being personally close, that would be enough to ensure his eventual selection.

In the end there was a very Trumpian beauty parade – although minus the swimsuit round, mercifully. Each potential running mate was brought out before the cameras to spend a day campaigning with Donald Trump. Trump wanted to test out the 'personal chemistry'; to figure out if they could get along. It was eventually whittled down to three names – Chris Christie, Mike Pence and the former Speaker of the House of Representatives, Newt Gingrich.

Christie, however, was being blocked by the powerful combination of Jared Kushner and Ivanka. Because there was bad blood, really bad blood, between Jared Kushner and Chris Christie, dating back many years. You see, over a decade earlier, Christie had been responsible for putting Jared's father, Charles Kushner, away in prison. Just so you don't think that all dramatic plot twists are monopolised by the Trump family, this too is quite something. Indeed, it probably eclipses any Trump drama.

Like the Trumps, the Kushners were also billionaire property people in New York. Charles Kushner, a huge Democratic Party donor, ran the business and had fallen out (in the way of family businesses) with his sister Esther and her husband Bill Schulder. So far so normal. They felt they were being pushed out, and were suing Charles. But Mr Kushner thought they were ungrateful parasites. He would deal with this in his own way, and teach them a lesson they would never forget. They would know never again to tangle with Charles Kushner. Kushner knew that Bill had a bit of a weakness for women. So, via a private detective, Kushner employs the services of a high-class blonde-haired prostitute from New York's Upper East Side called Susanna. He had set up his own brother-in-law with a hooker as a way of scaring off his sister from interfering in the business.

The call girl's job was to entrap Bill at a motel in Somerville, New Jersey. She goes to a diner where he is a regular, says her car has broken down and needs help. He gallantly offers to help, and she wants to express her 'appreciation'. A miniature camera is placed in an alarm clock in her room at the Red Bull Motel (cue easy jokes). Bill succumbs to Susanna's undoubted charms, and hey presto, a highly compromising XXX videotape is born. On the day that Bill and Esther's son is due to get engaged, a brown manila envelope plops onto their doorstep, with some action photos from the video. There's no message, but Charles Kushner's sister is convinced it has all the vindictive hallmarks of her brother. It is the spring of 2004 when she decides to put this in the hands of her lawyer. He contacts a federal prosecutor by the name of Chris Christie, who takes the case. The FBI get involved and eventually the trail leads straight back to Charles Kushner. After much haggling over plea deals, in 2005 Charles Kushner pleads guilty to a wide array of charges and is sentenced to two years in prison. Something that Jared would never forget Chris Christie's role in – or, it seems, forgive.

With Christie having been given the 'black spot' by the Ivanka and Jared axis, and Gingrich – for all the talk –

never really a contender, the path was clear for Mike Pence. When Christie was eventually told by Trump that he was no longer being considered, Trump lauded Pence by saying he was straight out of central casting. He would be the 'balance' on the ticket. If there were Republicans out there who thought that Donald Trump was just some New York liberal, mouthing conservative platitudes on abortion and guns just to get himself the nomination, that was never an accusation that would be levelled at Mike Pence. He is the real deal, Bible Belt Christian – and was a smart, strategic addition to the Trump campaign. Another attraction was that he was never going to compete with Trump for the limelight, as Christie might have done. He would be happy to be in the shadows. And there was something else too. With his grey hair went a reassuringly grey image, another good counterpoint to the erratic and unpredictable man at the top of the ticket.

They are not soul-mates; it's not the kind of buddy-buddy 'bromance' that Barack Obama and Joe Biden sometimes gave an impression of. Pence is not a man with whom Trump would choose to spend his down time. For one thing, he is not a golfer – and nearly all Donald Trump's leisure time is spent on one or other of the golf courses he owns. To think he berated Obama for the amount of time he spent going from tee to green. If there's a weekend that goes by without the President taking off to play golf, it's only because the weather is too bad for him to go out. Anyway, that is an aside. Trump and Pence is a perfectly workable businesslike relationship, and that hasn't always been the case.

For unlikely characters brought together out of necessity, the decision by John F. Kennedy to ask Lyndon B. Johnson to be his running mate in 1960 after Kennedy had won the nomination is a remarkable story. The privileged northern, liberal, highly educated circle around the young JFK looked at LBJ (quite important, it seems, in US politics to have three initials that just string together) with a mixture of contempt and fear. Lyndon Johnson had been the main challenger to Kennedy for the Democratic nomination. As he travelled around, LBJ would refer to JFK as 'Johnny' or 'the boy' – terms deliberately designed to belittle the junior senator from Massachusetts. The circle around the senator from Texas – who was also the majority leader, a position that confers immense power – were even more disparaging about the young Catholic senator from Massachusetts, born to that storied and wealthy family. Kennedy was a 'silver spoon' liberal who had had it easy. He didn't know what life was about. LBJ's people also spread stories about Kennedy's health, saying he suffered from Addison's disease. The Kennedy camp fiercely denied what was then seen as a smear against their man. A Kennedy physician was wheeled out. She insisted that the candidate's adrenal gland was functioning normally. History would show that the fake news was not the allegation, but the Kennedy camp's response to it. He did have Addison's; and he was taking large doses of cortisone.

The Kennedy cabal could barely disguise their contempt for the Democratic Party leaders from the South. They were a different party, a different breed. Remember this is 1960; the Civil Rights Act had not been passed. In 1956, ninety-nine Democrats in Congress signed the 'Southern manifesto' – a policy document that expressed unswerving support for segregation– and opposition to the Supreme Court ruling in Brown vs Board of Education, the landmark case that ended segregation of black and white children in schools. Today the Democratic Party may be known for its progressive policies; back then in the South – where it still held political sway – it was anything but. It was redneck and socially conservative, working class, blue collar and less well educated. A very different party from the smart, young, preppy, cosmopolitan, polo neck jumper wearing brigade around Kennedy. They regarded those keeping company with Lyndon Johnson as little more than Neanderthals, their white knuckles scraping along the segregated streets of Georgia, Texas, Alabama, Mississippi and Tennessee. This went way beyond the normal antipathy of rival candidates jostling for power. This was deep-seated and visceral. The two sides really detested each other. And Robert Kennedy's loathing for LBJ knew no bounds.

When Kennedy had sewn up the party's nomination at the Democratic Convention in Los Angeles in July 1960, both men had suites at the Biltmore Hotel where the gathering was taking place. JFK's people were wary about their man making any offer to LBJ, and LBJ's people wanted nothing to do with 'boy' Kennedy. But when the victorious Kennedy went via a back staircase from his ninth-floor rooms to LBJ's suite – away from the prying eyes of the media – he went with an offer that had been framed in a way that he felt certain LBJ would not entertain, and flatly reject. A *pro forma* offer to the older, far more experienced senator to be Kennedy's running mate. LBJ said yes without hesitation – which would later cause a total meltdown in both men's circles. But there was logic to it, if little warmth.

Kennedy had to deal with the backlash of those closest to him about this unlikely development, and try to convince them of the wisdom of the move. He told his aides, 'I'm 43 years old, and I'm the healthiest candidate for President in the United States. You've travelled with me enough to know that I'm not going to die in office. So the vice-presidency doesn't mean anything.' An argument that would turn out to be horribly and poignantly inaccurate.

His other argument was far more compelling. The whole focus of the Kennedy campaign team had been to get enough delegate votes to win the nomination at the Democratic convention. But if you are to be more than a footnote in history, as someone who ran and lost, then you need very quickly to move towards working out how you are going to win enough electoral college votes to win the main prize – the presidency. Having LBJ on the ticket would help guarantee Texas's 24 electoral college votes, and should ensure that Kennedy would pick up other Southern states, that might otherwise have shunned a Roman Catholic liberal from Boston. In the 1960 election, Kennedy narrowly saw off his Republican rival, Richard Nixon, and shaded the popular vote.

It's hard to find exceptions to the rule that the running mate is primarily there to reach parts of the electorate that the principal on the ticket is unable to. Perhaps the only exception to that in modern times was the 1992 election when Bill Clinton chose Al Gore as his running mate. Another youthful, dynamic and good-looking figure, Gore seemed more of a mirror to Clinton than a counterbalance; this was about a Democratic Party that had been out of power for 12 years wanting to project an image of youth and vitality – at both ends of the ticket.

But if you go back to the founding of the United States, the President did not get to choose his deputy. The job went to the runner-up in the electoral college. After George Washington stood down as America's first president, in the 1796 election John Adams was running to succeed him for the Federalists; Thomas Jefferson, Washington's former Secretary of State, was the favoured candidate of the Congressional Republicans. Adams won the election and became America's second president; Jefferson, from a rival party, became vice-president by dint of being runner-up. Just imagine that in today's context. President Trump and Vice-President Hillary Clinton. Okay, agreed, unimaginable.

The fact is, the position of the vice-president was an afterthought. No consideration had been given to the possibility – as happened with Adams and Jefferson – that you might end up with two men, yoked together, who had sharply differing views on the world. It was an issue that would only be addressed by the 12th Amendment. There were only two constitutional functions ascribed to the number two. They would succeed the president in the event of death; and they would preside over the Senate – the vice-president having a casting vote in the event of a tied vote. As if to underscore how little the VP had to do with the executive branch of government, his salary was paid for by the legislature.

But gradually presidents increasingly wanted a vice-president who would be a political aide. Andrew Jackson, who became president in 1832, chose his chief political strategist Martin Van Buren as his deputy, and relied heavily on his counsel. During the American Civil War, Abraham Lincoln chose to drop Hannibal Hamlin, his first-term vice-president, who came from Maine, in favour of Andrew Johnson. Lincoln feared that without support from the South he would not be able to see the war through to victory and save the Union. Johnson, who at the time was the military governor in Tennessee, opposed secession, but he had a much more sympathetic attitude to the southern states than many of Lincoln's supporters. They went on to win the election together, but soon afterwards Lincoln was assassinated, while at Ford's Theatre in Washington. Johnson succeeded him and promptly went about reconstruction in a way that many believe Lincoln would have never supported. President Johnson would go on to carve his own little niche in the history books: he became the first president to be impeached for high crimes and misdemeanours.

For the first half of the twentieth century the ceremonial role of the vice-president and position as president of the Senate was to the fore. Incredibly, Harry Truman who was Vice-President to Franklin Roosevelt during the Second World War, was unaware of much of the wartime planning. So isolated was he, in fact, that he knew nothing about the Manhattan Project, the research programme that would lead to the development of the first atomic bomb. He would only learn of it when he was 12 days into his own presidency following FDR's death in April 1945 – and he would order its use in Japan a few months later to bring the war to an end. Indeed, he knew so little of what was going on that he described the day after Roosevelt's death in the following terms: 'I felt like the moon, the stars and all the planets had fallen on me.'

After Truman took over the presidency from FDR – having been so ill prepared for the role – he sought to change the functions and the responsibilities of the vice-president. He brought his number two, Alben Barkley, much more into the centre of decision making. The next step change in the vice-president's role came at the end of the 1950s when Richard Nixon was VP to Dwight Eisenhower. Nixon had a more formalised set of duties – diplomatic trips – and almost acted as the envoy of the president, chairing executive commissions and being a lobbyist for the administration. He also moved into the building next door to the White House – then known as the Executive Office Building. And that was more than a mere question of geography. Remember that a whole school of academic thought grew up in Soviet times in which who of the party *nomenklatura* was sitting next to whom at the Red Square parade would be carefully studied for indications of who was on the rise and who was on the wane: Kremlinology. And so it is in Washington, with WhiteHouseology. The closer you are physically, the more face time you have with the president, the more you are brought into decision making, the more powerful you are.

And so it would develop when John F. Kennedy took over from Eisenhower. Despite the unpromising start to their relationship, the irascible, insecure and egotistical Lyndon B. Johnson formed an important and productive relationship with his charismatic and youthful boss. Kennedy valued his counsel on questions of legislation, public opinion and political strategy. He also made sure that LBJ was included in all major meetings taking place at the White House. Robert Caro, in his towering series of biographies on LBJ, quotes Jack Kennedy telling a political aide and appointee how important it was to keep the vice-president sweet: 'He thinks you're nothing but a clerk. Just keep that right in your mind. You have never been elected to anything by anybody, and you are dealing with a very insecure, sensitive man with a huge ego. I want you literally to kiss his fanny from one end of Washington to the other.' JFK would tell his chief of protocol to make it her priority to keep an eye on LBJ and Mrs Johnson: 'I want you to watch over them ... and see they're not ignored. Because I'm going to forget. My staff is going to forget. We're all going to forget. We've got too much to do around here ... but I want you to remember.' Theodore H. White, the great contemporary chronicler of US elections, would write in 1964, 'The president made of Johnson as much as any President can make of his Vice President, a working participant in national affairs.'

Of course, this relationship worked because John F Kennedy chose to make it work: he invested the time and effort into managing LBJ – and thus drawing the best out of him. He became an invaluable asset to JFK, and contemporaries noted how remarkably close the two became, given where the relationship had started. But this, in a sense, depended on Kennedy choosing to give LBJ the political space to exert his muscle. There was nothing pre-determined (aside from LBJ's force of personality) that would *require* the President to cede power to his number two. It was a choice.

That next important change would come with the election of Jimmy Carter in 1976, and the appointment of his Vice-President, Walter Mondale. The two men had a shared vision of, in effect, how to share the presidency; how to allocate roles to each other, and how to integrate the two jobs. And again, don't ignore physicality. For the first time the vice-president was brought into the White House itself. Mondale would have his own office in the West Wing, but a few steps away from the president. It would mark a serious 'upgrading' of the power of the office – and as in any organisational structure where the greatest enemy is stasis

and resistance to change, this required institutional imagination, engineering, imagination – and determination to push it
through. Mondale had talents and experiences that comple-
mented those of the Georgia peanut farmer, Jimmy Carter.
He would be senior counsel and chief trouble-shooter. There
is a fascinating memorandum written by Mondale to Carter
on 9 December 1976 – just weeks before the inauguration –
setting out how he saw the role of the vice-president in the
Carter administration.

To achieve the role as a general advisor to the president
he would need to receive frequent and comprehensive briefings from the CIA and other intelligence agencies. He would
receive advance warning of major issues to be discussed at
the National Security Council. He would travel the world
and deal with major global issues affecting the administration. And if he asked for information/research help, 'I would
hope that I could expect the same or nearly the same level
of responsiveness from key administration officials in seeking
information that you would receive.' In other words when the
VP asks for something, you'd better sit up and take notice.
Not only that, but the staff appointed by the vice-president
would also be included in White House meetings.

It is only in the final paragraph of the 11-page memo that
Mondale talks about the role for which the VP position is
famed: 'The role outlined above would, in my judgement,
clearly fulfil the most important constitutional obligation of
the office – that is, being prepared to take over the presidency
should that be required.' The transformation of the role
of VP was nearly complete. It was a model that would be
accepted and adopted by all presidential and vice-presidential
successors, whether Democrat or Republican.

If we are being unkind, the one vice-president who stands out a bit from the line of successors to Walter Mondale is Dan Quayle, who was Vice-President under George H.W. Bush. He was one of those vice-presidents who failed to impress. In fact Quayle turned out to be a bit of a turkey. Famously during the 1988 campaign when he was George H.W. Bush's running mate he went to a school where there was a Spelling Bee competition being run. Spelling Bee commands enormous attention in the US, as children compete against each other in what leads to a grand televised final for who has the best spelling. Mind-bogglingly clever children end up spelling out words that you've never heard of with meanings you don't know. Dan Quayle's intervention was not in a grand final, but at a school he was visiting in New Jersey during the campaign. The 12-year-old child had been asked to spell 'potato'. He went up the blackboard, wrote it out, and stood back to admire his work. It was then that Quayle intervened and told the boy that it was incorrect, and added an 'e' so that it was spelled 'potatoe'. His place on the ticket had been designed to bring some youth and good looks to the long-in-the-tooth Bush senior's campaign. It brought unintended comedy as well.

It was his appearance in the vice-presidential TV debate that brought one of the great put-downs of all time. Quayle, then aged 41, repeatedly tried to compare himself in his stump speeches to John F. Kennedy for his vitality and vigour. In the debate against the Democrat vice-presidential hopeful, Lloyd Bentsen, Quayle when questioned about his comparative inexperience insisted he had more congressional experience than JFK. His older and wilier Democrat opponent was lying in wait, ready to pounce. Lloyd Bentsen moved in, slowly, for the kill. 'Senator,' he said to Quayle. 'I served with Jack Kennedy. I knew Jack Kennedy. Jack Kennedy was a friend of mine. *(Pause)* Senator, you're no Jack Kennedy *(crowd erupts into shouts and applause).*'

There was also a whole series of gaffes and malapropisms from Quayle that brought a vice-presidential running mate rare attention. For example, 'One word sums up probably the responsibility of any vice-president, and that one word is "to be prepared".' Or: 'Republicans understand the importance of bondage between a mother and child.' And then there's this: 'The Holocaust was an obscene period in our nation's history. I mean in this century's history. But we all lived in this century. I didn't live in this century.' The list goes on and on, and it just becomes an exercise in cruelty to keeping adding to them. What? You'd like a couple more? Oh, alright then, but against my better judgement. Looking ahead he once said: 'I believe we are on an irreversible trend towards more freedom and democracy – but that could change.' And again, with rare prescience: 'We are ready for any unforeseen event that may or may not occur.' He spent four years as vice-president. For the past twenty years he has been working at a private equity firm, his head rarely appearing above the parapet.

The vice-presidency that aroused the most controversy was that of Dick Cheney, the number two to George W. Bush. Or was it the other way round? Was Bush the subordinate to Cheney? George W. Bush was the oldest son of George H.W. Bush – and in his youth a rather wayward son. He was the classic privileged child who had slightly gone off the rails. He drank a lot. In 1976 he was prosecuted for drink/driving. During his presidential bid he would recount that after waking up with a hangover following his fortieth birthday celebrations, he resolved never to drink again. He became Governor of Texas in 1995. That would be his launchpad for the presidency. But his surname was the most impressive thing about his résumé. It would unlock untold millions, the essential lubricant for all presidential campaigns

The same was not true of Dick Cheney. He was steeped and marinated in government, politics and the Republican Party. Only a few years older than Bush, he seemed to belong to a different generation. He had worked in a junior capacity for Richard Nixon – his boss at the time was Donald Rumsfeld, who would go on to be Defense Secretary in the Bush administration. He had been chief of staff to President Gerald Ford. He'd served in Congress for a decade, had become the Chair of the House Republican Conference, the House Minority Whip, then Defense Secretary to W's father. You name it, he'd done it. He knew how Washington worked, how Capitol Hill functioned, what kept the wheels of the White House turning. He knew where the bodies were buried, and who had buried them – and who might need to be buried if they stepped out of line. He was a bad enemy to have.

He matched that with great organisational skill, and intricate knowledge of the mechanisms of government. Building on the changes that Walter Mondale had brought, in his suite of offices in the Eisenhower Executive Office Building he constructed, in effect, a shadow White House. Whatever President Bush had staff for; he would have a team doing the same. There would be no issue on which he would be blindsided. And then there was the presence of the man himself – Cheney was an all-seeing, all-knowing force within the White House.

But his power wasn't confined to the Executive branch of government. He made sure his tentacles reached everywhere. In addition to the West Wing, he maintained his expansive suite next door in the Eisenhower Building; and the Speaker of the House of Representatives made sure Cheney had offices near the House floor, while maintaining two offices in the Senate. In all aspects of policy making, Cheney's reach was long. It was a similar story when it came to appointments at the highest level of the administration.

The presidency of George W. Bush was defined by one event – 9/11. It was the most traumatic event for America since Pearl Harbor, which brought the US into the Second World War, and truly shook the kaleidoscope. It was also a catalyst for a 'war on terror' whose repercussions are still felt to this day. At the centre of all decision making was Dick Cheney: the talk of an 'axis of evil', the war in Afghanistan and, more controversially, the 2003 invasion of Iraq, with 'shock and awe'. Cheney repeatedly sought to justify the latter on the grounds that the Al Qaeda bombers of 9/11 had links with the regime in Baghdad. In 2004 the 9/11 Commission concluded there were no such links. He would continue for a decade afterwards to repeat the same discredited claims. Where Cheney was vindicated was in his prediction that on the battlefield victory would be swift and overwhelming; what he and the rest of the Administration never anticipated was the quagmire into which the United States would become sunk. One policy blunder would follow another: the naïve de-Ba'athification of the Iraqi army, which left thousands of unemployed, highly trained soldiers to wage a war against the occupying forces; the under-estimation of the civil war that would erupt between Shias, Sunnis and Kurds; the total lack of thought that would go into nation building. It was textbook how to win the war, and lose the peace.

In the wake of the war we started to learn a new language. Questions would be asked about 'enhanced interrogation' techniques – aka torture. Then there was 'extraordinary rendition' – the policy of shifting prisoners from country to country as a means of circumventing those places where the laws on detention and torture might be less forgiving. Cheney was hugely influential in what policies should be followed on the detention of suspected terrorists and what legal limits should apply to their questioning. A couple of years after leaving office, Cheney was still defending the use of waterboarding and the torture of terrorist suspects. Cheney would tell ABC News, 'I was and remain a strong proponent of our enhanced interrogation programme.'

There was another troubling aspect at this time. Beginning in 2003 – the year of the invasion – Cheney's staff made an important decision. They stopped filing required reports with the National Archives and Records Administration, the office which protects classified information. Cheney's staff also refused to allow inspection of their record keeping. Some news outlets started talking about a new, fourth branch of government, that had declared itself above the law of the land, and beyond the reach of democratic accountability.

What I have concentrated upon here is the lead-up to and aftermath of the Iraq war – but Cheney's influence extended way beyond foreign policy. On budget and tax policy – and critically environmental policy – he played a leading role, invariably tilting US policy in favour of business over environmental protection. In July 2008 a former official from the federal Environment Protection Agency stated publicly that

Cheney's office had pushed for significant deletions from a document detailing the effects of global warming, 'fearing the presentation by a leading health official might make it harder to avoid regulating greenhouse gases'. Shortly before leaving office, Cheney's approval ratings stood at a miserable 13 per cent.

Mike Pence is no Dick Cheney. Pence would not presume to override the President. The overall impression you get with Pence is that he knows his place. One memorable meeting after the midterm elections in November 2018 saw Donald Trump playing host in the Oval Office to the new Democratic Party Speaker of the House, Nancy Pelosi and the Senate minority leader, Chuck Schumer. It was a testy meeting – throughout which Pence never said a word. More than that, it was mesmerising. It almost seemed that he was playing statues. There was not a twitch of a facial muscle, barely a flicker of his eyes. If he had been painted head to toe in silver and was standing on a soapbox in some Italian piazza, you would have definitely chucked a couple of euros into his tin for the street art performance. Pence looked as though he had spent a few days at a taxidermist beforehand.

In public pronouncements he will never get ahead of his boss. He will never seek limelight for himself at the expense of his master – that would be a criminally stupid thing to do. But he will seek to influence President Trump's agenda and priorities behind the scenes. He is also the smoother of ruffled feathers – a job that has rarely been more important than under this crockery-breaking president. He is like the trained FBI negotiator whose job is to talk suicidal staffers and senior administration officials off parapets and tall buildings when they think they can take no more of the President's antics. After Donald Trump had repeatedly undermined the Director of National Intelligence, Dan Coats, it fell to Pence to persuade him not to jump. It would be a pacifying role he would play again and again.

As well as pushing social conservatism – particularly when it comes to abortion – Pence has behind the scenes been a vocal support for the tough line that the administration has taken on Venezuela and Cuba. Fighting communism in America's backyard has been a core conservative issue for decades. He's notably taken a tough line with China and Russia – even if he can appear as a slightly obsequious toady. Meanwhile, for all the public professions of loyalty, you get the impression that there is a certain mistrust that pertains. Stories which appeared at critical times suggesting that Pence was biding his time, and was ready to step up if Trump stumbled, will have caused a certain amount of twitching in the White House. And when Donald Trump was asked whether he would back a Pence tilt at the presidency once he had left office, he very notably refused to give his number two that endorsement.

Which is tough on Pence. In public he has never done anything that would allow anyone to think there was even so much as a cigarette paper's width between him and the President. My favourite demonstration of this was in June 2019, when tensions with Iran were at a dangerous, flashing red on the dashboard high. American sanctions were trying to cripple the Iranian economy. The Iranians according to the US had attacked a number of tankers in the Strait of Hormuz. That was denied by Tehran – but when a $130 million dollar American drone was shot down over these contested waters by a surface-to-air missile, Iran was happy to claim responsibility. The President declared in the Oval Office that Iran had made a very big mistake. 'Will America retaliate?' reporters screamed. 'You'll see, you'll see,' said the President. And went on: 'This country will not stand for it, that I can tell you.' The omens were not good. Some kind of US response seemed inevitable.

After that the lights burned late into the night as national security officials met to consider the US response. It was agreed there would be a limited but firm, no-nonsense response. And we waited. And waited. But nothing happened. That morning the *New York Times* reported that the President had got cold feet. He'd aborted. The Twitter tiger had become a policy pussy. Something that was later confirmed by the President himself, when he tweeted: 'On Monday they shot down an unarmed drone flying in international waters. We were cocked and loaded to retaliate last night on three different sights when I asked, how many will die. 150 people, sir, was the answer from a General. 10 minutes before the strike I stopped it. Not proportionate to shooting down an unmanned drone.'

This left the President open to a certain amount of criticism from all sides: Republican hawks thought he had allowed Iran to get away with an act of aggression where there were no consequences. This was like Obama over Syria, when a red line was crossed and no action was taken. Trump had done a grand old Duke of York. Democrats saw this as a crisis of the President's own making: he'd pulled the US out of the Iran nuclear deal without a plan B. The Europeans who were still part of the deal were even more scathing. One senior official said to me that the episode showed how comprehensively this administration's Iran policy was failing.

And where did Mike Pence stand on this? His position was clarified by a spokesman: 'Vice-President Mike Pence supported those plans to strike Iran, but also agreed with the President's decision to abort them.' Two men creating only one shadow.

# CHAPTER 8

# Air Force One

Air Force One is not a building or a room, I freely acknowledge – but if there is one thing that projects unmistakable American power around the world it is the pale blue 747 jumbo jet with 'United States of America' written along the fuselage. I remember being in Cuba ahead of Barack Obama's historic first visit to the Caribbean island, and watching Air Force One coming in low over the Havana slums before landing. It is a plane that turns heads. It is an aircraft which says the world's pre-eminent superpower is on its way. On Donald Trump's first overseas visit after he became president we travelled to Saudi Arabia, Israel, Rome and Brussels before ending up in Sicily for the G7 summit. I had to return to London and managed to hitch a ride on Theresa May's plane. As we taxied out to the runway, all the journalists aboard and a lot of the officials were taking photos of Air Force One, which was parked nearby on the tarmac.

The British equivalent of Air Force One, conversely, projects frugality. The RAF Voyager is used as a tanker for mid-air refuelling when it is not ferrying British dignitaries around the world. When I flew back from Sicily the plane had just returned from the skies above Syria, where it had been instrumental in refuelling fighter aircraft engaged in the battle against ISIS. And it looks like a military plane. It has 'Royal Air Force' written along the side, and the paintwork is a matt, gunmetal grey. Or it might be more accurate to describe it as hair-shirt grey. Because heaven forefend that the British government should have a plane at its disposal, as every other leading nation has.

For years the easiest way to whip up a tabloid fervour against the government was to report that plans were being drawn up for the purchase of a British Air Force One. And so for years there was no prime-ministerial plane. In the days when I travelled with John Major and Tony Blair, Downing Street would charter a British Airways jet. Tony Blair had advocated that the British get their own version of AF1 – a project inevitably named Blair Force One, but that was scuttled by his nemesis, Gordon Brown. The famously dour Scot took delight when he eventually succeeded Tony Blair in cancelling the 'vanity project' of his more flamboyant predecessor. When David Cameron became PM he steered the middle path – a plane, yes, but one that would double as an RAF workhorse. That didn't satisfy everyone. Anticipating a post-Brexit era in which Britain would have to project an image of dynamism around the world, Boris Johnson as foreign secretary complained about its grey drabness.

In the US there are no such qualms or hand-wringing about Air Force One. It is a muscular expression of America's place in the world. And Donald Trump loves it. No, it doesn't have the gold fittings, shag pile carpets and white leather seats of his own plane that he used during the presidential campaign, but there is nothing quite like travelling on Air Force One. In the 2018 midterm elections he used it as a prop. The plane would draw up to an aircraft hangar where thousands of Trump supporters would have been waiting for hours. And a podium would have been erected between the crowd and AF1. It is an unbeatable backdrop, even if controversial. The jumbo is US government property, not an 'accessory' of the Republican party.

And as he does with the Oval Office, Trump loves to show it off. Friends from Mar-a-Lago have been invited to look around the plane; there have even been occasions when the 13 members of what is called the 'protective press pool', which travels at the very back of the plane, have been invited to come up front to the President's quarters to see his office suite – I am yet to be on the aircraft when that has happened. Travelling with him is a distinct mixed blessing. It can give you extraordinary access to the President and his entourage. When you fly with them, you move as the President moves. You are witnessing up close who he is meeting and what he is doing. But because you are 'pool' you are not working for your own media outlet, you are there representing *all* outlets. So the 13 seats reserved for the media are divided between newspapers, news sites, radio, television and the wire services. When the BBC is on the plane we only ever get the radio seat. The US networks will always be the TV pooler. And each seat is allocated – so you will always sit in the same seat. And your job is to report for all the radio networks who aren't on the plane.

It sounds fabulously glamorous. And it can be. First the glamour – and the obvious. Who wouldn't want to travel on Air Force One? I have never seen my BBC colleagues so jealous as when I waltzed into New Broadcasting House having just flown into London from the Middle East with President Obama, with my pockets full of packets of M&Ms – the small boxes of sweets given out on the plane that bear the presidential seal on one side and the president's signature on the other. They are top swag. We also get handed printed out cards from the flightdeck telling us the route, likely flying time and weather conditions. The food on board is terrific. There are trained United States Air Force chefs, who actually cut up fresh vegetables, and the meals are served on bone china with the presidential seal. Air Force One is the exclusive province of the 89th Airlift Wing at Joint Base Andrews in Maryland – charged with safely moving the president, his deputy and senior cabinet officials around the country and around the world. Being a part of the approximately 1,100 strong unit is considered one of the most plumb assignments of the Air Force.

Also, and this may seem an odd thing to say, it is the nearest thing I have seen to travelling in an Uber. When the president arrives to board Air Force One, we are invariably at the foot of the steps filming him or recording him as he walks up to the aircraft. But the moment he is on board we are rushed along to the back of the aircraft where secret service personnel are urging us to race up the steps – and before we've even found our seats, the plane is on the move. There is no safety drill: no one checking that your seat is in the upright position, your tray table is stowed and your seat belt is securely fastened. The doors shut and away you go. And the press cabin has a bulkhead running down the centre of the plane, bisecting the rows of seats – there are no proper overhead bins, so most of your kit sits at your feet and not safely stowed. But waiting our turn to take off? Air traffic control permission to push back? Loading the last of the bags? Held in the stack? Fifteen minutes of circling? None of those things ever happen aboard Air Force One.

This is also the nightmare of travelling on Air Force One. What if the president has said something as he boards? Then, you have literally seconds to file your report to the members of the White House Correspondents' Association who are waiting anxiously for your dispatch. Fat thumbs going berserk on an iPhone trying to complete your report, invariably full of comedic typos, as the plane is climbing into the sky, knowing that the signal is about to disappear. On this ancient jumbo jet, the media don't have access to the aircraft's wi-fi. Also, if you imagine it is all flat-bed luxury, forget it. The press cabin is high-class economy.

The last time I flew with the President, it was when Donald Trump had travelled to Florida. The 'wranglers' who are there to act as sheepdogs to us – a potentially wayward flock – had guided us to the vans where we would be part of the convoy going to Mar-a-Lago. But then we see that the President has gone to greet supporters at the airport. Out we charge to hear what he is saying – boom microphones being connected as we run, headphones on, machines set to record, phones to take photos. It is chaos. We are a tangle of wires, cables and recording devices. And then we are loaded back onto the vans, wedged in tight.

The convoy moves at a fair lick, but we are sitting in our press van trying to connect recording machines to laptops. Mine sits precariously on my lap as I fiddle with connections and type in necessary instructions so that I can upload the audio, and then feed the material via the internet, which I'm trying to connect to with a mi-fi device. We are seemingly taking corners on two wheels as we have to keep pace with the police outriders and the Beast. We are also trying to write some copy that will accompany the audio of the President, to help set the scene. And obviously tweet out the pictures. It is claustrophobic and stressed. Also, I'm trying to look out of the window so we can witness whether the crowds on the roadside are cheering or booing his arrival.

I swear, by the time we get to Mar-a-Lago I am ready to hurl the beautifully presented Air Force One meal, served on the finest bone china, with the freshly cut vegetables, all over the carefully manicured lawns of the President's country club. Which would, I am thinking, be an unwelcome *faux pas*. Indeed, my face has turned the colour of the grass, and I am as clammy as a clammy thing. This is not the journalism of Hemingway, sitting with a large tumbler of whisky at a clickety clack typewriter in an exotic hotel room, cigar smoke curling upwards to be dispersed by the whirring overhead fan. And then ambling down to the night manager to ask him to wire his copy to the *Toronto Star*. This is feeding-the-machine, fast food journalism – and as someone who is a little technologically challenged and clearly of a delicate disposition it is an ordeal which I barely survive. And I vow that I am never going to do it again. But then I wouldn't get to fly on Air Force One ...

The first presidential flight took place during the Second World War when Franklin Delano Roosevelt flew to the Casablanca Conference in Morocco, aboard a commercial Boeing Clipper Flying Boat. But defence chiefs were alarmed about the security implications of the President flying commercially, so it was decided there should be a dedicated aircraft run by the US Air Force. It came into service in 1944 and was nicknamed by journalists 'the Sacred Cow'. The Douglas C-54 Skymaster made its inaugural flight taking Franklin D. Roosevelt to the Yalta Conference, that would bring together FDR, Stalin and Churchill to discuss the shape of a post-war Europe. The plane was fitted with an elevator to lift the wheelchair-bound president into the cabin. But that didn't stay in service long. It also had a range of 4,000 miles and could land at virtually any airfield. It had a conference room and a stateroom, and the picture windows were fitted with bullet-proof glass.

'Air Force One' became the call sign for the presidential aircraft after an incident in 1953 when a Lockheed Constellation, named Columbine 2, carrying President Dwight D. Eisenhower, found itself in airspace with a commercial aircraft with the same flight number. After that moment, whenever the president was on board, the call sign would be Air Force One (when the vice-president is using the plane, it is Air Force Two). John F. Kennedy's Boeing 707 was the first plane to be specifically tailored for the Commander in Chief. Designs for the aircraft were leaked, and the French designer Raymond Loewy – who'd been behind iconic brands like Coca-Cola and Lucky Strike cigarettes – told a White House aide that he thought they were amateurish and gaudy. When Jackie Kennedy heard about this she insisted that Loewy be brought in to assist with the design. And so it was that John F. Kennedy ended up sitting on the floor of the West Wing with a French designer to pore over sketches and designs. That is when the iconic baby blue and slate was chosen. The plane's markings were changed from 'US Air Force' to 'United States of America'. The presidential seal would be placed near the nose; the Stars and Stripes on the tail. But JFK's use of the aircraft would be brief.

The plane would play an unwitting part in a desperate moment of US history; America's darkest day since Pearl Harbor and a day of maximum trauma and distress. The shocking moment in Dallas when President Kennedy, travelling in an open-top car with his wife, Jackie, at his side, was killed by an assassin's bullet. At Love Field Airport that November in 1963, Air Force One had been waiting to fly them back to Washington. Now it would fulfil a function that its designers – in fact, anyone – could scarcely have imagined. It would be the setting where the new president would be sworn in.

A federal judge, Sarah T. Hughes, hastened to the plane to administer the oath of office. Members of the presidential and vice-presidential parties filled the central compartments of the plane to witness this extraordinary moment of history. At 14.38 Central Standard Time, Lyndon Baines Johnson became the 36th president of the United States. Jackie Kennedy was there to witness it too, unchanged in her bloodstained pink Chanel suit. They would then all fly back to Washington together – the now *former* first lady refusing to leave Dallas until her husband's body had been loaded in its casket onto the plane. A decade later the same plane would bear the coffin of LBJ back to his home in Texas, after his State Funeral in Washington. That day in 1963 there were pool reporters present to provide a record of what happened. And getting the coffin aboard turned out to be anything but straightforward.

One of the reporters was a man called Sid Davis whom I met a couple of years ago for a documentary I was making.

Though 89 years old when I went to see him, his memories were vivid. He still had the black-and-white photos of him in the party witnessing the swearing in. He told me how, in the midst of this extraordinary moment of national drama, there were prosaic workaday issues that had to be dealt with. US Secret Service officers had to find an axe, because the coffin was too wide to get through the narrow hatchway onto the plane. The officers were having to use brute force to hack the big, ornamental handles off the casket. Davis was due to broadcast for the Westinghouse network when he got back to Washington, and having covered Kennedy extensively on the road, he remembered how JFK would often end his campaign speeches by quoting Robert Frost, the American poet who had died earlier that year. And that terrible night Sid Davis used those lines as well to end his report: 'The woods are lovely, dark and deep. But I have promises to keep, and miles to go before I sleep.'

The aircraft has extraordinary capabilities – some of which are kept secret, some of which are well known. The upstairs of the jumbo is out of bounds to visitors. It is where all the communications people are ensuring that the plane can function as a fully mobile West Wing, able to connect the president to anyone he needs to speak to. It is public knowledge that the plane can be refuelled mid-air, and stay flying indefinitely. On 9/11 it looked as though some of those capabilities would be tested. After President George W. Bush was given word that America was under attack, the plane took off from Florida as senior advisors and national security officials argued over where was the best place for the President to be.

The plane's departure is as dramatic as anyone can remember. By the time the convoy reaches the foot of the aircraft, the plane has been ringed by heavily armed secret service officers. Even the President's most senior staff are searched before they can get aboard. Two of the plane's engines are already running.

Those who were aboard described the scene later as though out of a movie. The plane took off like a rocket, one would recount. The pilot that day, Colonel Mark Tillman, rejected the gradual easy ascent and just pointed the nose up. All the fittings on the plane were shaking as they climbed almost vertically. One of the White House stenographers would recount that she thought they might need oxygen, they were climbing so high and so fast.

Then comes word that 'Angel' itself might be a target. This was the codeword for Air Force One, known only to a few insiders. Colonel Tillman takes the aircraft to 45,000 feet – about as high as a jumbo can go. His calculation is that if any plane came anywhere near that altitude you would know immediately it had bad intent. After the attacks on the twin towers of the World Trade Center in New York, came confirmation that a plane had crashed into the Pentagon. President Bush had been growing exasperated at being unable to reach his defence secretary, Donald Rumsfeld. Now he understood why. Another thing was clear: they were not going back to Washington, and the crowded airspace over the US was shut down in an unprecedented move. With rumours swirling there could be similar attacks on the White House or the Capitol from the handful or so of planes that had not yet landed, the decision was made that the President would stay in the air.

Soon the grey and blue jumbo with the tail number SAM (Special Air Mission) 28000 is the only plane along the eastern seaboard of the United States, except for its escort of F16 fighters that had been scrambled to protect the President and the 65 or so passengers (White House staff, secret service personnel and journalists) who are on board. Despite the President insisting the plane return to Washington, the Commander in Chief is overruled by his chief of staff, the pilot and the secret service. They head instead to a USAF base in Louisiana.

Ari Fleischer, who was the President's press secretary, comes back to speak to the journalists to brief them on what is going on. One of them is a longstanding White House correspondent for ABC television, Ann Compton. She would later tell *Politico* magazine: 'Ari came back to the press cabin and said, "This is off the record, but the president is being evacuated." I said, "You can't put that off the record. That's a historic and chilling fact. That has to be on the record." It was a stunning statement, about the president trying to hold the country together but facing a mortal enemy. The president cannot be found because of his own safety. That sent chills down my spine.'

At the airbase they are on an annual drill and exercise when the real world intervenes. The base commander recalls they were in receipt of a Code Alpha – a high priority incoming aircraft. The demand was for 150,000 pounds of fuel, 40 gallons of coffee, 70 lunch boxes, and 25 pounds of bananas. The plane wouldn't identify itself. It didn't take the airmen at the base long to figure out that the Code Alpha was Air Force One.

This airbase now becomes the centre of operations for a US under attack, as George Bush is able to talk to Washington and key advisors and allies around the world. The other passengers are told they can make one call home to tell loved ones they were safe, but there were strict instructions that they could not disclose their location. A slightly absurd demand, seeing as a Louisiana television station had sent a film crew to the perimeter of the base to get the 'local angle' on the huge national story: 'US military here in Barksdale have been put on a heightened state of alert following, etc., etc.' They were doing their somewhat predictable live news reports when, stone the crows, what should descend from the sky, and into the viewfinder of the cameraman's lens but a great big jumbo jet painted blue and grey, with 'United States of America' written along the fuselage. The 'Where's the president?' question was a mystery no longer.

One of Donald Trump's first jobs when he became president was to decide on the replacements for the two identical ageing jumbos SAM 28000 and SAM 29000, which each functioned as Air Force One when he was on board. And he got immersed in the detail. Bargaining and haggling with Boeing over how much they intended to charge for the new aircraft; and just like Jackie Kennedy over half a century earlier, also taking a deep interest in the colour scheme and décor. And like Jackie he has very firm views on what he wants. Out will go the iconic robin's egg blue or baby blue – he called it a Jackie Kennedy colour – for something that would be bolder and more 'American'. He told CBS, 'It's going to be the top of the line, the top in the world … and it's going be red, white and blue, which I think is appropriate.'

Donald Trump has a highly distinctive foreign policy, and as he criss-crosses the globe on the presidential plane, he has occasionally delighted, sometimes alarmed and often bewildered friends and foes alike with his mantra of 'America First'. In the US itself even the Republican foreign policy establishment has looked on aghast. If you take a sweep of the American presidents since the Second World War, of course you see big variations in how one president will prioritise a country or a region. Often the foreign policy of one is dictated by what are perceived to be the mistakes of a predecessor.

Take the obvious example of the Middle East. The post-9/11 landscape came to define the presidency of George W. Bush and the premiership of Tony Blair. There had been terrorist training camps in Taleban-run Afghanistan used by Al Qaeda to equip their fighters to take jihad to the West. The regime of Mullah Omar needed to be swept away, and in the emotional aftermath of the September 11 attacks, there was consensus in the international community that this had to happen. Attempts were made to introduce western-style elections to the country. And so was born the idea of 'liberal interventionism'. Next stop would be Iraq and the brutal regime of Saddam Hussein and his stockpiles of weapons of mass destruction – except, of course, he didn't have any. Support for this military adventure was much more difficult to drum up. Opposition, particularly in Britain and Europe, was massive. American weaponry took no time at all to get rid of the Iraqi leader, but the total lack of thought over what would come next, and how you would manage the tensions between Shias, Sunnis and Kurds, plunged the country into the most brutal civil war. So when Barack Obama became president, you could see him very deliberately trying to press the reset button. American adventurism would stop. The country had new priorities.

These are the policy adjustments that are the norm when a new president takes office. But they had always been made within a broadly agreed framework of America's place in the world: the role of multilateral institutions, the responsibilities that went along with being the world's pre-eminent superpower, and the alliances that would serve to achieve a certain stability. The architecture that had grown from the rubble of the Second World War, and which had – largely speaking – preserved the peace and seen nations grow more prosperous, had not been questioned: NATO, the European Union and the World Trade Organisation. The mixture of overwhelming military might through NATO, and the European economic area acting as a bulwark against the destructive nationalism that had been the spark on the continent for two world wars, and the WTO acting as a policeman – albeit an imperfect one – to govern and foster trade would keep a rules-based order on track. The UN – another imperfect policeman – would seek to set rules on acceptable and unacceptable behaviour of its members. These would be the pillars on which the new world order would be built.

But two events in 2016 demonstrated how those tenets were being challenged by a surge of nationalism and dissatisfaction with the existing edifice. The Brexit vote in the UK in June of that year, as the British people voted narrowly to withdraw from the EU, and the November election in the US of Donald Trump, who made clear during his election campaign that he felt no particular affection towards any of those institutions. More than that, here was a presidential candidate advocating nativism and isolationism. America could no longer be the world's policeman; America had to deal with its own problems. The US had to defend itself from globalisation and the forces that were sending American jobs overseas. The EU was ripping America off. Similar forces were at play in elections and protest movements that were springing up across Europe: the rise of the far right in Germany, the 'gilets jaunes' in France, the populists seizing control in Italy – and authoritarian rulers across the world seizing their moment to crush dissent in their own countries while America was gazing at its navel. What is certainly true is that these multilateral institutions now find themselves threatened by the very powers that constructed them – most notably, the United States under President Trump.

The extent to which Donald Trump was merely reflecting the voice of ordinary Americans in expressing disenchantment with the liberal international order, or was actually leading the way, can be debated. His dislike of these institutions did not seem to be based on a historic assessment of their role and some kind of intellectual rejection. It seemed to me much more instinctive than that. President Trump is allergic to multilateral bodies as a whole. His business career was built on bilateral deals, with just one person or institution sitting across the table from him. It was *mano a mano*, eyeball to eyeball. And there was something else as well, that his advisors despite their best efforts could not shift him from. He would express a common critique of every multilateral institution he looked at – they were all bad for America. If America was paying more than another member it was a bad deal. And there was no dissuading him from that view, even if the facts and the 'soft diplomacy' gains that US involvement brought pointed in a completely different direction.

Though criticism of the Trump approach to foreign policy and his view on America's place in the world is quite common, it would find an unlikely voice in June 2019, albeit quite coded, from a 93-year-old woman. But a woman not to be messed with. Donald Trump had come for his three-day state visit to Britain – and had brought nearly all the family along too. Senior White House officials had been blown away by

Buckingham Palace – one advisor said to me, 'It is a useful reminder of what a young country America is.' They were also, it has to be said, in awe of the Royal Family, and touched by the warmth of their welcome. A number of the White House women who were off to the Buckingham Palace banquet were putting on long, white gloves for the first time, and were fretting about not making a mess of the etiquette and protocol. One rather touchingly asked me if I knew when they came off and whether rings had to be worn over the top of the gloves. I had to confess to not having the faintest idea.

The state visit coincided with the 75th anniversary of D-Day, a time when the cooperation between the US and the UK was at its most existentially vital. In their respective toasts the US president and the Queen paid homage to the extraordinary valour of those young men who stormed the Normandy beaches, and the bonds forged between the two nations in what would later become known as 'the special relationship'. So far, so safe. But then the Queen went further: 'As we face the new challenges of the twenty-first century, the anniversary of D-Day reminds us of all that our countries have achieved together. After the shared sacrifices of the Second World War, Britain and the United States worked with other allies to build an assembly of international institutions to ensure that the horrors of conflict would never be repeated. While the world has changed, we are forever mindful of the original purpose of these structures: nations working together to safeguard a hard-won peace.' It looked like a very carefully worded, though deliberate rebuke to Donald Trump's America First rhetoric.

As I mentioned above, I travelled with the President on his first overseas tour. It is worth going through the trip in detail – and what has happened since, as each leg of the journey was instructive for what it told us about the new American foreign policy. Having never previously been to Saudi Arabia, this was now my second visit in a year. In 2016 I had accompanied Barack Obama on a very scratchy visit to the kingdom. There was no red carpet, no member of the Saudi royal family to greet him at the airport. The President lectured his hosts about their human rights record, and they lectured him on how disastrous the Iran nuclear deal would be. There was a strong mutual disrespect which neither side did much to cover up. When he arrived, he helicoptered in to the Ritz Carlton hotel where the presidential entourage was staying. I remember going into the city by bus on a drab, unremarkable journey. So when I flew in with President Trump I noted that on his itinerary it had him being driven into the city. It was a tiny thing, but I remember being surprised.

There was calculation. At least on the part of the Saudis. Every half a mile along the route, giant gantries had been erected with huge pictures of a thoughtful looking Donald Trump and signs saying 'Saudi Arabia welcomes you' and 'Together we prevail'. Genius. The new president loved it. Never mind that candidate Donald Trump had caused huge offence in the Islamic world with his plan to ban all Muslims from entering the United States; in the country which is home to Islam's holiest site, his hosts were giving him the warmest of all welcomes.

And Donald Trump went all in with the Saudis. They would be the pivotal country to deliver his ambitions for the region. The person he had tasked with delivering peace between Israelis and Palestinians, his son-in-law, Jared Kushner (never mind that he had zero experience, and his background as an orthodox Jew and family friend of the Israeli prime minister, Benjamin Netanyahu, hardly enhanced his credentials as an honest broker) was a WhatsApp buddy with the rising star of the house of Saud, the young tyro, Mohammed bin Salman, who would soon take over the reins of power from the ailing king.

Donald Trump did not arrive in Saudi with lofty ambitions, or with some over-arching vision of the future of a post-Arab Spring Middle East. He came with practical ambitions. He had come to sell US products to the kingdom – mainly military hardware. He wanted to exert maximum pressure on Iran. And the Saudis and Israelis both agree that Iran, with its nuclear ambitions and support for groups like Hamas and Hezbollah, is the major destabilising force in the region. The Saudis would put pressure on the Palestinians to agree to peace talks; the US would withdraw from the Iran nuclear deal, even though Tehran was in compliance with the terms of the Joint Comprehensive Plan of Action that had been agreed by the previous administration; and a back channel was opened up between Israel and Saudi to coordinate on peace talks. The US bizarrely allowed itself to be drawn into an internal Gulf states dispute, siding with the Saudis as they and the UAE tried to engineer a coup in Qatar – seemingly unaware that the US had a huge military base in the country.

But, having placed all his chips on the Saudi square and the wunderkind Crown Prince, Mohammed bin Salman, that gamble suddenly became a lot more complicated for Donald Trump with the murder of a Saudi journalist who was resident in the US and working for the *Washington Post*. Jamal Khashoggi went into the Saudi consulate in Turkey in

October 2018 and never re-emerged. He would face torture and murder that would have made King Ferdinand and Queen Isabella during the Spanish Inquisition wince. It was barbaric and medieval. Agents from Saudi had arrived in Istanbul on private jets and gone straight to the consulate. One of them was armed with a bone saw. It seems that, after brief resistance, the writer was overpowered and cut up into little pieces. The perpetrators then flew straight back to Riyadh. The UN Human Rights rapporteur, Agnes Callamard, said Khashoggi had been the victim of a brutal and premeditated killing, planned and perpetrated by officials of the Saudi Arabia state. The CIA assessment was said to be even more problematic. They apparently concluded that this couldn't have happened without the direct blessing of Mohammed bin Salman. Cue crisis in the relationship between the Saudis and the US.

Despite the immense pressure, Trump wasn't buckling. The US needed Saudi Arabia economically and geopolitically, and the President made clear from the beginning he wasn't going to jeopardise multi-billion-dollar arms deals to the kingdom when there were plenty of other countries who would be happy to fill the void. I suspect every other US president before him – yes, even Barack Obama – would have reached the same conclusion; they would have just couched it in more weaselly, condemnatory words. Donald Trump does not do hand-wringing. Khashoggi butchered, protestors imprisoned, criticism leading to diplomatic sanctions (as happened in Canada), a disastrous military adventure in Yemen – the US administration just shrugged.

When, early in 2019, the US declared it wanted to over-throw the Maduro regime in Venezuela because of its brutality and the way it treated protestors and stamped on dissent, it was hard not to point at US policy towards Saudi Arabia, and say, 'Spot the difference.'

Back in May 2017, Donald Trump flew from Saudi Arabia to Jerusalem. A small piece of history was made – Air Force One was able to fly direct. That may seem, alongside the invention of penicillin, the splitting of the atom and the ending of apartheid in South Africa, not really that significant. But in its own way it was. Saudi air traffic controllers handed Air Force One directly over to Israeli ATC. The two spoke to each other. Remarkably, that hadn't happened before. But just so no one came away thinking this was in any way normal, the press plane on which I was travelling physically had to touch down in Cyprus for a few seconds before it could take off again and continue to Tel Aviv. The Saudis passed our plane on to Cypriot air traffic controllers for the few moments that we entered and exited that country's air-space; and the Cypriots passed us on to their Israeli counterparts. The Israeli prime minister had planned a relatively modest arrival welcome for the US president, but having seen what the Saudis laid on, he ordered his entire cabinet to be present at Ben Gurion Airport to be there to greet their guest.

Since Israel's foundation in 1948, the United States has always been the country's most stalwart friend, though again – just like the Saudis – the Likud-led government of Benjamin Netanyahu were not too enamoured with the Obama presidency, and his pursuit of the Iran nuclear deal (among other things). But American muscle has always been seen as crucial – diplomatically, militarily. To get any peace-deal over the line between Israelis and Palestinians, there is a recognition that it is going to require the input of the United States. Nearly all American presidents have given it a go – Jimmy Carter and Bill Clinton made progress; most didn't. Donald Trump talked about it as being the greatest deal that he could possibly pull off. And during his visit, President Trump went to the West Bank to visit Mahmoud Abbas, the Palestinian leader, to show his seriousness about the subject.

But then came a decision that upended decades of US policy that had been followed by successive administrations. The US embassy would be moved from Tel Aviv to Jerusalem – a decision that not only alienated Palestinians but the Arab world as a whole. The future of Jerusalem was one of those key 'final status' issues that would have to be resolved in any future deal, containing as it does holy sites for Judaism – the Western Wall – and holy sites for Islam, most notably the Al-Aqsa mosque. It wasn't until the Six-Day War, in 1967, that the Israelis annexed Arab East Jerusalem. Both Israelis and Palestinians claimed Jerusalem as their capital. By moving the embassy to Jerusalem, Donald Trump was accepting that the historic city was the capital of Israel. He described it as a 'long overdue step to advance the peace process'. But it was anything but. On one of the most controversial issues of all, the US president had put his thumb on the scales in favour of the Israelis. How could America be the honest broker when it had seemingly taken sides?

In early 2019 came another announcement that seemed to catch the US State Department and the rest of the Arab world by surprise. With Benjamin Netanyahu facing a difficult re-election battle, and mired in scandal, Donald Trump attempted to ride to his rescue. He would tweet:

'After 52 years it is time for the United States to fully recognise Israel's sovereignty over the Golan Heights, which is of critical strategic and security importance to the state of Israel and Regional stability!' This again was a seismic change in settled US policy. The future of the Golan would be something that would be negotiated in future peace talks. But at a stroke, the US president had declared in Israel's favour. It was a dramatic change in US policy. Mike Pompeo, who was in Israel when the President put out his tweet, had not said a word about the Golan Heights. Indeed, appearing on Israel's Channel 12, a couple of hours before the President had decided to exercise his Twitter thumbs, Pompeo had been defending American decision making, and the careful and deliberative approach taken. 'No. I don't think we're seeing diplomacy by Twitter,' he tells the interviewer. 'It still requires thoughtfulness, it requires resources, it requires capability and determination.' And then up popped the President's tweet, completely undercutting the Secretary of State.

Back to Donald Trump's first overseas trip. From Israel he flew to Rome (briefly to meet the Pope) and then on to Brussels for his first appearance at a NATO summit. Here, too, he seemed intent on overturning decades of US policy. No, I am not talking here about the diplomatic faux pas of the new US president's determination to barge out of the way the hapless prime minister of Montenegro who had dared to stand in front of the US president as he pushed through to get to the front of the 'family photo'. A truly comedic moment. Instead I am talking about his general disposition to the North Atlantic Treaty Organisation – what it was set up for, what it was doing, and in particular Article 5, the doctrine that an attack on one NATO member is an attack on all. Collective security is the underpinning of the treaty, and the warning to an aggressor who might think about picking off an individual member.

In public the President had limited his expressions of unhappiness to talking about how the US was shouldering too big a burden of the NATO budget, and that other European nations needed to pony up more. But in private he and his aides were questioning the very existence of NATO itself and whether the US should leave. Several times over the course of 2018 the President said privately that he wanted to withdraw; that he didn't see the point of the alliance. All he could see was that it was a drain on the US, and that America put in far more than it got out. This utterly terrified Europeans, particularly the former Soviet bloc countries whose nations abutted a Russia growing more aggressive and more expansionist in its actions.

We had been briefed ahead of his speech in Brussels that the President would commit the US to Article 5 and collective security. When he came to deliver his remarks, that bit was strangely missing. Officials travelling with the President sought to play down the significance, stressing that of course the US stood fully behind Article 5. Yes, but not for the first time a nagging question returned which has gnawed at policy makers since Donald Trump's arrival at the White House – whose voice should be listened to: the administration's, or the President's? Too often they were badly out of kilter. A disjunction that must have had them celebrating with an extra shot of vodka in the Kremlin. Sowing discord has been a central part of Russian strategy.

The NATO summit a year later was equally fractious. Trump called an emergency meeting to address his grievances over the financial contributions made by other countries. The president was mad with the other leaders. I'm told the prime minister of the Netherlands, Mark Rutte, took him aside and pointed out that actually over the past couple of years other NATO countries had increased their military spending – it was in fact an agreement reached at a NATO summit in Wales when Barack Obama was still US president, but Mr Rutte didn't dwell on that part of it. He suggested to Donald Trump that rather than carping, he should go out and claim the credit for these increased contributions. And that's exactly what the President did. He called a news conference at which he took 'total credit' for NATO members increasing their budgets 'like they have never done before'. To Donald Trump's US audience it looked like he had gone in, read the riot act, and squeezed a lot of extra cash out of those recalcitrant Europeans. The Rutte ruse had worked a treat – in spite of nearly being undermined by the French and Italian leaders coming out and saying 'What spending increase?'

Meanwhile in Europe faith that the US under Donald Trump was still a dependable ally of other NATO members was plummeting. A poll conducted in Germany found that only 10 per cent of those questioned felt the US could be relied on. And from his tweets it appeared that he wasn't relying much on his allies. There were barbs at different times aimed at Angela Merkel, Theresa May and Emmanuel Macron. At the G7 in Quebec in 2018 – another bitterly divided summit – one photo, beautifully composed, captured the tension. Donald Trump sits arms crossed looking defensive at a table, while around him are the other members of the rich nations club berating him. I had left the Quebec summit early to make the long journey to Singapore, where the world's most unlikely summit was about to take place – that between the US president and the North Korean leader.

Before we come to that, let's just finish up with what happened at the G7. I had flown from Quebec to Toronto and then on to Hong Kong, where I had a three-hour layover. News of the agreement came just after we landed in Hong Kong. My newsfeed was full of stories of success-against-the-odds in Quebec. I had a shower, got some breakfast – and before I took off on the last leg of the journey, Donald Trump, who was on Air Force One on his way to Singapore, withdrew his signature from the communiqué. Boom. The President was watching on the plane the Canadian prime minister, Justin Trudeau, at his news conference. In it he said that he found the US decision to impose tariffs on Canadian aluminium and steel by invoking national security 'insulting' to all Canadians. 'Canadians are polite, we're reasonable,' he said, 'but we also will not be pushed around.'

That, apparently, was beyond the pale for the President. From his office suite on the plane as it was going over the top of the world, the President was arguably going over the top on Twitter. 'Based on Justin's false statements at his news conference, and the fact that Canada is charging massive Tariffs to our U.S. farmers, workers and companies, I have instructed our U.S. Reps not to endorse the Communique.' In other missives he called Trudeau 'very dishonest' and 'weak'. In G7 history had a communiqué ever been as short-lived?

For the rest of the journey to Singapore, I am told, the President was fixated on one thing, and one thing only. No, not the details of what any denuclearisation deal would look like with North Korea; nor what confidence building measures would need to be agreed on both sides to measure progress. And not much thought was given to when the US would lift sanctions. No, Donald Trump wanted to see mock-ups of the stage where the first handshake would take place between him and Chairman Kim; what the backdrop would be (alternate US and North Korean flags); who would enter from which side; where the cameras would be; whether there would be cameras in elevated positions as well as at eye level.

Indeed, when he got to Singapore the President was frustrated to learn that a day had been set aside for prepping before his historic meeting. Trump was impatient. He spent the morning tweeting about a whole range of topics that had nothing to do with the summit. He even tried to persuade his chief of staff, John Kelly, to ring the North Koreans to see if they could just get on with it, and bring the summit forward a day. The President was told that wouldn't be possible.

If that was unorthodox, everything about this coming together defied orthodoxy. And that is where credit needs to be given to Donald Trump. I don't believe any conventional US president would have dared go ahead with a summit with the leader of a pariah nuclear state when so little groundwork had been done – and when in all likelihood it would result in a major PR victory for the North Koreans for simply turning up and sounding normal (as indeed it did).

Only a few months before this summit, all the talk was of the likelihood of nuclear war between the North Koreans and the US; now it was about what the prospects were for peace. At the United Nations General Assembly the September before, the US president had talked about totally destroying

North Korea – not the sort of language one normally associates with speeches at the UN. But no longer was the US president talking about weapons being locked and loaded and of raining down fire and fury onto North Korea. No longer was he calling Kim 'little rocket man'. And conversely Kim Jong-un wasn't calling Donald Trump a 'mentally deranged dotard', as he had been. More importantly, North Korea had stopped its highly provocative missile tests.

For all that foreign policy experts in Washington predicted the summit wouldn't go ahead, and shouldn't because of the sheer unpredictability, it did – and was in a limited way a success. Yes, there was a whole pile of unanswered questions, but the two sides had opened lines of communication. What politicians of all stripes agreed was that the single most serious national security issue facing the United States, which had been in a state of impasse for years, was seeing progress under the presidency of the most unorthodox and inexperienced commander in chief the US had ever had.

Their second summit in Hanoi, though, showed the limitations of that approach. The months of talks beforehand hadn't narrowed differences sufficiently; what would a communiqué look like? The questions that could be ducked in Singapore by simply saying it was a 'get to know you' summit, could not be avoided in Hanoi. We were given a White House schedule of the day – after the talks there would be a lunch and then a signing ceremony, before the President would come to the Marriott Hotel on the outskirts of the city to hold a news conference. I was on a White House bus awaiting security clearance to go into the hotel when one of the Secret Service guys said timings were shifting. The presser was going to be two hours earlier than had been scheduled.

In other words, no lunch and, more importantly, no signing ceremony. The whole thing had imploded. Kim Jong-un had overplayed his hand in demanding all sanctions be removed; Donald Trump had over-estimated his persuasive powers. A summit that most definitely shouldn't have gone ahead had ended in failure.

At the news conference after the Singapore summit, it was Donald Trump who made all the concessions; this time he had been more cautious. In Singapore he suddenly announced to the press that the US would stop military exercises with the South Koreans on the peninsula, describing them as provocative. Seeking to justify the decision the president used talking points that were straight out of the Chinese playbook. It was hard to see what he had got in return for this major concession. Not only did that halt to exercises come as news to the South Koreans, it came as a total shock to the Pentagon, and Defense Secretary General James Mattis.

This wouldn't be the final straw for Mattis in his troubled relationship with the President. That would come eventually over Syria. The President was keen to stay out of the civil war; his principal concern was to erase the Islamic State caliphate from the map. But with the Damascus regime's use of chemical weapons that would change. He wasn't going to 'do an Obama' and let a red line be crossed with no repercussions. The pictures of children choking to death, foaming at the mouth, eyes bulging, led Trump to order action. Firm action. And immediately. Even targeting the Syrian ruler Bashar al Assad. According to Bob Woodward's book, the President said: 'Let's fucking kill him! Let's go in. Let's kill the fucking lot of them.' And with the firepower that US had, the decapitation of the Syrian leadership was well within US capabilities. General Mattis, the US Secretary of Defense, told the Commander in Chief that he would get right onto it. And apparently put down the phone and said to his senior staff, 'We're not going to do any of that.' He told them to prepare a more measured response. And sure enough, that's what came to pass. A volley of cruise missiles was fired at the Al Shayrat airfield where the Syrian jets had taken off from to deliver the chemical weapons. Fighter jets, the runway, radar installations, hardened aircraft shelters and ammunition bunkers were hit. No other action was taken. General Mattis had done things his way. The President's order had been heard, but not acted upon. If one of the common themes of the Trump presidency has been the chaos and noise, don't be gulled – there are areas where the state is still operating with cold efficiency, as I would discover.

The second use of allied cruise missiles against Syria came in April 2018 after President Assad was held responsible for the use – again – of chemical weapons against his own people. This time dozens were killed outside Damascus, in the suburb of Douma. The President had repeatedly made clear that the use of chemical weapons was a red line. Three sites were targeted.

In Washington there was no great mystery that the attack was going to take place. It was very much a case of when not whether. On the Friday evening I got a tip from a source that it was indeed going to be that evening. I put out a tweet saying that I had heard action would be taken in the coming hours; and then a little later another one saying that the President would address the nation.

The normal thing at times like this is for the White House to simply say they had no comment to make; that they never comment on matters relating to national security. Except they didn't this time. My tweets were widely picked up around the world – and of course at the White House, where in the Briefing Room journalists were told I was wrong, what I had written was factually incorrect and that they should go home. Nothing was going to happen this Friday evening. I have to say I spent a sweaty few hours thinking I had screwed up, and that I had been given duff information, by someone usually reliable.

Sure enough the missile strikes did take place, and the President addressed the American people from the Treaty Room of the White House, as I had predicted he would. There were lots of recriminations, with journalists furious that they had been deliberately lied to by the press team. It's one thing to deflect, to obfuscate, to play a dead bat, to say you don't know; it's another to tell a downright untruth.

Anyway, I didn't think much more about it, except that I was out at a dinner a couple of weeks later and I noticed that on my iPhone I had a text message from someone who could have been construed as my source. But despite trying to open the message repeatedly, it wouldn't open. I thought it was just a glitch on my mobile device. But a little later I ran into this person and asked whether they had been trying to reach me, and explained about the text message I couldn't open. This friend had had the same thing happen: a text message from me, which they were unable to read. Neither of us had sent a text message to the other. I took advice from people who know about these things. Our phones had been tampered with. I was told my phone had been compromised. It certainly looked like someone was very keen to know where my information had come from and who my source was.

Meanwhile US forces and their partners, particularly the Kurds, were making progress all the time in the fight against Islamic State. The caliphate would be declared over in March 2019, as the last scraps of land were surrendered. But at the Pentagon they had long understood this would not be the end of US involvement. The great mistake in Afghanistan after the expulsion of the Taleban in 2001 was to think it was job done. As America switched its focus to Iraq, the Taleban regrouped and came back. US forces would need to remain vigilant, and boots would have to remain on the ground.

So imagine the surprise for General Mattis when, from nowhere, he saw the President tweet that he was withdrawing all US forces from Syria. Just as the decision to stop military exercises on the Korean peninsula had been a decision heavily influenced by President Xi, so it looked as though the decision to pull the American military out of Syria had been taken after a telephone conversation Trump had had with the Turkish leader, President Recip Tayep Erdogan. Remember the fight against IS had been led by the Kurds, with the US providing air cover and special forces support. To abandon them, with a Turkish leader who had his own agenda against the Kurds, was unconscionable to Mattis. It was wrong every which way Mattis looked at it. The lack of orthodoxy, the impetuous decision making, the policy on a whim, the confusion over who were friends and who were foes, had finally become too much. He quit.

His resignation letter is worth quoting in more or less its entirety – not because it says things that hadn't been said in any number of critical articles from foreign policy think-tanks or political enemies. No, it is worth quoting at length because this is, very politely but determinedly, the most thinly disguised repudiation of Trump's foreign policy from someone who had been on the inside and had been working to make the 45th presidency a success.

Dear Mr President:

I have been privileged to serve as our country's 26th Secretary of Defense which has allowed me to serve alongside our men and women of the Department in defence of our citizens and our ideals.

I am proud of the progress that has been made over the past two years on some of the key goals articulated in our National Defense Strategy: putting the Department on a more sound budgetary footing, improving readiness and lethality in our forces, and reforming the Department's business practices for greater performance. Our troops continue to provide the capabilities needed to prevail in conflict and sustain strong U.S. global influence.

One core belief I have always held is that our strength as a nation is inextricably linked to the strength of our unique and comprehensive system of alliances and partnerships. While the US remains the indispensable nation in the free world, we cannot protect our interests or serve that role effectively without maintaining strong alliances and showing respect to those allies. Like you, I have said from the beginning that the armed forces of the United States should not be the policeman of the world. Instead, we must use all tools of American power to provide for the common defence, including providing effective leadership to our alliances. NATO's 29 democracies demonstrated that strength in their commitment to fighting alongside us following the 9–11 attack on

America. The Defeat-ISIS coalition of 74 nations is further proof.

Similarly, I believe we must be resolute and unambiguous in our approach to those countries whose strategic interests are increasingly in tension with ours. It is clear that China and Russia, for example, want to shape a world consistent with their authoritarian model – gaining veto authority over other nations' economic, diplomatic, and security decisions – to promote their own interests at the expense of their neighbours, America and our allies. That is why we must use all the tools of American power to provide for the common defence.

My views on treating allies with respect and also being clear-eyed about both malign actors and strategic competitors are strongly held and informed by over four decades of immersion in these issues. We must do everything possible to advance an international order that is most conducive to our security, prosperity and values, and we are strengthened in this effort by the solidarity of our alliances.

Because you have the right to have a Secretary of Defense whose views are better aligned with yours on these and other subjects, I believe it is right for me to step down from my position.

The President was incensed by this public dressing down, and the way it was received. But it didn't change his modus operandi – over the period I have been writing this section of the book, the Treasury department announced new sanctions against North Korea in coordination with the White House national security team; the President's own National

Security Advisor said they were an important step in turning the pressure up. The following day the President announced on Twitter he was cancelling them, undercutting his own Treasury Secretary and his NSA. Why, we asked Sarah Sanders, the President's spokeswoman. Because he likes President Kim, we were told. Growth figures came in that were lower than expected. The President put the blame entirely on the chairman of the Federal Reserve for his mismanagement of the economy. The education secretary was going to cut funding for the Special Olympics, and went to Congress to defend the move. The President told reporters she'd got it wrong and he was reversing that. On anything and everything the President marched to his own drumbeat.

Nowhere was that more evident than in his relations with the Russian leader Vladimir Putin. When Jim Mattis wrote in his letter, 'My views on treating allies with respect and also being clear-eyed about both malign actors and strategic competitors are strongly held and informed by over four decades of immersion in these issues,' it felt as though he was saying to Donald Trump, you don't really know what you're doing. The confusion between allies and adversaries; the gap between how the administration might act and what the President might say was never more evident than when it came to Russia.

There have been two meetings and one summit, each peculiar in their own way. The first, in Hamburg, came during the G20 summit. At that meeting the President was joined by his Secretary of State, Rex Tillerson, but after it ended, Donald Trump demanded that the translator on the US side hand over his notes, and not breathe a word of what was said to anyone else. They would meet again at the G20 a year later in Buenos Aires. What was remarkable about this was that it had been announced just beforehand that their scheduled meeting had been called off by the Americans in protest at the Russian detention of Ukrainian sailors and vessels in the Black Sea. But it would later emerge they did meet, and the only people present aside from the two presidents were the first lady, Melania, and Putin's translator – in other words there is no US record of the meeting.

At their summit in Helsinki in the summer of 2018 it was even more bizarre. For nearly two hours the two men met alone with only translators present. It is hard to exaggerate how unusual and how abnormal this is. It just doesn't happen. Even if the British prime minister is on the phone to one of the UK's closest allies, the principal private secretary, the Foreign Office and the ambassador of the country concerned would be on the call. Officials should *always* be present so there is an official record of what is said.

A joint news conference took place afterwards. I was sitting next to someone who had clearly planned to disrupt it in some way. He was writing out slogans on large sheets of paper. I suddenly had Finnish security and Secret Service agents clambering over me to remove my neighbour from the room. The news conference was equally unexpected. President Trump was asked if he believed his own intelligence agencies or the Russian president when it came to the allegations of meddling in the US presidential elections. 'President Putin says it's not Russia. I don't see any reason why it would be,' he replied. In other words, given a straight choice between accepting the unanimous assessment of the CIA, FBI and the director of National Intelligence, Donald Trump chose the word of the Russian leader. It caused a furore back in Washington. In a strongly worded statement, the Republican Speaker of the House Paul Ryan said Mr Trump 'must appreciate that Russia is not our ally'. Senator John McCain weighed in too: 'No prior president has ever abased himself more abjectly before a tyrant.'

The President returned to Washington under serious pressure to clear up the mess he'd left behind in Helsinki. So what did he do? Without batting an eyelid, the president called the cameras in and explained that when he said he didn't see why it *would* be Russia interfering in the elections, what he meant to say was that he didn't see why it *wouldn't* be Russia. Those pesky double negatives. It was an explanation that didn't really hold water, as throughout that news conference with Vladimir Putin it was clear that the US president had bought the assurances given by his Russian counterpart.

In the copious output of the Trump Twitter feed you will find attacks on anyone and everyone – allies like Theresa May, Justin Trudeau, Macron and Merkel. You will even see him piling into cabinet colleagues if he feels they've fallen short; he goes after sports stars and TV personalities. Even Meryl Streep was told she was an overrated actress by the President after she had said something disobliging. And, of course, he goes after political enemies with a rare gusto. But Vladimir Putin? Try to find a critical word that he's ever said about him. You won't: there isn't one.

And this is where the gap between what the administration does and how the President acts is so striking. After the Salisbury Novichok attack, the US administration acted as it always had in support of an ally. And remember this was a chemical weapons attack on the soil of a NATO ally. Russian diplomats were expelled from the US, statements of condemnation came thick and fast. Donald Trump did sign a joint letter condemning Moscow – and that there was 'no plausible alternative explanation' for the poisoning of Sergei Skripal and his daughter, Yulia, other than Russian action. But when he found himself in front of a microphone or a television camera, or when he was on his own Twitter feed, he seemed to be rendered mute.

In many of its actions this administration has been tougher on the Russians than previous ones. Look at Ukraine. Where Barack Obama supplied Kiev with blankets and weapons (not what the government wanted), the Trump administration has supplied them with offensive weapons to thwart Russia militarily. They have expelled diplomats, they have issued stern warnings to Moscow over Russian involvement in Venezuela. It may be that Donald Trump's uniquely accommodating approach to Putin is part of some elaborate tough cop/soft cop routine that the administration is performing.

Or maybe it is something altogether different. To misquote Churchill, Donald Trump's approach to Russia was a riddle, wrapped in a mystery, inside an enigma. And unravelling it would become the overwhelming, all-encompassing issue of this presidency.

# CHAPTER 9

# A federal building somewhere in Washington

Twenty-two months into the Mueller investigation, word finally starts to seep out that his investigation is wrapping up. It is the middle of March 2019. Throughout the week rumours had swirled about when and how. The report would be delivered to the new Attorney General, William Barr, and then it was anyone's guess what would happen next. It is now Friday, and still nothing. But by mid-afternoon rumours start to intensify that it could come at any moment. Finally, we thought, Mueller would deliver his report and reveal his hand. At about 4pm the skies suddenly darkened. There was a tremendous thunder clap and then crazy lightning, our TV screens flashing severe weather warnings. And, as one in perfect harmony, everyone in the newsroom in our Washington office called out 'Mueller!' And then mirth. An hour later, though, came confirmation:

his 400-page report had indeed been delivered to the Attorney General. In literature I think they call this pathetic fallacy.

The stakes could not have been higher. The fate of the presidency was in his hands. Mueller's report was the result of hundreds of interviews given on oath by those who had been closest to Donald Trump, who had seen his ways of operating, and it would thus offer the sharpest – and most testing – light yet shone on his administration. Donald Trump had raged against the Special Counsel from the day he was appointed. There were literally hundreds of tweets about this being the greatest hoax of all time, an unacceptable witch-hunt, persecution, a Democrat plot. He declared himself to be the most persecuted president ever. Mueller was variously an investigator who had gone rogue, and a man who was deeply compromised. His investigators were angry, Trump-hating Democrats. For a man who repeatedly claimed he had nothing to hide and was guilty of no wrongdoing and was entirely sure of vindication, he behaved in a way that suggested he was anything but.

William Barr now had the report, and holed up in the Department of Justice he plotted the next moves. While his predecessor, Jeff Sessions, had earned the president's undying disdain and scorn by setting in train the set of events that would lead to the establishment of the Special Counsel investigation, Barr proved himself to be a figure much more to Trump's liking. Forty-eight hours after taking delivery of the report he boiled down the 400-plus pages to four, and released his verdict to an agog American public.

At face value it seemed to give Donald Trump the vindication and clean bill of health that Trump had insisted he deserved. The Mueller report was broken down into two distinct parts. The first question his team investigated was whether there had been collusion between the Trump campaign and the Russians. On that, the Barr summary said that Mueller had been emphatic: there had been none. The second question the investigators looked at was whether the President by his actions had sought to obstruct justice by interfering with issues arising from the presidential election that the FBI had been looking at. Obstruction of justice is one of the 'high crimes and misdemeanours' in the US Constitution that can lead to impeachment.

On that issue Barr quoted one tantalising line from the Mueller report: 'While the report does not conclude that the President committed a crime, it also does not exonerate him.' What did that mean? We would have to wait a few weeks to find out. But here Barr and his deputy stepped in and made the adjudication that Mueller had apparently ducked: 'Deputy Attorney General, Rod Rosenstein and I have concluded that the evidence developed during the Special Counsel's investigation is not sufficient to establish that the President committed an obstruction of justice offence.'

It looked like Trump was in the clear. No collusion, and the Attorney General saying no charges to answer on obstruction. Happy days. I reported that this had to be the best day of Trump's presidency. Democrats who had put so much faith in the work of Robert Mueller were feeling decidedly deflated. The week before the report came out I had been in Paris with the former CIA Director, John Brennan, who was confidently predicting that it was going to be a disaster for the President; that Donald Trump junior was certain to be indicted, that the whole house could come tumbling down. But in the White House, nothing had tumbled. Donald Trump and those closest to him were dancing a happy dance.

But was that it? After the endless speculation and anticipation had Mueller served up a whitewash of a report? Barr had delivered a prebuttal. And this wily operator knew exactly what the effect of that would be. It gave the President exactly the headlines that he had spent two years craving. It would hopefully have the effect of satisfying the American public that the whole investigation was a 'nothingburger' and that they need detain themselves no longer with the intricacies of the matter. Barr's four-page letter was of inestimable value to the President. It wouldn't be the only time that Barr would give the appearance of being more Trump's personal defence attorney than the senior law officer of the United States.

The truth was in fact far more complicated than the Barr summary indicated. Mueller had done his work meticulously and exhaustively from one of the drab, slightly dreary federal government office blocks.

For 22 months, Mr Mueller and his team dug into the fertile soil of the Trump family, and the President's associates, many of whom had been through only the most scant vetting. Robert Mueller, the man tasked with this assignment, had been a director of the FBI, a decorated Vietnam veteran and a lifelong Republican. And he had a reputation for granite-like integrity. Serious. Independent-minded. Unflappable. From the moment of his appointment, through to the completion of his investigation, Mueller became a spectral figure. His modus operandi was to say nothing, reveal nothing, reply to nothing. And in a town where the exchange currency is how often you are seen and how much you're heard, this was startling. Visibility is everything. But he was the Scarlet Pimpernel *de nos jours* – 'They seek him here, they seek him there ...' But

Mueller's brief was not to save the élite from the guillotine's blade; his job was to see who should face justice.

Many found this disquieting – there were no leaks, no whispers, no unmarked manilla envelopes falling into journalists' grateful hands. There was just the deafening sound of silence. And the person who found this most disquieting was the President himself. He likes to have an enemy he can visibly punch at, an enemy he can intimidate and stare in the eye. But though Donald Trump kept on swinging, his haymaking right hooks were doing nothing but disturbing the air around him. They were not landing on their target. More infuriating still, despite all the provocations from the President, not once did they yield a response. Trappist monks have been more raucous.

There were occasional reports of sightings. Mueller was spotted at Reagan National Airport waiting to board a flight to New York – ironically Donald Trump Jr was a passenger on that flight too. There was an Italian restaurant he would go to in Spring Valley – but he would slip in via a rear entrance and disappear into the night equally quickly. There was also a fish restaurant in Palisades that he would go to with his wife. But photos? None. Clips of him speaking? Zilch. And then that weekend in March 2019, when his report had been delivered and his work was done, an apparent apparition: he was seen with his wife emerging from church. And not just any church. He was seen coming out of St John's Episcopal, just across Lafayette Park from the White House. The church the President traditionally attends on the weekend after his inauguration. Mueller had resurfaced, and in the heart of establishment Washington.

This has been an epic drama in which the two principal actors were Donald Trump and Robert Mueller. But there were two important co-stars of the show – the director of the FBI and his first Attorney General, Jeff Sessions. Remember Donald Trump is extremely conscious of his own height, and is very conscious of the physical demeanour of those around him. It was reported he wouldn't appoint John Bolton to a senior position because of his moustache, while his first press spokesman was too fat and was ordered to get better fitting suits. The former New Jersey governor, Chris Christie was told by the President that he ought to change the way he tied his tie, so that it didn't emphasise the width of his sturdy girth. He comments on the appearance of women freely (and some would say inappropriately). So, it was an almost clichéd piece of casting that the FBI director, James Comey, was a lofty 6 feet 8 inches, while the Attorney General was physically diminutive, standing at just 5 feet 5 inches in his little stockinged feet. And each was to the President's distaste. Trump didn't like that he had to look up to the slightly imperious and supercilious Comey – that grated; while Sessions was too small, and quickly became a punchbag for Trump's withering contempt towards the former Alabama senator, who had done so much to help get the New York tycoon elected (he was the first senator to come out and endorse him).

The Comey character was killed off early, stripped of his directorship of the FBI without warning as he was addressing federal agents on the West Coast. He was holding a town-hall meeting, TVs were on in the office but muted, when the breaking news strap appeared across the screens informing them that the boss they were listening to attentively had been fired by the President. Sessions would live on for much longer but it was a painful existence, in a near permanent state of being half alive and half dead politically. The President would ridicule him, demean him, taunt him and provoke him – on Twitter, and at rallies, where he would mock Sessions's southern drawl. As a political spectator, it was like spending every Thursday night in the same wine bar with a friend who keeps telling you she's about to dump her useless boyfriend, but never gets round to it. And you want to scream, 'Just chuck him then.' But instead the presidential mithering went on and on. It would take until November 2018 before Donald Trump moved decisively against him.

But before we get to the detail of the personalities and the meat of what Mueller investigated and what he found, in the interests of clearer understanding, forgive me if I set out a bit of a timeline of what unfolded and why. And then we can get back to the compelling and gripping psychodrama that has been the continuous and dominant thread running through the Trump administration. I am making the starting point the beginning of 2017, two weeks before Donald Trump is sworn in as the 45th president of the United States.

**6 January:**
American intelligence agencies release a report outlining why they believe Russia was behind the hacking during the election campaign. Comey and others go to Trump Tower to brief Trump about the intelligence community assessment concerning Russia's efforts to interfere with the presidential election. Comey pulls Trump aside for a one-on-one meeting to brief him on the contents of the unverified Steele Dossier, with its lurid and unproven allegations that the Russians have kompromat of a

'pee pee' tape, in which prostitutes allegedly hired by Mr Trump urinate on a bed in the presidential suite at the Moscow Ritz Carlton where Barack Obama had once slept and where Mr Trump was staying after a Miss Universe pageant.

**10 January:**
The Director of National Intelligence James Clapper and the heads of the FBI, CIA and the NSA brief Congress on their findings on Russian influence in the 2016 US presidential election. They say in explicit terms Putin was directly involved and that the Russians sought systematically to interfere in the 2016 election.

**20 January:**
Trump inauguration.

**27 January:**
Comey and Trump have dinner together. Comey recalls that, at the dinner, the President said, 'I need loyalty, I expect loyalty.' Comey testified that he replied, 'You will always get honesty from me.' Trump apparently paused and then said, 'That's what I want, honest loyalty.' Trump says he never asked for loyalty. Comey made a contemporaneous note of the meeting, which given his standing as an FBI officer would make it admissible as evidence in a court of law.

**13 February:**
Michael Flynn resigns as National Security Advisor over lying to the Vice-President about his contacts with Russia's ambassador to the US, and what he said to him. Flynn who had led

the anti-Hillary Clinton chants of 'lock her up' at Trump rallies would soon face being locked up himself as he is charged and pleads guilty to a single charge of lying to the FBI.

## 14 February:

Trump and Comey meet in the Oval Office following a larger meeting. Trump says to Comey, 'I hope you can see your way clear to letting this go, to letting Flynn go.' Trump has denied asking for the investigation to be alleviated. In later testimony, Comey said that given the setting and the fact that Trump asked to see him alone, he took the President's words as a directive. 'It rings in my ear as kind of, "Will no one rid me of this meddlesome priest?"' Comey said, referring to Henry II's alleged words that led to the murder of Thomas Becket.

## 2 March:

Jeff Sessions the Attorney General recuses himself from overseeing the Russia Investigation being led by the FBI. Because he had been so closely involved in the Trump presidential campaign, he felt he couldn't also be the referee of what went on during it. Another complication was that he had been – how can one put this – less than forthright in answers to the committee overseeing his confirmation hearings about his own contacts with the Russian ambassador.

## 20 March:

Comey testifies before the House Intelligence Committee and, for the first time, confirms the existence of an investigation into Russian hacking and possible links to the Trump campaign.

**9 May:**

Comey is fired. In his note to Comey, Trump says, 'I greatly appreciate you informing me, on three separate occasions, that I am not under investigation.' The letter dismissing him, written by the Deputy Attorney General Rod Rosenstein, states two reasons – one, his handling of the Hillary Clinton e-mail saga, and two, that Comey had lost the confidence of the FBI.

**10 May:**

Trump meets with Russian officials, including Foreign Minister Sergei Lavrov and Ambassador Kislyak at the Oval Office. Knowledge of this meeting only emerges after the Russian Foreign Ministry release photographs. No US press were allowed. The *New York Times* is leaked an official minute of the meeting in which Trump says, 'I just fired the head of the FBI. He was crazy, a real nut job … I faced great pressure because of Russia. That's taken off.' In other words the reason for firing Comey was *not* as stated in the Rosenstein letter; it was because of the Russia inquiry.

**11 May:**

The President now confirms this publicly, telling NBC's Lester Holt that the firing was because 'this Russia thing with Trump and Russia is a made-up story'.

**17 May:**

Because Sessions has recused himself from anything to do with Russia, and with the scandal not going away, Deputy Attorney General Rod Rosenstein appoints Robert Mueller as Special Counsel to, in effect, take over the FBI investigation into Russian interference in the 2016 election. Mueller a month later asks Rosenstein whether he can widen the scope of the inquiry to look into whether Donald Trump once he had become president might have obstructed justice as well – Rosenstein accedes to that request.

This is not part of the timeline, but I would add one other date, just for its jaw dropping, eye popping, head swivelling extraordinariness, and that is 11 January 2019. That is when the *New York Times* had on its front page a story with this headline: 'FBI Opened Inquiry into Whether Trump Was Secretly Working on Behalf of Russia.' Hold on. Hang on a sec. Say that again. The FBI opened an investigation into whether the president of the United States was actually a Russian agent? Are you kidding me? That has to be fake news, I thought, when I read it. Either that, or a plotline from a sub-standard espionage novel that no publisher would ever put into print. But it was true (true that the FBI launched that investigation, not that the President actually was an agent). After the firing of Comey and the Lavrov meeting, and the earlier dissembling of Flynn and Sessions, law enforcement officials were spurred into action. According to the *NYT* report, 'They began investigating whether he had been working on behalf of Russia against American interests ... the inquiry carried explosive implications. Counterintelligence investigators had to consider whether the president's own actions constituted a possible threat to national security. Agents also sought to determine whether Mr Trump was knowingly working for Russia or had unwittingly fallen under Moscow's influence.'

Wow. Even more amazing, given the febrile atmosphere, was that the President's communications team felt he couldn't just ignore it – he had to address it. The President had been posed the question about whether he was a Russian spy by a super-friendly Fox news anchor the weekend after the report appeared. He called it 'the most insulting thing I've ever been asked'. But that didn't shut anything down. It was a non-denial denial. So, a couple of days later as he was preparing to fly to New Orleans, Trump answered the question directly of whether he had worked for the Russians: 'I never worked for Russia,' he told the gathered media on the South Lawn of the White House. In the history of the United States of America has a president ever had to deny being an asset of a foreign adversary?

There is a scene in one of the episodes of the evergreen TV drama *The West Wing* where the chief political advisor character, Josh Lyman, is prepping the President for a news conference. A couple of staff are pretending to be journalists, and the fictional President Bartlet repeats a part of the reporter's question during his answer. Lyman tells Jed Bartlet never to do that. 'Don't repeat the phrase, sir, that will be the soundbite.' Someone could have done with telling the real-life President Trump that. 'I never worked for Russia' most definitely became the soundbite.

So why was there such suspicion over the President, over the Trump campaign? Where did it all start? The genesis of the concern over Moscow's involvement is actually a wine bar in London. And as plot lines go, like so much to do with the Trump campaign and presidency, there is much that strains credulity. A young foreign policy advisor to the Trump campaign, George Papadopoulos, finds himself in the Kensington Wine Rooms. It is May 2016, with just six months to go until polling day. And this man has a huge amount of swagger and consumes the alcohol to match, an unwise combination in a political operative. He brags about the dirt that the Russians have on Hillary Clinton, and how the Trump campaign are going to be able to access it and weaponise it.

Except the person he is shooting the breeze with is Australia's High Commissioner, Alexander Downer. Downer is so alarmed by what he hears that he gets in touch with US contacts based at the embassy in London; these people then report back to FBI HQ, and, hey presto, a counter-intelligence operation is born. According to former FBI Director James Comey, this report – and not the Steele dossier, written by the former MI6 agent, Michael Steele, and ultimately paid for by the DNC and the Clinton campaign – was the seminal event that raised concerns about Donald Trump's ties to the Russians and the major reason it launched its counter-intelligence investigation of the Trump campaign.

I should say there is a counter-narrative which portrays a deep state and rotten establishment and 'bad cops' (a phrase Donald Trump regularly uses) encouraged by a president who hated him (Barack Obama) abetted by foreign agents (the British secret service) doing their all to scupper the Trump campaign. In this version of history, the FBI illegally spied on members of his team, lying to the courts to get the authorisation to eavesdrop on campaign members. Let me add that this account is long on assertions and conspiracy theories and short on facts. But in the wake of the conclusion of the Mueller report there are many Trump allies – along with Trump himself – insisting this must be investigated by the Department for Justice.

But that wasn't part of Robert Mueller's remit; he had to look into whether there was collusion between the campaign and the Russians; and if there was, why. What motivated it? There was a whole series of events which were decidedly odd, and would lead to charges being laid against various individuals. He found dots. What he didn't find was a thread that joined them.

Papadopoulos was the first to be indicted. He pleaded guilty to lying to the FBI to conceal his contacts with Russians and Russian intermediaries during the presidential campaign. A federal judge also sentenced him to one year of supervised release and imposed a fine of $9,500. The operatives whom Papadopoulos met offered him 'dirt' on Hillary Clinton that he fed back to the Trump campaign. His lawyers said Papadopoulous acted out of a 'misguided sense of loyalty to his master' and to preserve his career options in the new administration.

He was a minnow in the Trump orbit – a young political operative who had just turned 30 when he found himself swimming out of his depth. However else you describe Paul Manafort, the word that would not attach to him is minnow. At the time he is picked to lead the Trump campaign he is in his mid sixties. A multi-millionaire, he'd made a fortune with a lobbying firm, representing a variety of unsavoury clients around the world. And with wealth came a certain ostentation: jackets made of ostrich skin or brown python. He had accrued around $30 million in real estate dotted around. He would be forced as part of his plea deal with prosecutors to give up a 43rd-floor condo in Trump Tower in New York, his 1890s Brooklyn brownstone, and a loft in SoHo. Another three-bedroom condo in Lower Manhattan would be put up for sale, as well as a ten-bedroom house in the Hamptons equipped with a pool, tennis court and putting green.

The Trump team never really asked any questions about where the money came from; they were just keen to get someone who had plenty of miles on the clock as a Republican political operative. And he had plenty, having worked on political campaigns going right the way back to President Gerald Ford in the 1970s. If they had followed the money they would have found that much of it had come from working for pro-Moscow politicians in Ukraine. He was in charge of the Trump campaign during the Republican convention in 2016 when the candidate's policy suddenly changed. The proposed weakening of US support for Ukraine was a policy shift that was very much to Moscow's liking.

He was also present for a meeting at Trump Tower on 9 June when he, Donald Trump junior and Jared Kushner met Natalia Veselnitskaya, a Russian lawyer with known links to the Kremlin who was offering 'dirt' on Hillary Clinton. The meeting had been set up by a British intermediary, Rob Goldstone. Goldstone was a publicist working mainly in the music industry who had helped the Trump Organisation bring the Miss Universe pageant to Moscow years earlier, and so had good Russian contacts. Post election, when details start to emerge about the Trump Tower meeting, Donald Trump Jr issued a highly misleading statement, saying that they were there to discuss policy around adoption of Russian children. It would later emerge that the statement had been written by President Trump, not Don Jr. But then emails emerge which cast a very different light on the meeting. The following is an exchange between Goldstone and Donald Trump Jr.

Goldstone: 'Emin just called and asked me to contact you with something very interesting. The Crown prosecutor of Russia met with his father Aras this morning and in their meeting offered to provide the Trump campaign with some official documents and information that would incriminate Hillary and her dealings with Russia and would be very useful to your father. This is obviously very high level and sensitive information but is part of Russia and its government's support for Mr Trump – helped along by Aras and Emin.'

Trump Jr responds: 'Thanks Rob I appreciate that. I am on the road at the moment but perhaps I just speak to Emin first. Seems we have some time and if it's what you say I love it.'

Steve Bannon, who would succeed Manafort as campaign chairman, described the meeting as 'treasonous' and 'unpatriotic'. But it was what Mueller found in Manafort's past that rang alarm bells. He had made millions from his work for pro-Russian groups in Ukraine, and never declared it. He was eventually sentenced for a variety of offences, including witness tampering when he was under house arrest, and will serve several years in a federal prison. Rick Gates, his deputy on the campaign and long-time business associate, pleaded guilty to conspiracy against the United States and making false statements in the investigation into Russian interference. But if those activities pre-dated their involvement in the campaign, they certainly got up to quite a bit that was crucial to the Mueller investigation. They provided sensitive internal polling data to a Russian oligarch, Konstantin Killimnik, who Gates understood to be a 'spy' for the Kremlin. And they engaged in various bits of subterfuge to meet him in New York.

The other person who fell afoul of the Mueller investigation was General Michael Flynn. He had been a prominent Trump supporter during the campaign and was rewarded after the election by being made National Security Advisor. It is, arguably, the most pivotal role in the administration that doesn't require Senate confirmation. But he was fired within weeks of the Trump inauguration. He had misled the Vice-

President over conversations he had had with the Russian Ambassador Sergey Kislyak. More telling is that for three weeks, Donald Trump knew that Flynn had lied to the VP, but it was only when it got out into the media that Flynn was forced to walk the plank. He had broken the eleventh commandment: thou shalt not get caught.

When the Mueller investigation started, Flynn was questioned about those contacts with the Russian embassy. Again he dissembled – but this time the FBI had phone intercepts to match against Flynn's account. He would plead guilty for having 'impeded and otherwise had a material impact on the FBI's ongoing investigation into the existence of any links or coordination between individuals associated with the campaign and Russian efforts to interfere with the 2016 presidential election'. The man who had led the chants of 'Lock her up!' against Hillary Clinton during Trump rallies was now the one looking at jail time. As many commentators noted at the time, karma's a bitch.

The other prominent Trump aide netted by the Mueller probe was the President's personal Mr Fixit, Michael Cohen. The New York lawyer had been at Trump's side for a decade and was his go-to person when there was something difficult or delicate that needed sorting. He had once said he would take a bullet for Donald Trump, but cornered by Mueller and cut adrift by Trump, Cohen now 'flipped' and started cooperating with the Special Counsel investigation. Far from taking a bullet, he was now aiming a gun at the President's head. He admitted to lying to Congress over the ambitions of Donald Trump to build a Trump Tower in Moscow. The President had consistently maintained that he had no business interests in Russia, but throughout the campaign his team was working on getting permission to build a flagship property in the capital, that could have made Mr Trump hundreds of millions of dollars.

The court filings were even more astonishing. Another of the crimes that Cohen pleaded guilty to was the breaking of campaign finance laws. And if that sounds dry as dust, it isn't. This relates to the hush money paid to the pornstar Stormy Daniels, and the former *Playboy* model Karen McDougal, both of whom had claimed to have had affairs with Donald Trump. Attorneys from the Southern District of New York state explicitly in their court submission that Cohen 'acted in coordination with and at the direction of Individual-1' in handling payments to the two women. In this and other filings by US attorneys 'Individual-1' is identified as the man who 'was elected President'. Just think about this for a second – these lawyers are federal employees. They work for the Department of Justice. And in their filing to the court they say – in terms – that Cohen broke the law 'in coordination with and at the direction of' the man who is now the president.

To summarise, a former head of the Trump campaign, his deputy, a foreign policy advisor, the national security advisor and Trump's personal lawyer had all been found guilty. And that is not to mention the pile of indictments against various Russians who had sought to interfere in the election.

The focus on collusion in legal terms has always been a bit of an oddity. There is no federal offence of 'collusion'. The criminal offence is conspiracy and that was the focus of Mueller's investigators: whether the Trump team purposefully worked with Russia to win the 2016 election. What he found boils down to this: yes, there were members of Trump's team at different stages who had deep and troubling links with Russia. The Russian government for its part was doing all it could to get Trump elected president. And as for the campaign team, they were keen as mustard to benefit from any embarrassing leaks that would hurt the Democrats – and no, they never thought it was necessary to alert the authorities to the source of the information they were receiving. Despite that, 'the investigation did not establish that members of the Trump campaign conspired or coordinated with the Russian government in its election interference activities,' the report said. That's the good news as regards the confidence that Americans can have in the integrity of the election. This is the bad: 'The Russian government interfered in the 2016 presidential election in sweeping and systematic fashion,' according to Robert Mueller.

Having covered the campaign throughout 2016, travelling extensively with candidate Trump as he clocked up the air-miles all over the country, it always seemed far-fetched to me, the idea that there was conspiracy/collusion. There was a compelling defence that Trump and those closest to him could have mounted, but would never make because it would require too much self-awareness and an acceptance of frailty (not the President's strongest suits). The campaign was simul-taneously wonderful and a total shit-show. It was as different as could be from the tightly controlled and disciplined (but ultimately useless) campaign of Hillary Clinton. Trump's was careering down a hill, extremely fast, with dodgy brakes and the possibility that anyone and everyone could be tipped over the handlebars at any moment. A conspiracy with Russian agents? You're having a laugh. The people in Trump Tower were making it up as they went along. There was no playbook, no bible that had to be consulted. Messaging was haphazard (but effective); travel plans changed regularly; command and control over the candidate was partial, at best. But as I say, this was a defence Donald Trump would never mount.

But if you look back at the names of the people who have been found guilty during the course of the Mueller investigation, what is the one thing that unites them all; what is the common denominator? They were all found to have lied over their contacts with Russia. Why did Michael Cohen lie about the Moscow building project? Why did Flynn feel it necessary to tell untruths about his conversations with the Russian ambassador? Why did Donald Trump instruct the participants in the Trump Tower meeting to invent a cock and bull story that it was about adoption, when it was really about getting dirt on Hillary Clinton? If you don't think you are doing anything wrong – and that has been Donald Trump's line throughout – why the almost industrial scale quantity of untruths?

The second part of the Special Counsel investigation looked at whether there was obstruction of justice by the President (as he was by then) in his efforts to halt the Russia investigation – whether being carried out by the FBI director James Comey, or later by Robert Mueller. But these, of course, are not two entirely discrete entities. They are overlapping circles. Nowhere more so than in how the President reacted to the indictments and charges laid against the individuals from the campaign – and in particular the extent to which Donald Trump felt they did or didn't cooperate with the authorities.

The President has previously said that two of his favourite films are *The Godfather* and *Goodfellas*. Certainly, the language he used at times seemed to borrow more from the Cosa Nostra than from the high-minded idealism of the founding fathers in *The Federalist Papers*. Michael Cohen, his long-time *consigliere*, was a 'rat' for having cooperated with the Mueller investigation. He was a 'flipper' for having done that. Trump told Fox News, 'I know all about flipping. For 30, 40 years, I've been watching flippers. Everything's wonderful, and then they get ten years in jail and they flip on whoever the next highest one is, or as high as you can go.'

But Paul Manafort, who initially refused to cooperate, was lauded by the President, even though he had committed serious crimes that might have caused him to spend the rest of his life in prison. He tweeted, 'I feel very badly for Paul Manafort and his wonderful family. "Justice" took a 12 year old tax case, among other things, applied tremendous pressure on him and, unlike Michael Cohen, he refused to "break" – make up stories in order to get a "deal." Such respect for a brave man!' Manafort had obeyed the mafia code of *omerta* and so was venerated; Cohen hadn't and so was vilified. This from the man who is there to uphold the laws of the land and be in charge of the justice system. The White House General Counsel, Don McGahn, was similarly lauded by Trump for keeping schtoom (although once the Mueller report came out and it emerged just how extensively McGahn had cooperated, that all changed). The President said he wasn't a 'John Dean type "rat"'. That's a reference to the former Nixon White House counsel who cooperated with Watergate prosecutors, helping to end Richard Nixon's presidency in 1974. Trump didn't argue that Dean got his facts wrong, just that he'd flipped – making him, in Trump's mind, a 'grass'.

This led Mueller to investigate whether there was more to this than met the eye. Was this intimidation in the case of Cohen; was Manafort being given a nod and a wink that if he stayed being 'brave' and kept stonewalling Mueller, there might be a presidential pardon at the end of it? Certainly, the President never ruled out the possibility. According to Mueller's report, 'In January 2018, Manafort told [Rick] Gates that he had talked to the President's personal counsel and they were "going to take care of us". Manafort told Gates it was stupid to plead, saying that he had been in touch with the President's personal counsel and repeating that they should "sit tight" and "we'll be taken care of". Gates asked Manafort outright if anyone mentioned pardons and Manafort said no one used that word.'

Did that amount to interference? In the case of Cohen, Mueller wrote that the evidence could 'support an inference that the president used inducements in the form of positive messages in an effort to get Cohen not to cooperate, and then turned to attacks and intimidation to deter' cooperation and undermine Cohen's credibility. Mueller went down a similar path with the treatment of Michael Flynn, who was also the beneficiary of a range of sympathetic messages from the President. Were they also code for 'limit your cooperation and there'll be a pardon at the end of it'?

The Flynn case was really the starting point for the obstruction of justice part of the investigation. The day after Flynn had been fired, President Trump calls the FBI Director James B. Comey to come and see him at the White House. It is 14 February, but there was not a lot of love around. Immediately afterwards, as had become Comey's MO in his dealings with the President, he made a detailed note of the meeting. Comey wrote that the President shooed everyone else out of the room so he could speak to the FBI director alone. Trump denies this. But Mueller finds that 'other Administration officials who were present have confirmed Comey's account'. Both Reince Priebus, who was then Chief of Staff, and Jeff Sessions, then the Attorney General, told the Mueller team that the President had 'asked to speak to Comey alone'.

Finally it is just the two of them and, as we've seen, Trump says to Comey, 'I hope you can see your way clear to letting this go, to letting Flynn go' – which Comey interpreted as an instruction to drop the investigation. The President would much later refute that, writing on Twitter, 'I never asked Comey to stop investigating Flynn. Just more Fake News covering another Comey lie!' But Mueller reports that this was contradicted by Priebus and the then White House counsel Don McGahn. Trump apparently told them that he 'spoke to Comey about Flynn' and called Flynn 'a good guy'. In any case, why would Trump need to have the room cleared and see Comey alone if it was merely to tell the FBI director what a good egg he was? Mueller also takes evidence from other White House officials who tell him that the President was furious that he couldn't simply instruct his attorney general who or what should be investigated.

Trump's judgement was that with the firing of Flynn he had put to bed the whole Russia investigation. It would be in the rear-view mirror. The former New Jersey governor Chris Christie recalls, in his book *Let Me Finish*, a telling lunch he had with Trump and Jared Kushner the day after Flynn had gone. According to Christie, Trump said to him: 'This Russia thing is all over now, because I fired Flynn,' and Christie starts to laugh – the former prosecutor told them it was nowhere near over.

Christie was spot on. This was going to go on and on. Christie also said he gave the President a piece of advice. He told Trump there was no way he would be able to shorten the process, but he could sure as hell lengthen it – and that was by continually talking about it. Christie's advice was that he should say nothing. It was advice the President was unable to take, and it was true the 'Russia thing' went on far, far longer.

The next stage in the decline of the Trump/Comey relationship came in March, when Comey testified in public that there was an FBI investigation going on into Trump and the Russians and the 2016 campaign – and it had been going on since well before the election. This was the first time it had been said out loud. It was fascinating to see how the same people presented with the same facts could reach such wildly differing conclusions. Trump supporters thought (and continue to think) this was 'bad cops' at the top of the FBI trying to engineer a coup against the President. Democrats who had seen Hillary Clinton's presidential ambitions go up in flames when Comey announced, just days before the election, that he was reopening the inquiry into her use when she was Secretary of State of a private email server, thought this was deeply unjust. Why reveal the Clinton investigation, but not the fact that there was one relating to Trump? How did that serve the American people? Wasn't that gross interference in the election? Those questions will stay with Comey for the rest of his life.

And when Trump decided it was time to dispatch the man at FBI HQ, this was the slightly risible pretext – because Donald Trump was so concerned about the treatment of poor old Hillary. Because of the implications over obstruction of justice, the Russia inquiry was not mentioned. The bureau, Trump asserted, was in turmoil. Comey was a general who had lost the confidence of his troops. Trump was claiming that hundreds of rank and file officers had contacted the White

House to pledge their support for the decision to fire Comey. I was at the White House briefing when the President's then deputy press secretary, Sarah Sanders, repeated it, saying, 'I can speak to my own personal experience – I've heard from countless members of the FBI that are grateful and thankful for the President's decision.' And she went on, 'I've certainly heard from a large number of individuals. And that's just myself.' But interrogated by Mueller, under the threat of perjury charges for lying, she would admit that her assertion 'was not founded on anything'. She had lied from the podium. She would later explain it as a 'slip of the tongue'. A slip of the tongue repeatedly made.

A memo drawn up by the deputy attorney general argued that Comey had overstepped his authority in the Hillary Clinton email investigation. Rosenstein said that Comey had been wrong to usurp the authority of the Attorney General to announce the reopening of the investigation, and had compounded that by giving 'derogatory' information about someone who was not going to be subject to criminal charge.

Of course, this explanation – concern over the way the FBI had treated Hillary Clinton – did not withstand any scrutiny. It soon became clear that was all a smokescreen. The President wanted Comey fired because – just as he had mistakenly calculated over the firing of Flynn – he thought this would end the Russia pain; it would put a stop to the questions. But this was an even greater misreading of the situation than in the case of Flynn. It only made things worse. Far worse. And set in train a chain reaction that would shake his presidency to the core. According to Mueller, the White House buried Trump's original termination letter, which exposed his true motives. According to notes discovered by his team, the White House counsel's office concluded that the letter should never see the 'light of day'.

As the outrage over the firing of Comey grew, so the Attorney General Jeff Sessions would make a hugely consequential decision on the way forward. He decides he has to recuse himself from overseeing the Russia investigation because of his involvement in the Trump campaign, and because of questions that had been raised over his own contacts with the Russian Ambassador. This sends Trump apoplectic. But then worse follows. The deputy attorney general, Rod Rosenstein, decides that the only way forward is to appoint a Special Counsel to oversee the investigation. Now add incandescent to apoplectic. The President was not a happy camper. And from that moment on he would launch lacerating attacks on Jeff Sessions until and beyond the day he fired him 16 months later.

My experience of reading official reports is that they tend to be extremely worthy, but immensely dull. The Mueller report is not that. It is a gripping page turner. From the interviews conducted with all the key witnesses to events – all conducted under oath – Mueller pieces together (with annotations and footnotes) what happened when Trump found out about Sessions standing aside from overseeing the Mueller report. Much of the report has this strong narrative thread – but here is the key paragraph, from page 78 of the report:

On May 17, 2017, Acting Attorney General Rosenstein appointed Robert S. Mueller, III as Special Counsel and authorized him to conduct the Russia investigation and matters that arose from the investigation. The President learned of the Special Counsel's appointment from

Sessions, who was with the President, Hunt [Jody Hunt was Jeff Sessions chief of staff], and McGahn conducting interviews for a new FBI Director. Sessions stepped out of the Oval Office to take a call from Rosenstein, who told him about the Special Counsel appointment, and Sessions then returned to inform the President of the news. According to notes written by Hunt, when Sessions told the President that a Special Counsel had been appointed, the President slumped back in his chair and said, 'Oh my God. This is terrible. This is the end of my presidency. I'm fucked.' The President became angry and lambasted the Attorney General for his decision to recuse from the investigation, stating, 'How could you let this happen, Jeff?' The President said the position of Attorney General was his most important appointment and that Sessions had 'let [him] down', contrasting him to Eric Holder and Robert Kennedy. Sessions recalled that the President said to him, 'you were supposed to protect me,' or words to that effect. The President returned to the consequences of the appointment and said, 'Everyone tells me if you get one of these independent counsels it ruins your presidency. It takes years and years and I won't be able to do anything. This is the worst thing that ever happened to me.'

As an aside, when the report was eventually published on the Department of Justice website there was an exercise in speedreading by journalists across Washington. It seemed only minutes after its publication that one of our colleagues working for CBS news came across the gemstone nugget: the 'This is the end of my presidency. I'm fucked' quotation. It was the stand-out phrase from the four hundred plus pages. But how to report it on the news? He used an expletive? He used the F word? Well, ladies and gentleman, I made broadcast history that evening by being the first person in BBC News to use the work 'fucked' on the flagship *Ten O'Clock News*.

But, this being the BBC, nothing is that straightforward. The decision to use it was relatively simple – then, however, came questions over context and what sort of 'health warning' you give before you ignite the F-bomb to the audience. The initial decision from London was that I should say the President used 'extremely offensive' language beforehand. But – hey – this is 2019. Isn't 'extremely offensive' reserved for the C-word? And back and forth it went. We eventually settle on very strong language.

Then came the debate about whether I say it live to camera, or do we quote it in graphic form in the body of the piece. I don't want to say it to camera, as I think that will look like grandstanding, or worse still accidental. So it was eventually decided I would say the word, but the graphic animation would say f*****. I went to the White House to do a 'live top' to my piece, and as per instructions I finished my introduction by saying, 'I should say my report contains very strong language.' I did wonder whether by the time I got back to the bureau it would be my career that would be f*****.

If you read the Mueller report you can see why the administration were so keen to pre-spin the verdict. What the report does is show that most of the 'exclusive' reports delivered by the *Washington Post* and *New York Times* in the near two years that the report was being conducted were spot on. Though nothing leaked from the federal office building where Mueller and his team were doing their work, there was plenty seeping out of the White House.

The report conveys a White House in meltdown during the summer of 2017, as an angry president seethes at the Mueller investigation and looks at ways of shutting it down. That is the Nixon nuclear option: the Saturday night massacre when he fired the special prosecutor Archibald Cox conducting the Watergate investigation. A move that ultimately led to the President's resignation (but more rapidly resulted in the memorable bumper sticker 'Nixon is a Cox-sacker'). Again, on what was unfolding within the White House, I can do no better than quote from the report itself.

McGahn's clear recollection was that the President directed him to tell Rosenstein not only that conflicts existed but also that 'Mueller has to go.' McGahn is a credible witness with no motive to lie or exaggerate given the position he held in the White House. McGahn spoke with the President twice and understood the directive the same way both times, making it unlikely that he misheard or misinterpreted the President's request. In response to that request, McGahn decided to quit because he did not want to participate in events that he described as akin to the Saturday Night Massacre.

At this point McGahn drove to the White House to pack up his personal belongings and prepare a resignation letter. He told Reince Priebus, then the chief of staff, that the President was asking him to do 'crazy shit', and that he had had enough. Mueller in his conclusions said that substantial evidence indicated that the President's attempts to have the Special Counsel removed were driven by Donald Trump's concern that he was being investigated for potential obstruction of justice. Or, to put it in layman's terms: Trump sought to obstruct justice because he was being investigated for obstruction of justice.

Since the report's publication, this is the one detail of the report with which the President has taken issue. He has said that he never ordered McGahn to contact the deputy AG and instruct him, in turn, to fire Mueller. And Trump has said that even if he had done that he would have been within his rights to do so. He has further added that if he wanted to fire Mueller he would have done so himself. The one caveat that needs to be added to this is that the President was not interviewed face to face by the Special Counsel, whereas the conclusions that Mueller reaches are based on those interviews with key members of staff like McGahn, Priebus and Bannon – which were all conducted under oath. The President, who has previously boasted of having 'one of the best memories in the world', would only agree to answering a number of written questions – and more than two dozen times in the published testimony the phrase 'I can't remember' or 'I do not recall' appears.

There is another reason why Trump has singled out this particular finding. What McGahn and others did was disobey orders. They ignored the President's instructions. And that makes Trump look weak, and not in command. Some days later he would tell reporters everyone obeys his instructions.

Mueller goes on to list a number of other ways in which the President might have obstructed justice, and the public learned of hitherto unknown attempts to neuter the investigation. But for all that the report is comprehensive and compelling in its research and its attention to detail, Mueller ducks making a determination of whether Trump crossed a line and actually broke the law. Yes, he lays out ten specific examples where there was an arguable case for obstruction of justice, but to use an American metaphor, it's as though he takes the baseball bat up to the plate, and leaves it for others to pick up and go for the home run. What he very clearly doesn't do – though some have tried to paint it otherwise – is give the President a pass. 'If we had confidence after a thorough investigation of the facts that the President clearly did not commit obstruction of justice, we would so state,' the Mueller report states. 'Based on the facts and the applicable legal standards, however, we are unable to reach that judgement.'

Mueller also made clear that he found many of the President's answers 'inadequate'. That begs a second difficult question for Mueller: if that was the case, having read the answers, why didn't the Special Counsel subpoena the President to appear before them? It would have been a high stakes roll of the dice, and the President might have resisted, thus setting up a constitutional showdown. But he chose to accept what he had been served up by the President.

The argument that Trump's legal team have made is to ask how there could be an obstruction of justice case when there was no original sin. In other words, because the Mueller report found that there was no crime of conspiracy or cooperation committed by the Trump campaign in its dealings with the Russians, how can you then find that the President obstructed an inquiry that was into something where no crime had been committed? There is a longstanding policy in the Department of Justice that you can't indict a sitting president. But Bill Barr the new Attorney General has a rather different outlook. He has a maximalist interpretation of presidential privilege. In other words, if the President is using his constitutional powers in the course of his duties, he can't commit obstruction. When Donald Trump said during the presidential campaign that he could go and shoot someone on Fifth Avenue in New York and get away with it, you sense that it might well be true.

Mr Barr claimed that the 'White House cooperated fully' with Mr Mueller, even though Mr Trump declined to meet with the Special Counsel's team, sought to have Mr Mueller fired and allowed – even encouraged – his administration to make repeatedly inaccurate public statements about the investigation.

The President in the days after the report was published claimed he had been exonerated. His tone was one of vindication mixed with vindictiveness. I am free, but I am going to get those SoBs who tried to set me up. He also reluctantly acknowledged that Mueller had behaved honourably. But with publication and the saturation media coverage that followed, so his mood darkened. There is a very fine line for Donald Trump between being a victor and a victim. He could sometimes feel both simultaneously. His pinned tweet on the day after publication was a *Game of Thrones* meme with the words 'Game Over'. But in his mind it clearly wasn't. He reverted to attacking Robert Mueller – as a rogue investigator who was compromised and a Trump hater. What is certainly true is that the Mueller report is not a clean bill of health. Far from it. The more you read, the more damning is the portrayal of Donald Trump as a stranger to the truth – the impression given is that the President seems to spread falsehoods as a first resort. And asks others to do the same, or to double down on the lies that have already been told.

At the end of May 2019, Mueller would eventually break his silence. He caught the White House by surprise by appearing before the lectern at the Department of Justice to make a statement. He would take no questions; he warned Congress that even if he was called to testify he wouldn't go beyond what was in his report. But then he said one or two things that stood out. He said that charging the President had never been an option because DoJ guidelines forbade it. And then this one sentence: 'If we had had confidence that the President clearly did not commit a crime, we would have said so.' The implication of that could not have been clearer. Did Robert Mueller think he had exonerated Donald Trump, as the President had claimed? Not a bit of it.

I was really struck by some polling that came out a couple of weeks after the Mueller report appeared. It was one poll, and the numbers might change, and I haven't gone into the details of the fieldwork or the sample size, or margins of error – but it seemed to tell a wider truth about America, the state of public opinion, the norm-shattering nature of this presidency, and how Americans were adjusting to it. The research done for the *Washington Post* and ABC found that 56 per cent of Americans were opposed to moves to impeach President Trump. A clear majority. While 58 per cent were absolutely clear in their view that the President had lied to the public. Only a third of Americans in this survey thought he had told the truth. To summarise – we know he's a liar, but let's not do anything about it.

Two years into his presidency, Donald Trump is being treated differently than anyone who has ever held the post. It is hard to think any of his predecessors could have survived some of the lacerating conclusions of this report. He feels himself to be the most persecuted president there has ever been – yet no one has ever been given the latitude that he has.

The reason his acolytes say he is exonerated, and in the clear, is that there was no determination that he had broken the law. Is that the height at which the bar is now set? So long as any behaviour falls short of criminal, it's OK? It seems a far cry from America's first President, George Washington, when he was at Mount Vernon setting out his seventeen rules for decency and civility to be expected of the post-holder.

The Trump haters had hoped the Mueller report would be the smoking gun that would finish him off. The kill shot from a sniper's rifle. It is not that. It has left a Democratic leadership fearful that if it moves to impeach him it will ultimately fail and just rally Republicans, and make Donald Trump even more popular. The US economy has been growing impressively, stock markets are booming and unemployment is at a record low. On trade, on immigration, on military spending the President is staying true to the pledges he made to the American people. Taxes have been cut. And for all the calamities and the division, living standards are rising, as is consumer confidence.

The President is still on the high wire, sometimes leaning precipitously to one side, then tilting horribly to the other. In politics there is no safety net to break the fall. There are wide-eyed gasps of oohs and aahs from the audience, some thrilled by the show, some covering their faces in horror. But with each precarious step that he takes out on the trapeze without coming crashing to the ground, so his confidence grows and self-belief surges that he is not going to be knocked off course. Not now. Not in 2020.

# Index